# Divorced.

# Catholic.

# *Now What?*

*Navigating Your Life After Divorce*

by Lisa Duffy and Vince Frese

3rd Revised Edition

A Journey of Hope Publication

D1056529

# Dedication

Lisa:

To all the men, women and children who are suffering because of divorce. I endured the most intense pain of my life when I divorced. I feel your pain and I know what you are going through. I offer my work for you and I pray for you every day.

Vince:

For Caroline, Kaitlyn, Emily, Riley, Austin, Maria and Vincent Peter. May you never experience the pain and sorrow of divorce.

# Foreword

## by Patrick Madrid

Everybody knows somebody who has been divorced. It's a tragic phenomenon that today affects practically every American family in some way, and Catholic families are no exception. Many who have gone through this painful experience are (or were) Catholic.

There are many reasons why marriages fracture and disintegrate. Each divorced couple went through a unique set of circumstances that led to that fateful moment when one or both spouses called it quits, turned, and walked away from the marriage forever. And for every wife or husband who abandons a marriage for selfish reasons, there is a husband or wife who was abandoned and was left to deal with the catastrophic aftermath of emotional, financial, and spiritual wreckage left in the wake of a divorce.

Is it any wonder, then, that God would declare, "I hate divorce" (Malachi 2:16)?

Countless wives, who committed themselves to their husbands wholeheartedly and for life on their wedding day, now find themselves in the agonizing position of having to file for divorce in order to protect themselves and their children from their husbands' mendacious, abusive, or vindictive behavior (sometimes all three). There are, of course, countless husbands, too, whose lives have been shattered by the emotionally lacerating and financially disastrous decision of their wives to seek a divorce — often, as the result of her sexual infidelity. The emotional toll on children, who watch their parents' divorce unfold, powerless to prevent the wrenching apart of their family, is simply devastating. No matter how it happens, no matter what the causes, the short- and long-term damage inflicted by divorce on individuals, families, communities, and our very civilization cannot be underestimated.

Nor can divorce be underestimated (much less discounted) as a common factor among Catholics who wind up abandoning their Faith. They often leave the Church after their marriage fails, and it's easy to see why. There is such discouragement and despair, a distrust of others, and a lot of misinformation about whether or not they are welcome in the Catholic Church.

Obviously, the widespread problem of divorce urgently requires solutions across many levels, emotional as well as spiritual. True healing requires God's grace, and in the Catholic Church you will find that grace and consolation your heart has been yearning for.

This is why I recommend so highly that you read and assimilate the excellent and insightful information contained in this book. It will present you with much clear, accurate information and advice for dealing well with your divorce (or the divorce of someone close to you). It will approach you with compassion and understanding, and it will provide you with practical, effective tools for healing. Perhaps most importantly, this book will offer you genuine and consoling reasons for hope. I believe hope is perhaps the most important remedy for any grieving heart.

Sacred Scripture tells us to, "Always be ready to give a reason to anyone who asks you for a reason for the hope that is in you," and to "do it with gentleness and respect" (1 Peter 3:15-16). That is exactly what you will find in this wonderful book: reasons for hope after divorce presented gently and respectfully.

I promise you my prayers that the Lord will bless and guide you as you embark with Him on this journey of hope.

— Patrick Madrid is an author and the publisher of Envoy Magazine. He and his wife Nancy have been married for 27 years and have been blessed with eleven happy and healthy children.

# Authors' Note

Experiencing a divorce is one of the most difficult things in life and there are so many people, all over the world, who are suffering the loss of their marriage and the breakdown of their family unit. Although circumstances vary - her husband left her, his wife left him, abuse, no abuse, children, no children - the common threads of divorce are the pain, loneliness, and wondering what the future will hold.

So many people who experience a divorce are searching—searching for love, for happiness and for peace. You are encouraged to look no further than the Catholic faith. Founded by Jesus Christ, its sacraments, its teachings and its 2,000 year history provide a rich treasure of spiritual reality, wisdom, and Truth. This book will help you tap into that richness and fullness of truth.

Before this book was published, it was the *Journey of Hope* program and it was offered in various parishes from 2002 to 2007. Through directing these groups, we have learned many things, but primarily that beginning each meeting with prayer was essential. We knew that everyone's time was precious and we wanted the meetings to be as fruitful as possible, so we began with prayer and put the Holy Spirit in charge of inspiring our thoughts and conversation. This way, every meeting was a good meeting.

The groups usually began by praying one decade of the rosary together, and the Prayer to the Holy Spirit, which is included on the next page. We strongly recommend doing the same before each chapter you read to invite the Holy Spirit to guide your thoughts and reflections, and ask Mary to obtain for you from her Son, the graces you need as you walk this path.

We also found that participants who actually acted on the resolutions at the end of each chapter and used a journal during their time in the group received far more benefit from the program than just by attending the meetings. We hope you can apply yourself in the same way, because your time, your life, your healing is very important – for you and for the ones who love you.

We will be praying for you. too.

# Prayer to the Holy Spirit

Come, Holy Spirit!

Replace the tension within us with a holy relaxation.

Replace the turbulence within us with a sacred calm.

Replace the anxiety within us with a quiet confidence.

Replace the fear within us with a strong faith.

Replace the bitterness within us with the sweetness of grace.

Replace the darkness within us with a gentle light.

Replace the coldness within us with a loving warmth.

Replace the night within us with your light.

Straighten our crookedness, fill our emptiness.

Dull the edge of our pride, sharpen the edge of our humility,

Light the fires of our love, quench the flames of our lust.

Let us see ourselves as you see us

that we may see you as you have promised

and be fortunate according to your word:

"Blessed are the pure of heart for they shall see God (Mt. 5: 8).

# Table of Contents

# Chapter One:

## Praying in Times of Distress

Pray, pray, pray! Christians say that all the time but when life is painful and full of strife, many people have a difficult time getting on their knees to pray. When life is harsh and stressful, prayer can be dry, hard to focus on, and yes, even painful to attempt. Many people abandon prayer when it becomes difficult.

What significance does the word "prayer" have for you? When you read that word – prayer – do you feel a sense of peace? Do you feel a sense of burden? Are you comforted by the thought of praying? Perhaps you feel a little guilty because it's been a while? By the time you finish this chapter, I believe the word "prayer" will be a source of consolation and strength for you.

God is often regarded as a foul weather friend. It seems we call out to him most when we are facing times of distress and uncertainty. For many, prayer is simply a scream for help when they find themselves plunged into the darkness of divorce. But not everyone has that kind of prayer life. Some people have very devout prayer lives and have a prayer regimen throughout their day. Some people pray once a week at church while others haven't prayed since they were required to do so as a child. Some use prayer as way to get closer to God, while others will pray just to cover all the bases. But prayer offers so much more then just a lifeline out of crisis!

> Is prayer your steering wheel or your spare tire?
> -- Corrie Ten Boom

In this chapter, we will discuss why praying during times of distress can be so difficult and address the importance of praying every day, not just when the storm clouds are gathering. We will look at different forms of prayer. You may be surprised to learn that prayer can be so much more than simply reciting written lines or verses you memorized when you were a child. We will examine the different ways to pray. And most importantly, we will describe how to develop a daily prayer routine that transforms your life, bringing the peace and healing you seek.

## The Case

Sometimes it can seem as if there is a mystique surrounding prayer – as if prayer is some magic formula requiring very specific words said in a precise order to be effective. The Catholic faith supplies us with a treasure of prayers, novenas, devotionals, etc., and at times, it can be confusing when trying to figure out which prayer we need to say. Who should we pray to? Jesus? Mary? The Saints? All of the above? This confusion can often to draw people away from prayer instead of toward it.

Here is how Craig feels about praying:

My divorce was the most difficult thing I ever had to go through. I had never experienced so much fear and pain in my life. The night my wife told me she was leaving, I dropped to my knees for the first time since I was a kid and begged God to make her change her mind. It felt strange to pray because it had been so long, but I believed it was what I needed to do. I wasn't sure what I should say; should I say the prayers I learned as a kid? Should I just make up something on my own? That night I threw in an Our Father and a Hail Mary for good measure.

For the next six months I prayed morning, noon, and night. Most of my prayers were the same: *Lord, please change her mind! Wake her up so she can see what she is doing!* While I didn't feel any different after I prayed, I didn't want to stop. I was afraid that if I stopped, none of my prayers would be answered.

Some of my Catholic friends encouraged me to keep praying and it seemed that each of them had a different suggestion as to how I should pray. One suggested I pray a novena, but I wasn't really sure what that was. Another suggested that I pray the rosary every day. I hadn't prayed the rosary since the nuns at school taught us how to recite it thirty years ago. Others suggested I pray to specific saints. My sister told me to make sure I went to adoration for an hour each week to pray. I knew they all meant well, but all they did was confuse me. I ended up doing most of my praying in the car to and from work. I would just talk to God as if he were my father. I was not sure if I was praying correctly, but it did make me feel better.

Frankly, I feel a little cynical about prayer right now. I prayed so hard for months during my divorce and it didn't change anything. In the end, my wife still left me. I sometimes wonder if things would have been different if I had prayed the way my friends had recommended. Maybe I didn't say the right prayers, in the right order, or at the right time? I still go to mass but I feel distant when I'm there . . . I have to admit I am feeling pretty disconnected from my faith. I hardly pray at all anymore and I am struggling to believe that my prayers really make any difference.

## Why Prayer is so Important

Where you go in life and how you get there, is determined by a series of endless decisions strung together. Each day offers the opportunity to take many different paths. Some will lead you to peace and joy and others to turmoil and sadness. This is the journey called life. Your life as a human being is comprised of both a physical and spiritual self, your body and your soul. You must nurture each one carefully and properly. If you don't, you will suffer the consequences and this is true for every human being. You know how to nurture your physical self; eat well, get enough sleep, exercise, and keep stress to a minimum if possible. The consequence of not doing so is also understood. To some degree or another you will get sick and be unable to live up to your full potential.

Since your spiritual self is not visible and with all that you are bombarded with each day it is easy to ignore the health of your soul and fail completely to nurture it. Unlike your physical self, you can't use physical instruments to take your spiritual vital signs. Only by looking inward can you gain a sense for how spiritually "healthy" you are. Often, it is only in looking back that you can understand the effects of poor decisions that resulted from a poorly formed conscience. Prayer is the means to nurture your spiritual life, allowing you to form a more sensitive conscience. This results in better decision-making and a happier life that is aligned with God's will. When your life is aligned with God's will, you find peace and joy each day, and become better equipped to meet life's challenges.

Unfortunately, prayer is often overlooked, or worse still, is ignored. In the crush of everyday life, many just "don't have the time" to pray. The result is a "spiritual couch potato" too weak to fend off worldly temptations and too ill prepared when called on to make sound decisions. When a major crisis comes into their lives, they are more apt to suffer a spiritual stroke than to handle it with any sense of poise and confidence.

## Spiritual Fitness Training

What physical exercise does for the body, prayer does for the soul. And like physical exercise, prayer must be done routinely to have a lasting effect. Unfortunately, many try to "pump up" during times of crisis with intense prayer, but fail to maintain a life of regular daily prayer. Once the crisis is over, the praying stops and the soul once again becomes flabby. This is not a program for a lifetime of spiritual vitality.

Simply put, daily prayer is the exercise program for the soul. It fortifies you spiritually and enables you to meet the challenges of each day with a positive attitude and with a sense of hope. It acts as a "spiritual immune system" allowing you to fight off temptation and avoid sin. And just as people who exercise regularly are more in-tune with their bodies, people who pray regularly are more in-tune to the promptings of the Holy Spirit. This allows them to better sense when they are veering off track from God's will and are more able to call on the spiritual strength they need to get back on track.

But why is it so difficult to pray in times of distress? Well, particularly, because the emotions you are feeling including fear, sadness, anger, depression and discouragement, are contrary to the peace and happiness that makes prayer easy to do. When you feel these intense negative emotions, your prayers, and every day life at that, can become dry, out of focus, and frustrating. It's normal to want to feel great after you pray; you want to see some fruit come from your efforts! So when prayer is difficult, it's easier to leave it aside with an attitude of discouragement. *My life is difficult enough right now. God knows I love him and that will have to be enough for the time being. I will try it again when I'm feeling better.*

This exact point is where you miss out on some huge benefits! Two major things happen when you persevere in prayer despite the challenge:

- First, if you lived your life simply at the whim of your feelings, basing all your actions on how you felt at the time, you would be living like an animal. An animal has no ability to reason and has no free will. But God gave humans these gifts, and when you use your free will to motivate yourself to do something good, especially during times of adversity, there is an ennobling effect that results in your personal growth and maturity. So many times, we see people who have suffered greatly during their lives and as a result have great character, integrity and strength. It is in taking steps like this, praying even when you don't feel like it, that those great virtues come into place.

- Second, true love is not an emotion, it is an act of the will . . . willing the good of another person. When you pray, even though everything in you would like to turn away, this is a perfect example of true love for God and it is something he will bless you for. You can decide not to pray because it's hard and doesn't feel good and God understands that. He will still be waiting for you to come to him, even so. However, if you decide to pray despite the difficulty, God is very pleased and the graces he rewards you with are innumerable.

## Never Give Up!

Here is a great analogy that illustrates these points:

Imagine a bridegroom waking up on the day of his wedding and much to his dismay he's late! The alarm clock didn't ring and by this time he should already be at the church! What will his bride be thinking? *I can't waste a second!* is what he thinks as he rushes to shower and dress. A short while later he runs out the door and gets into the car. As he drives away from the house, he realizes he has forgotten his cuff links. *I can't stop now, I need to get to the church so my bride will not think I've changed my mind. Better late with no cuff links than miss my own wedding to go back and get them*, he rationalizes. Suddenly, there is a loud noise and the car begins to bump violently. *Flat tire! How can this be happening?* The bridegroom gets out of the car and getting out his tools and spare, begins to change the tire. Now, he is really, *really* late! *But I will do this and get to the church still in time to marry my bride.*

About fifteen minutes later, he has tightened the last lug nut and put away his tools. Closing the trunk, he turns to get back in the car and as he approaches the driver's side door, a bus drives by, splattering him with mud. The bridegroom looks at his clothes, utterly distressed, but then looks at his watch. *If I don't stop for anything else, I might make it. I hope my bride hasn't given up on me!*

Finally, the bridegroom arrives at the church only to find the parking lot empty. Everyone has gone home. He hangs his head as he walks inside the church to see what he missed. He is sorrowful and afraid of what his bride might be thinking. As he walks up the aisle, the bride sees him from the altar where she had been sitting on the steps. She certainly had felt he had changed his mind but when she sees him and his dirty clothes, his wrecked hair and the sadness on his face, she is filled with love for him. She doesn't care about the way he looks or the flat tire. She can see what he's been through and the fact that he persevered, he never gave up the fight to reach her, made her love him all the more. *He didn't give up on me!* The bride and the groom run to each other and kiss.

This is so much the way God loves us. We struggle, we're distracted, we're late, stuff happens. But our muddy clothing or flat tires are not what God takes note of. He is pleased by the fact that we don't give up. That's all he asks of us, that we persevere.

## The Freedom to Choose

Oftentimes, if you are used to praying in a certain way, for example, if you are used to saying traditional prayers such as the Our Father, Hail Mary and Glory Be, you might find it difficult to focus your thoughts on your prayer. You might feel too angry, too numb, or whatever the emotion may be that is becoming a stumbling block to praying. But the beautiful thing about prayer is that there's not just one way, but many ways to communicate with God, thus you have options. Who doesn't like to have choices? If one form of praying doesn't work, try another. The important thing, of course, is to pray because prayer is how we remain connected to Christ, who is our life. Without prayer, we cannot remain connected to him.

Well, what is prayer exactly? Prayer is conversation . . . simple and loving communication with God. In thoughts, words, and even actions, such as when you offer what you do to God for his glory. The best disposition for prayer is to put yourself in God's presence meaning, wherever you are and whatever is going on at the time, imagine God with you and believe that he is present. Acknowledge him as being there by your side, listening to you, for he always is. And once you have put yourself in his presence, you can begin to communicate with him.

Prayer should be heartfelt and not contrived. God wants your heart to be open to him. It's the same as holding a conversation with someone you can see . . . if you were distracted and focused on other things, the other person would be aware of that and know you weren't really focused on him. Well, there is no difference here, either. So, find whatever disposition you can that is the most conducive to being in God's presence and use that for your regular prayer. However, when you cannot find that place or when life is just too demanding, simply imagining God with you, walking beside you, listening to you is the perfect time to talk to him. You can do it riding the bus or sweeping the floor. You can do it in an Adoration chapel or riding your bike.

St. Teresa of Avila, one of the greatest saints of the Church, had a beautiful way of praying that she referred to as "the interior castle." Saint Teresa described the interior castle as her innermost self and her method of praying was this: of all the many rooms in the castle, there was one particular room reserved for meeting with God. When she entered the room, she would be alone with Christ and felt free to tell him everything, hold back nothing, and receive all that he gave her. She would go to that room often to meet with Christ and there, she would find all the strength and hope she needed to continue her work. For people who are visual, this is an effective form of prayer, especially during times of great distress.

But there are many other forms of prayer as well. All of them are good and a powerful means to keeping you connected to Christ. It's simply a matter of finding which one works for you during your time of difficulty.

1. **Rote prayer** is praying the standard prayers we may know or have grown up with, such as participating in mass, reciting the Rosary, praying novenas to any of the saints, praying litanies of the saints or the litany of

Mary, or praying devotionals such as the Chaplet of Divine Mercy. Of course, mass is the most excellent form of prayer because it allows us to participate in Christ's sacrifice for us. These types of prayers may be the perfect route to communication with God for you, especially if your prayer life thrives in the structure and guidance that these formulated prayers provide.

2. **Spontaneous prayer** is a beautiful form of prayer, and it involves speaking sincerely with God from your heart without any pre-written formula; simply speaking to God as the words come to you. For people who are angry or dealing with powerful emotions, sometimes this is the best form of prayer because it allows them the freedom to speak frankly with God. This type of spontaneous conversation with God is just as effective as any other form of prayer. Spontaneous prayer is praying in the moment, conversing as you go through the day, doing your work or taking time to sit quietly and enjoy the silence. In addition, if finding time to be silent and reflect is difficult, any activity that is offered up to God for his glory and honor is a beautiful prayer as well. So taking one moment to say, "Lord, I offer you this work I am about to do," and then performing it to the best of your ability is an excellent prayer.

3. **Meditation**: Some people find that when they are in great distress and cannot focus on other types of prayer, doing a meditation is their best form of conversation with God. Doing a meditation is simple and consists of choosing a gospel passage to read, meditating on it by picturing yourself in the story and conversing with Christ as he was in the passage. An example of this would be meditating on the gospel passage of the beatitudes ( Matthew 5: 1 – 11) . . . imagine yourself sitting on the hillside on a sunny, breezy day, listening to Jesus preach to the crowd. You hear his words and you can see his face, you can sense the love with which he speaks. You are sitting close to him, so talk to him; ask him the questions that burn in your heart. And then listen to him . . . what is his response? Sometimes when you are in great pain, try placing yourself in one of the scenes from Christ's passion . . . read about his scourging and torture and place yourself in the crowd watching; meet him on the road as he carries his cross to his death, or place yourself at the foot of the cross . . . listen to his mother and Mary Magdalene weep as they watch him die, hear the taunts of the drunken soldiers and the jeers from the angry crowd . . . feel

the blood drip onto your face as the flies buzz around. As you kneel there at the foot of the cross and experience this scene, look up at Christ and talk to him; tell him about your suffering, tell him how you feel and listen to his response . . . he will give you one.

4. **Prayer in song** is yet another great way to pray. A simple, silent song inside yourself, like humming the tune to "How Great Thou Art," or driving and listening to Christian music is an excellent way to pray because the music and lyrics lift our hearts and minds to God. Singing to the Lord has often been described as praying twice!

5. **God's creation**: Finally, a simple and exhilarating prayer is in experiencing God's creation and responding to him with praise for his works. And here, the possibilities for praise are endless. The desert, the mountains, flying in an airplane, taking a boat ride . . . isn't it amazing that we can have 300 cable channels to watch and become bored, but sit down on the beach and stay there for hours? That's no mistake; it's the glory of God's creation. He made it for us so we can know him. Going to the mountains for a hike or canoeing on the lake will easily bring the Creator's greatness to the forefront and as we take in the fantastic beauty of it all, we can respond with gratitude for the glorious creation and for giving it to us humans, stewards of nature. So many people feel at peace with God when they go to find him in nature. It is yet another way to lift our hearts and minds to God and speak with him.

> For me, prayer is a surge of the heart; it is a simple look turned toward heaven, it is a cry of recognition and of love, embracing both trial and joy.
> – St. Therese of Lisieux

## How to Develop a Daily Prayer Life

We have addressed why daily prayer is the cornerstone to a peaceful and fulfilling life and the many ways we can pray. Now let's talk about how do develop a regular prayer routine. Like an exercise program, to be successful, you need to identify a time slot each day that will help ensure success. If you try to cram it in between two other priorities, chances are very good one of the other priorities will win out. It is better to find the time each day where you are most likely to have 20-30 uninterrupted minutes. It can be first thing in the morning before you start the day. It can be during the drive into work or during lunch, or in the evening. It really doesn't matter when it is, just make sure that it is the same time each day and that you are not too tired.

Once you have identified the time you are going to pray each day, determine how you are going to pray. We have previously described many types of prayer. Choose the one that seems to suit you best. Again, as with exercise, don't try and overdo it. While it might seem that praying two rosaries is better than praying one, and praying three better than two, it does no good if you can't keep it up every day. Once you have firmly established your prayer routine, you can begin to try other forms of prayer. It is very effective to incorporate other forms of prayer into your routine to keep from getting spiritually stale.

It is also very important to prepare your mind for prayer. An effective way to do this is to create a special place to pray. The use of candles, statues, a crucifix, or other spiritual icons will help put you in a good spiritual posture. You will find yourself relaxing and more readily opening your heart and mind to God than by creating a physically spiritual place. This is why prayer in front of the Blessed Sacrament is so effective. There is no better way to open your heart and mind to God, than by being physically present with him.

Another effective way to complement your daily prayer is with prepared meditations and daily devotionals. There is an abundance of these materials in bookstores, via subscription, and on the Internet. (See the suggested reading for a list of some of these resources.) Typically, they provide a daily scripture reading along with a prepared mediation and prayers. These are very good at providing you with a framework in which to pray. They are also very helpful for those days when you are feeling spiritually dry or can't find the words to pray. What you will typically find is that starting out with these prepared mediations and devotionals will "kick start" your daily prayer allowing you to better identify and dig into those issues that are most important to you.

No matter how diligent you are in your prayer routine, there are going to be days that don't go as planned. Be ready for those. Keep a rosary in the car. Keep spiritual meditations on your iPod or on a CD. Keep a book of devotionals in your briefcase or purse. This will allow you to take advantage of prayer times that might open up during the day.

Once you get into the habit of daily prayer, you will receive the fruits of a vibrant spiritual life, including more peace, less anxiety, more confidence when dealing with difficult issues, a deeper sense of purpose, better decisions, more resolve to battle temptation, and less sin. All of these come from God and the Holy Spirit. And as with exercise, you may not see these results right away. Stay with your prayer program. Once you tap into the power of prayer, you will be transformed. You will have opened up a pipeline directly to God and he will continually nurture your spirit and guide you.

# Meditation

## Luke 11: 9 – 13

So I say to you: Ask, and it will be given to you; search and you will find; knock and the door will be opened to you. For everyone who asks receives; everyone who searches finds; everyone who knocks will have the door opened. What father among you, if his son asked for a fish, would hand him a snake? Or if he asked for an egg, hand him a scorpion? If you then, evil as you are, know how to give your children what is good, how much more will the heavenly Father give the Holy Spirit to those who ask him!

**Opening prayer**: Dear Lord, I come before you with many concerns, many deep pains and I seek healing. I want to know you better, and hear what it is you would like me to know. As I spend this time with you, help me to leave behind anything that might get in the way of our conversation. I trust in your mercy and your love.

**Petition**: I ask you, Lord, for the grace to open myself to you in faith and hope.

1. *Confidence is the key.*

   God wants you to have confidence in him. When Jesus was on earth, he taught us how to pray, both in word and example. When he prayed, Jesus referred to the Father in heaven in a term that the Jews were not accustomed to using in prayer. He called the Father, "Abba," which means "daddy." Christ was showing us how to approach God in prayer; with the affection and trust that a child has for his daddy. Even when Christ was beginning his passion and went to the Garden of Gethsemane, he walked into the garden, knelt down by the rock and cried, "Abba" (*cf.* Mark 14:36). In this, your suffering and passion, approach God with confidence and affection, believing he hears you and will help you.

2. *Ask, search, knock.*

Life is not just a box of chocolates! That old saying is a quaint way of addressing the surprises of life, but if you believe in the goodness of God, "Abba," and his desire to help you, that saying falls short of the truth. God doesn't sit passively up in heaven and watch life hit you from all angles nor does he sit idly by while you struggle to deal with your difficulties. God wants you to come to him with your sufferings, your concerns, your requests, your desires and plans. He wants you to know that he is waiting for you, every moment of the day and at every turn. And if it is true you should approach God as a trusting child approaches his father, it is even more true that "Abba" will give you what you need. He is waiting for your permission to help you; he is seeking that open heart that welcomes him in and allows him to work. Are you open to allowing God to help you?

**Closing Prayer**: I am consoled, Lord, to know that you love me and want to help me. Increase my trust in you, Lord, and my desire to speak to you more often, for I know that you are the one who can truly help me. I pray for these and all things in your name. Amen.

# Resolution

Before you move on to the next chapter, review the "Freedom to Choose" section of this chapter again and select a form of prayer you would like to practice. Try and incorporate that new way of praying into your day and set aside a time for prayer.

# Suggested Readings

<u>Magnificat</u>, published monthly www.magnificat.com

<u>The Word Among Us</u>, published monthly www.wau.org

A. J. Russell, *God Calling*, Jove (June 27, 2006)

Thomas a Kempis, *The Imitation of Christ*, Vintage; Rev Sub edition (March 24, 1998)

Nan Merrill, *Psalms for Praying,* Continuum International Publishing Group; 10 Anv edition (December 18, 2006)

# Chapter Two:

# Anger with Your Spouse, Yourself, and God

In this chapter, let's take a look at anger and how it is manifesting itself in your life at this time. Do you wake up and go to sleep angry? Are you short on patience? Is anger an excuse to do things you wouldn't normally do? Do you forget about praying because you are angry? There may be many different manifestations of anger in your life right now, and some that you may not recognize. But it is important to begin to recognize the warning signals that are associated with anger because the sooner you can get a firm handle on this powerful emotion, the sooner you can plant your feet firmly on the road to some true, meaningful healing.

Anger is a God-given emotion and is a completely normal reaction to things or circumstances that threaten our physical, emotional or spiritual well-being. It is normal to want to defend ourselves and our loved ones from these threats. For most people, the typical way to respond to hurt and anger are indignation and strong words. Many people report feeling remorseful after communicating angrily toward the person who hurt them.

However, there are many angry people in the world who have extreme difficulty controlling their emotions. Terrible things happen when anger is allowed to skyrocket into rage and the rage goes unchecked, and people allow their rage to become the excuse for bad behavior. Road rage, abuse within the family, substance abuse, and much larger, serious crimes occur as a result of anger and rage.

Many people never realize they don't have to be victims of their own emotions. Unless there is an actual mental disorder involved (such as bi-polar disorder) you don't have to allow your emotions to run your life. You have choices and you can choose to be in control of your emotions, even rage.

The goal of this chapter is to identify some of the key symptoms of anger, identify how this emotion may be manifesting itself in your life, and equip yourself with positive, healthy ways to deal with your anger and to set out on the road to forgiveness. Let's also consider the examples Jesus has given that can help you in this difficult time.

## The Case

You probably never imagined that you would find yourself in this position, yet here you are, separated and in the process of the civil dissolution of your marriage. You gave your word at the altar! Your marriage was supposed to last forever, but something went wrong.

Maybe you are past this stage and everything has been divided, finalized and legalized, and now you're beginning to build a new foundation for your life. Maybe many years have gone by since your divorce and you have done a lot of different things by this point, but still feel the need to revisit some issues related to your divorce. Whatever stage you happen to be in, it won't take much effort to vividly recall the circumstances that got you to this place in your life.

Here's what Kayla, a woman divorced for one year, says about her experience:

Looking back at those first three months or so, I remember how I was simply permeated with shock, horror and sadness. It was unconscionable for me to think that my twelve-year relationship with my spouse would end. On my wedding day, I didn't stand at the altar before God, family and friends, pledging my life to another, only to think, "I can always get out if I want to," or, "You don't have to stay together if you find you don't love each other anymore." Nor could I have imagined that my spouse would ever dream of thinking these same thoughts. Despite this commitment I had made for the rest of my life, I watched my marriage fall apart and there was nothing I could do to stop it.

I was angry for being lied to, for being played as such a fool, for giving my husband the benefit of the doubt. I was angry because he never told his family the real story and they believed his lies. Most of all, I was angry because I didn't stand at the altar in front of family and friends the day I got married and pledged my life to him just so I could leave when things got uncomfortable or inconvenient. I married for life. It was my world, my future, my dream!

As the days advanced, I realized my anger was not only directed at my soon-to-be ex-spouse, but also toward God. How could God let this happen to me? Didn't he hear my prayers? Didn't he see me in pieces on the floor? Didn't he hear me crying out to him? Didn't he know the anguish in my heart? I was a good Catholic! How could he let this happen to me?

So, there I was alone in my empty house. Abandoned by my husband and no hope of him coming back, it seemed. I had cried my tears dry, I couldn't eat a thing, I had drunk a lot of wine that night to get myself to fall asleep. And there were much deeper emotions that had been brewing and bubbling during that first week after he left and now they were beginning to erupt. So what was I going to do? Would I face my anger or avoid it?

With each day that passed, I came to a deeper realization that my life would never be the same. Even though I was able to put a smile on my face around other people—fake as it was—I was crying out to them on the inside, holding my hands out for them to grab and support me in some way, but knowing the whole time that there was absolutely nothing anyone could do. It was a terrible feeling, but with each experience I was forced to recognize this change—this awful change.

I was embarking on a long and difficult journey and the decisions I make from this point forward would probably have a profound impact on who I would be in the future. These decisions—all these many decisions I would have to make from that point forward—they hurt, but they were certainly opportunities to change. I tried to think of the bad things in terms of choices I could make: Will I cry myself sick today or will I be strong and try to take a step forward, even if it's just a small one? Will I at least try to eat lunch or some sort of dinner, or will I allow my grief to completely consume me and destroy any appetite I may have had? Will I think angry, horrible thoughts about my ex-spouse or his family, or will I say one small, short prayer and ask God to forgive him, to help him?

In the very depths of my heart, I understood that even though I didn't reach that far down very often, I knew each decision essentially equated to this: Will I allow my divorce to drag me down, lose all hope, all trust, and become bitter, or will I let my pain motivate me to move forward, to learn some lessons about life, to search for hope in my future? Will I allow myself to become a victim, or will I use my pain in a positive way?

Anger and disillusionment were clouding my vision, distorting my perception of what was happening. I needed direction, advice, understanding and consolation.

## Recognizing the Signs of Anger

Sometimes, the ways that intense emotions can take over are not easily recognized, particularly in their subtle forms. Does anger make you lose control of your temper when you talk to your ex-spouse? Does anger make you moody, shy away from social situations or do things you wouldn't normally do (drink in excess, over-eat, shop without limits, react to people or situations in a "knee-jerk" fashion, etc.)? Does anger make you feel guilty? All this may stem from years and years of built-up resentments that have never been addressed. Possibly, the anger stems from painful feelings of betrayal – deliberate lies that shredded the mutual trust agreement essential to marriage. No matter what the circumstances, many times the anger results from what your heart perceives to be a "lie": that your marriage was supposed to last forever, and it didn't.

Anger is a natural human emotion that stimulates you to respond to danger, hurt or threatening circumstances. Therefore, anger in and of itself is not wrong, but useful. But it's what you do with it that makes it wrong. Many experts agree that intense anger serves as a flashing light or warning sign that you need to pay attention to because if left unattended, the building emotions could become a problem and possibly get out of control. It is very important to be able to recognize some of the warning signs of emotions that are unchecked. The following are some warning signs:

- muscle tension and pinched nerves not caused by physical stress
- accelerated heartbeat
- upset stomach, knots or aching
- breathing rapidly and feeling intense anxiety
- flushed in the face

More serious signs of anger that need to be addressed include:

- loss of temper on a daily basis
- a beginning or an increase in abusive language, which may include swearing and using profanity
- an "I just don't care" attitude toward daily life and people
- an increase in risk-taking behavior
- the start of or increase in drinking alcohol in excess or using illegal or prescription drugs for the sole purpose of altering feelings
- becoming physically aggressive towards others
- loss of appetite and weight

Most of these symptoms accompany two or three others at a time and result in dangerous behavior. This doesn't mean a person reacting this way is suddenly a criminal; it simply means the anger needs to be recognized, acknowledged, and addressed before it becomes destructive.

In your case, the anger is real and most likely justifiable because either you were abandoned by your ex-spouse, or you filed for divorce and feel that you were pushed into taking your absolute last resort—the one thing you never believed you would ever do. Especially if you see your ex-spouse on a regular basis (for the sake of children, etc.), anger can resurface and remain longer than it might otherwise.

## What does Scripture Say?

In order to begin to focus yourself on the future and not remain stuck in the past, you need to address this issue of anger from a different perspective—a positive one. You want to understand this problem and learn to control your anger so it doesn't control you.

Let's take a look at how Jesus would handle a similar situation. It's so easy to think of God as some cloudy, distant figure who has little interest in our lives and only stands in judgement. While it is true that Christ is our Judge, we need to recognize that he is first our loving Savior; the one who sacrificed everything for our sake. And so look to him in his humanity because he understands your anger perfectly. Let's read from the Gospel of John:

When the time of the Jewish Passover was near Jesus went up to Jerusalem, and in the Temple he found people selling cattle and sheep and doves, and the money changers sitting there. Making a whip out of cord, he drove them all out of the Temple, sheep and cattle as well, scattered the money changers' coins, knocked their tables over and said to the dove sellers, "Take all this out of here and stop using my Father's house as a market" (John 2: 13- 19).

Jesus was equally God and equally man; 100 percent human and 100 percent divine. The emotions he experienced were the same that you experience. In this passage, note how Jesus had righteous anger and there was no mistaking what he was trying to say: *stop!* Stop this horrendous behavior! But it is important to note that this image of an angry Christ is not the primary depiction the gospels give us of him. Although it's certain that he had many frustrations, heartaches and miseries, Jesus' primary teaching was charity.

Your anger is most likely of the same nature as Jesus'—righteous anger. You may feel the same way Jesus did, and want to shout: "Stop! Stop this behavior! Give me back my wife! My husband! Give me back the one I fell in love with!" But in dealing with it, you can't go yelling and screaming and turning over tables. And so you need to approach dealing with your anger in a way that helps you preserve (or find) charity. It might be difficult, but it is possible.

## Managing Anger

What if you could use your anger in a constructive fashion? What would your life look like if you were able to make positive changes out of such a negative emotion? Being in control of your anger—instead of allowing anger to control you—is a major step toward healing.

So, let's look at how you can "manage" your anger. It's important to understand that manage doesn't mean ignore or suppress. In this sense, "manage" refers to "channeling."

For example, instead of acting aggressively on your anger by speaking hurtful words or breaking something, use your overwhelming emotion as energy to fuel a positive action. Don't stay inside and break the dishes—go play a hard and fast game of racquet ball with a friend. Do some yard work or go jogging. Any activity that will allow you to release your anger in a constructive fashion is good.

St. John Vianney was known for channeling his anger. He would take great care in the presence of whoever was frustrating him to be calm and charitable. Yet, if you looked closely you would see a twisted and knotted handkerchief in his hands that received all the punishment—never the people around him.

In conjunction with channeling, forgiveness is also highly important in managing anger. FORGIVENESS?? Does your spouse deserve it? Could it ever be possible?

> **Any activity that will allow you to release your anger in a constructive fashion is good.**

This issue of forgiveness will be discussed further in an upcoming chapter, but for now let's take into consideration some good reasons to try to begin letting go of anger.

- Anger is a complete waste of your energy.
- Anger is a complete waste of your time—precious time that you cannot regain.
- Anger distorts your perception of things.
- Anger does not promote love—the love you profess to have in your heart.
- Anger does not promote peace—the peace you can't live without.
- Prolonged anger can take a physical toll on your body.
- Anger prohibits healing.

*Wouldn't you rather heal?*

## Concluding Thoughts

It may be difficult to envision forgiving your spouse and letting go of anger. Particularly when a marriage ends, forgiveness is something that is not accomplished overnight. It takes constant effort. Again, you are feeling righteous anger and you may believe you have been unjustly hurt, especially if you have done everything in your power to keep your marriage and family together.

You may also feel reluctant to forgive, because that would mean your ex-spouse gets away with hurting you; as if suddenly, the offender is just let off the hook, relieved of all responsibility for what he or she has done. It may seem that way to the casual observer, but it simply isn't true. The reality is that everyone has to stand before God in judgement and be accountable for their lives; you do as well as your spouse. And you know that nothing escapes God. Another important reason to consider forgiveness is that when you cling to anger and resentment, you are the one who is unhappy. You can't make the offender feel as bad as you do, although you might think that would bring you some relief. Holding on to the anger simply prolongs your own unhappiness. So despite the pain, work on letting go of your anger so you can stand before God with a clean heart.

It is precisely at this point that you need to turn your heart towards the true Victim—Christ. He is the one who, above all other humans, suffered unjustifiably. And he suffered willingly because of the sins of everyone. And despite the injustice, he loves you with a love bigger and deeper than you can ever understand. When you think of Jesus on the cross and realize how he forgives you for your own failures, you can come to the realization that you must forgive (even if it's eventually). Therefore, you must set out on that road to forgiveness, however rocky, and take the journey day-by-day.

Forgiveness, anger, divorce, moving forward—these are all painful issues and certainly not things that you take lightly. Forgiveness won't come in a day, nor will the disappearance of anger; the only way to move forward is one day at a time. So go chop some wood or paint that room that's been needing a new look. The options for releasing your anger in a constructive manner are endless. But take note that the way you handle your suffering right now will shape the kind of person you will be in the future. You can become bitter and resentful, but your divorce can change you for the better. In the midst of your pain and difficulty, if you open your heart to God he will make you stronger and wiser.

> The way to overcome the devil when he excites
> feelings of hatred for those who injure us
> is to immediately pray for their conversion.
> - St. John Vianney

# Now What?

After reading this chapter, hopefully you are able to understand the importance of managing and channeling your anger. It is quite possible you are thinking, I'm so mad right now, I don't want to manage or channel it constructively—I want to take it out on my ex-spouse! I want him or her to know how bad the pain is that I am feeling! And maybe nothing would make you feel better—that is, at this moment. Chances are any action you take in the heat of anger will be regretted later. There is a better way. That is what this section is about. It's about finding ways to help you take all the pent-up emotion and energy and use it in a constructive fashion—some way that it will help, not hurt. Here are a few ideas:

1. **Journal**: Maybe you had a diary as a kid and figured that journaling was something you grew out of in the 10th grade. Now is the time to rethink that. Journaling is a great way to be totally honest with yourself. It is the perfect place to say exactly what you are thinking and make yourself feel better without hurting anyone. The Workbook companion contains all you need to get started. Whenever you feel the emotions building, get out this handy journal and just start writing. Say everything you want to say, exactly as you want to say it. No holds barred. The key is NOT to censure your thoughts. Your journal needs to be that one safe channel where you can let it all hang out. Try it, it works.

2. **Write a letter:** Write a letter to your ex-spouse telling him or her exactly how you feel, how mad you really are at them, how much they have hurt you, etc. This is not something you will ever give to them, but simply an opportunity to get rid of some of the toxic feelings that are poisoning your heart. In this letter, give yourself the luxury of telling your ex-spouse everything you really want him or her to know. Again, the key is to get it all out, holding nothing back. Once you are done with the letter, take it over to your shredder and shred it, or go over to your fireplace and burn it. It is fine to tuck the letter away in your files, or sit on it for a few days before destroying it. But, whatever you do don't send it to your ex-spouse.

3. **Vent:** Go to a place where you know you are alone and no one can hear you. Good places for this are in your house when no one is home, in your car, or on a nature trail. This is basically verbal journaling, but you are by yourself and no one can hear what you are saying. Pretend your ex-spouse is right in front of you and, just as in writing a letter, you have the luxury of saying everything you really want to say. If you feel like yelling at the top of your lungs, then yell! Cry! Allow yourself to have an emotional outburst and start releasing the anger—letting go of the emotional pollution. You have extremely valid reasons to be angry. It is healthy to get those feelings of anger out in this way.

4. **Exercise:** When you are angry, your body creates adrenalin. At a base level, that adrenalin is preparing you for a fight. Since physical fighting is not a healthy way to deal with the anger, yet there is all this adrenalin racing through your veins, a great way to expend that adrenalin is through vigorous exercise. This could be fast walking, jogging, bike riding, racquetball, etc. The key is that it is vigorous enough for you to work up a sweat. A leisurely stroll is not going to do it. Of course, make sure that whatever you do, you are in the proper physical shape to do it. Make exercise a regular habit and not only will you find yourself less angry, you will be healthier. That can only be a good thing.

5. **Find peace:** Think back to those times in your life when you were more carefree, when life was simple. What types of things did you really enjoy doing? How did you really enjoy spending your time? What hobbies did you have? What activities did you do? What music did you listen to? Pick one of these things and do it. Even if it brings you just one minute of peace in the midst of your turmoil, it is productive. The idea is to find that one thing that brings you peace and make that part of your daily routine. Not only will you find your anger will diminish, but those moments of peace will grow in duration and frequency.

6. **Pray:** This is easier said than done sometimes, especially when you are angry. This is where devotionals can be so helpful because you don't need to think of the words to say, they are already written for you. Also, picking the right time to pray is key as well. You may find that you are less tense and anxious after you have exercised or after journaling. In any case, the best time to pray is always when you can. Here are some ideas:

- Pray the rosary with an intention before each decade:

  1st Decade: Prayer for patience
  2nd Decade: Prayer for fortitude
  3rd Decade: Prayer for trust
  4th Decade: Prayer for peace
  5th Decade: Prayer for forgiveness

- Pray the Divine Mercy Chaplet, offering an intention before each decade.

- Go to a private place or a church (ideally with the Blessed Sacrament present) and "vent" to God. Really pour yourself out to God. Tell him how much you hurt. Tell him how mad you are. Know that he loves you more than you can ever imagine and wants to help you. Ask for his help and believe that help will come, remembering that he will never abandon you.

7. **Hug your child** (or family member): It is easy to get consumed in your own anger and hurt when a divorce or separation occurs. One way to help alleviate that is to focus on those around you who love you unconditionally. Your children, family and friends are true gifts. They are a channel of God's love to you. When you take time to recognize and appreciate that, a sense of balance returns to your life. This helps take the intensity out of the anger and pain.

# Meditation

## Matthew 5: 38 - 48

"You have heard that it was said, 'An eye for an eye, a tooth for a tooth.' But I say to you, do not resist an evil person; but whoever slaps you on your right cheek, turn the other to him also. If anyone wants to sue you and take your shirt, let him have your coat also. Whoever forces you to go one mile, go with him two. Give to him who asks of you, and do not turn away from him who wants to borrow from you.

"You have heard that it was said, 'You shall love your neighbor and hate your enemy.' But I say to you, love your enemies and pray for those who persecute you, so that you may be sons of your Father who is in heaven; for He causes His sun to rise on the evil and the good, and sends rain on the righteous and the unrighteous. For if you love those who love you, what reward do you have? Do not even the tax collectors do the same? If you greet only your brothers, what more are you doing than others? Do not even the Gentiles do the same? Therefore you are to be perfect, as your heavenly Father is perfect."

**Opening Prayer:**  Dear Lord, Father, Son and Holy Spirit, I thank you for this time to spend with you. I come to you today with a heart full of concerns and a mind distracted by details. I put them all in your hands, Lord, and pray that you will guide me and bring me closer to you.

**Petition:** I pray you will grant me peace of heart and mind Lord, that I may gain the clarity and simplicity I need to deal with all I have at hand.

1. *Turn the Other Cheek?!?*

   What is it that God is really asking of you in this passage? Is He asking you to be a doormat, letting anyone and everyone walk all over you, abuse you and become a victim? No. God is asking us to love in a way that is contrary to the way society loves. Society preaches a "feel good" love, so as long as it feels good, love, and when it doesn't feel good anymore, stop. This definition is false, for love is most vividly displayed when things are difficult and painful, yet a person still remains loyal, still seeks the good of the other, and still does not allow angry sentiments to rule his thoughts. It is easy to look at someone who has hurt us and say, "That person doesn't deserve my love." But contemplate Christ on the cross . . . the torture, the whipping, the insults, the spitting, the pain! That couldn't have felt good, yet Christ endured his torture and pain out of sheer love for us, even though we do not deserve it.

2. *Love your enemies and pray for those who persecute you.*

   It is easy to love and care for those whom you like; those who make you happy or whom you feel comfortable with. It is certainly harder to want to do anything for someone you dislike or have bad feelings toward. But it is hard to find the reward in simply "taking care of our own." If you truly want to find healing and peace in your life and move forward to a better place, you need to step outside your comfort zone.

You need to ask God for the grace to forgive others, to find love where there is none, to remember that He loves every one of us and wants us to be in heaven with Him for eternity. He wants each of us to be saints, including the people you can't stand or harbor resentment toward. Ask God for the grace to love.

**Closing Prayer:** Lord, you know all things. You know my heart and all that I have suffered. I pray for the grace to love others, despite how I may have been offended by them. Please help me, Lord. I trust in you.

# Resolution

Set aside thirty minutes sometime this week to be alone. The place is not extremely important, but choose a place with few or no distractions, such as a park, a church, etc. Don't bring a cellular phone! Use this time to really speak to God about your situation. If you get angry or upset, this is fine. He is the right person to share your anger with. If you find it becomes too difficult, just remember that Christ wants to help us, but he can't unless you allow him. Try to imagine how much he loves you. Pray for his help in your life.

# Suggested Reading

Conrad W., M.D. Baars, *Feeling & Healing Your Emotions*, Bridge-Logos (February 2003)

Jordan Aumann and Conrad Baars, *The Unquiet Heart: Reflections on Love and Sexuality*, Alba House (December 1991)

# Chapter Three:

# Why Did God Allow
# This to Happen to Me?

In this chapter, let's consider the possibility that there is more to your situation than what you see. This can be difficult because there are so many details that have your attention right now, and for good reason. The changes in your life have given you more to deal with than you bargained for, and the stress of the situation can filter the way you see things. Despite all of this, there is a bigger picture. It's time to take a step outside of yourself, stand beside Christ, and try to see what he sees. He already knows the whole story, so take this time to ask him the questions you have about what is happening.

Does God really have a plan? Was this divorce part of his plan? It seems difficult to believe that he would want such terrible pain and suffering to be a part of his great design. How about the way in which divorce affects children? They suffer tremendously for so many reasons; could that really be part of God's plan too? How could a loving God allow these terrible things to happen?

Some people don't believe in God, and instead believe that life is simply what you make of it. They believe each individual is in control of his own destiny and things that happen are either something he made happen, or are just a bunch of unrelated circumstances and occurrences.

Other people believe that God is present and watching over everyone, but does not have a plan because that might constitute predestination and be an infringement of our personal freedom of choice. With this perspective also comes the assumption that whatever happens in life is either something we made happen or simply a coincidence, accident or some other non-related occurrence.

There are also those people who believe God has a plan. They believe that at all times, good or bad, easy or difficult, God is not only aware of what is happening, but is involved as well. They believe that their own actions create consequences, and after that everything else that comes their way during the course of the day is brought forth by God's hands. Even when bad things happen, their perspective is that God will take it and bring forth good from it.

The major difference between the perspective of the last group of believers and the first two is hope. Sometimes, particularly in the face of disaster and distress, our beliefs are challenged and it is difficult to find a reason why God has allowed bad things to happen to us. If you are able to find hope, you are able to light your path through the darkness. Hope gives you the ability to rise above the despair and confusion and set your feet firmly upon the path you need to walk, even though you may not understand why things are happening.

The goal of this chapter is to realize that, although it is difficult to see how, God is working in your life, and throughout all this difficulty he is closer to you now than ever before.

## The Case

Sometimes, you may think that you just can't understand why God has allowed your marriage to end; why has he allowed all this pain? If he intended marriage to be forever, why hasn't he done something to stop all the hurting, the fighting, and the breakdown? Even before the separation took place, how could he allow the relationship to become so broken? Doesn't he hear my prayers?

Michael remembers:

I have always been faithful to God and faithful to my wife. I've worked hard and always did the right thing, even if it meant others didn't like my decision. But I'm not trying to be a martyr here; I've always been in love with my wife and had a strong relationship with God, so it was easy to be that way. I've struggled to build my career for my family's benefit and raised my kids as good Catholics. But when Kathryn left me, I kept wondering—after being true to God and my family—how could God take away my marriage? How could he allow my children to suffer so much? It was my whole life and now I feel all my hard work has gone to waste.

When it all happened and I was left alone, trying to understand and get a grip on things, I had to—absolutely had to—believe there was some bigger reason for what was happening. Nothing made sense to me at that point, not even going to work in the morning. I always had blind faith, but when my wife filed for divorce, my world was crumbling all around me and I couldn't buy into that theory anymore. I needed more than that because if I didn't find a real reason to sustain hope for my future, I saw very little value in continuing to practice my faith at all.

That was almost nine months ago and I have to admit, I don't have any better answers now than I did back then. I continue to practice my faith because when I think about it, I want to believe that God has a reason for what happened, but I certainly don't have clarity on the situation.

## A Loving God or a Stone God?

Despite the agony of your situation, God does not want your life to be miserable. God is not sitting up in heaven, aloof, like some cold, distant observer, unmoved and unloving. Quite the contrary, God is so close to you now, closer than you know.

There have been many books written on the subject of suffering, and it's safe to say this issue could be discussed and debated endlessly and you still won't have full understanding of it. Why? Because suffering is one of the mysteries of life that you won't have complete knowledge of until you reach heaven. However, you can use your ability to reason, coupled with faith, to understand at least some of it.

### Freedom of Choice

First, let's talk about the issue of free will. You don't always make good choices, and the same applies to everyone else in the world. But God will not force us to choose one way or another. That is his gift to us as human beings and you are free to choose what you want in life. Killing, stealing, rudeness, lies, gossip, abandoning your spouses and children, substance abuse, etc.; it's all your choice. So if you are free to choose what you want in life, and you know for a fact that you don't always choose wisely, it's safe to say that suffering will be caused as a result of poor choices made. And in the realm of divorce, there are lifetimes of suffering caused by one person's decision to have an affair and cheat on their spouse, or to allow an addiction to ruin their family or any of the many other reasons why divorce is so rampant in our society. So you can at least understand that God allows suffering because he will not take away our freedom of choice.

## When Bad Things Happen to Good People

People often wonder, "I am a good person! Why did this terrible thing happen to me? I pay my taxes, go to church, teach my kids right from wrong; I even point out when the cashier has given me too much money back at the store! Why am I suffering so much?"

Peter Kreeft, PhD., a well-known Catholic author and professor of philosophy at Boston College, directly addresses this question in his book, *Making Sense Out of Suffering*, and brings incredible insight to this question. In it, he makes the case that the question "Why do bad things happen to good people?" is valid, but will not lead to much understanding of the issue. Rather, Kreeft proposes the question should be, "Why do good things happen to bad people?" Let that question sink in for a moment. Again, one might revolt and cry, "But I am good!" Of course you are good, God made you that way, and he gives us the grace to do the good things we do. But the point that Kreeft illustrates so well is that we are all, every one of us, sinners. We are not perfect human beings and we all have our faults and failings. But God is perfect, and moreover, God is perfect Love. We offend him daily with our sins, yet he continues to bless us with many good things, hence the new perspective, *Why DO good things happen to bad people?* And here is the best part of that point; even the crosses you bear are blessings because when you suffer, you learn, you grow, you change, you become wiser and more loving. You become more like Christ. Suffering can be the door to new life. You become gold purified by the fire.

# What does Scripture Say?

Let's listen to St. Paul's exhortation in his letter to the Romans:

So then, now that we have been justified by faith, we are at peace with God through our Lord Jesus Christ; it is through him, by faith, that we have been admitted into God's favor in which we are living, and look forward exultantly to God's glory. Not only that; let us exult, too, in our hardships, understanding that hardship develops perseverance, and perseverance develops a tested character, something that gives us hope, and a hope which will not let us down, because the love of God has been poured into our hearts by the Holy Spirit which has been given to us.

When we were still helpless, at the appointed time, Christ died for the godless. You could hardly find anyone ready to die even for someone upright; though it is possible that, for a really good person, someone might undertake to die. So it is proof of God's own love for us, that Christ died for us while we were still sinners (Romans 5: 1 - 8).

St. Paul, with all that he suffered during his life, found great peace and joy in the fact that Christ died for him so he could have eternal life and that was the hope that outweighed every suffering.

What else can you know about this issue of suffering? Only good things can come from God; bad things that happen are due to the absence of God. Bad things happen among people because somewhere in the situation, God's presence is lacking. Somewhere in your marriage God's presence was lacking. When you look closely at your circumstances, you can detect the trouble . . . did you practice your faith as a family? Was either of the spouses holding back some truth from the other? Maybe the lack of God's presence was really from the beginning, from the day your relationship with your spouse began. Only you, your spouse, and God know the true details of the relationship.

## A Golden Opportunity

Here's the flip side of that coin . . . we know for a fact that God brings good things out of suffering. That is, if we allow him to enter our lives and give us his grace. The fact is that God has allowed this to happen to you because he respects the gift of free will he gave you, but it doesn't mean he doesn't love you or that he wants you to suffer needlessly. But it is precisely at this point—when bad things have happened—that Christ is ready to create new, good things for you. He is simply waiting for your permission to take the situation and bring good out of it. Imagine it this way: you can take your broken heart to the foot of the cross and say to Christ, "Why, Lord? Help me!" And Christ comes down from the cross, puts his arms around you and says, "I know you are suffering. I love you, and now I want to show you the way through your suffering into happiness." And so in trying to make sense out of what happened, you also need to look at what good things you can find in it all.

> Can you not buy two sparrows for a penny?
> And yet, not one falls to the ground
> without your Father knowing.
> Why, every hair on your head has been counted.
> So there is no need to be afraid;
> you are worth more than many sparrows
> (Matthew 10: 29 – 31).

It is awesome to think that God knows us so well; he knows every single hair on our head. He knows everything we've ever thought or done and he knows every desire within our hearts. God was present through the years you were married and saw every good time, every argument, every laugh, every tear.

## Concluding Thoughts

Then suddenly from behind him came a woman, who had been suffering from a hemorrhage for twelve years, and she touched the fringe of his cloak, for she was thinking, "If only I can touch his cloak I shall be saved." Jesus turned round and saw her; and he said to her, "Courage, my daughter, your faith has saved you." And from that moment the woman was saved (Matthew 9: 20 – 22).

Male or female, it is easy to identify with this woman in the passage. Your pain is the "internal bleeding" you experience as a result of your divorce. But Christ heals the deepest wounds, the most painful hurts in life. Place yourself in the shoes of this woman. Her faith is so great that although it seems impossible, she believes Christ can heal her. She believes Christ can bring good things out of the bad. She knows all she needs to do is extend her hand out in faith and she will be healed. She was healed, and you can be healed too. There is a future waiting for you, and a great one at that.

There comes a time in your life when you have to take a step out in faith and really believe that God has a plan for your life. Believe that when you love God and place your trust in him, your life is not just a bunch of unrelated circumstances that happen by accident. Everyone you know and everything that happens is God's hand trying to bring you closer to him.

To take a step further, you need to believe that God's plan will make you happy. This may seem contradictory to your current situation, but remember, things are not always what they seem. You are in the thick of the situation. You are filled with anger, resentment, grief, loneliness . . . but God knows your pain! He knows what you are going through, he is very aware of what is happening in your life, and he is trying to help you learn and grow through these circumstances. It may all seem a jumbled mess now, but if you allow God access to your life, he will take it and make it something wonderful. He will make you happier than you could ever imagine.

In addition to being present in your life, God has a plan. It takes hope for the future to survive the devastation of divorce, and hope is possible, even on the darkest of nights. It also takes faith—trust in God.

## Now What?

Here are some things you can do that will help you endure the suffering as well as restore a sense of hopefulness to your life:

1. **Pray**: (Hardships are the pathway to peace!) The Serenity Prayer is a very powerful prayer that speaks to the peace that comes from accepting and enduring hardships. Recite this prayer daily, especially when you are feeling overwhelmed or abandoned:

---

### The Serenity Prayer

God grant me the serenity to accept the things I cannot change;
courage to change the things I can; and wisdom to know the difference.
Living one day at a time; enjoying one moment at a time;
Accepting hardships as the pathway to peace;
Taking, as He did, this sinful world as it is, not as I would have it;
Trusting that He will make all things right if I surrender to His Will;
That I may be reasonably happy in this life
and supremely happy with him forever in the next. Amen.
–Reinhold Niebuhr

---

2. **Plan**: (Focus on the future) It is easy to get caught up in the pain of today and lose the hopefulness that tomorrow can bring. While you can't change the past, you can certainly shape your future. On page 26 of the Workbook companion, you will find the following column headings: Tomorrow, Next year, Three Years From Now, Five Years From Now. In each column, write down how you want your life to be at that point in time, and this should include your goals, dreams and aspirations, etc. Be as detailed as you would like. The key is to try and move beyond today's hardship.

3. **Change**: (Offset negative changes with positive changes) Make a list of all the things in your life you would like to change. It could be the obvious things like your weight, your hairstyle, or your income. Or, it could be the more subtle things like developing a new skill, being more consistent in a particular area, taking on a new activity you've been meaning to do, or breaking a bad habit. Pick the one thing that you can commit to doing and start doing it, everyday. Don't begin to work on the other items on your list until you have mastered the

current item or reached a specific goal. Resist the temptation to start doing too many things at once. You will wind up getting frustrated and not getting anything done. While there is a lot of turmoil in your life, much of which you have little or no control over, there are still many things in your life you can control, starting with you. So, take that karate class, start that exercise program, start going to mass every Sunday, join that scripture study, or quit smoking. There is no reason the negative changes in your life cannot be used as motivation to create some positive changes as well.

4. **Charity**: (Acts of kindness restore hope) When bad things happen to us, it is easy to allow ourselves to be consumed by the negativity. When you shift your focus away from your challenges and onto others and their needs, you gain a better, more rounded perspective. Helping others in need not only makes us feel better and makes the world a better place, it helps us understand that you are not the only one suffering—that there are other people suffering badly too. Consider doing random acts of kindness for someone you know who is in need, or volunteer to do charity work at your church. Sometimes, the smallest acts of kindness can have the biggest impact on restoring your sense of hope.

5. **Reflect**: (Overcoming past struggles provides hope) Think of a different time in your life when you were really struggling. Did the situation seem hopeless at the time? How did you overcome that struggle? Reflect on the lessons you learned from that struggle, how it changed the course of your life, and how life is better because you endured that hardship.

6. **Trust**: (God has a great plan for you!) Divorce can bring a tremendous amount of suffering and uncertainty. In a moment, a lifetime of dreams and plans can be destroyed. It is during these times that it can feel like you were dropped in a foreign land—with no map—in the dark. It can be a very scary feeling! Scripture repeatedly reassures us that God will never abandon us and that He has a tremendous plan for us. Try to trust in that for it is through that trust that a sense of hopefulness will return. While you may not have a clue as to what God has planned for you in the future, you can rest assured that it is going to be better then you can imagine.

Trust wholeheartedly in Yahweh
put no faith in your own perception;
acknowledge him in every course you take,
and he will see that your paths are smooth.
Proverbs 3: 5-6

"And look, I am with you always; yes, to the end of time."
Mark 28: 20

# Meditation

### Mark 10: 46 - 52

"Then they came to Jericho. As Jesus and his disciples, together with a large crowd, were leaving the city, a blind man, Bartimaeus (that is, the Son of Timaeus), was sitting by the roadside begging. When he heard that it was Jesus of Nazareth, he began to shout, "Jesus, Son of David, have mercy on me!" Many rebuked him and told him to be quiet, but he shouted all the more, "Son of David, have mercy on me!"

Jesus stopped and said, "Call him." So they called to the blind man, "Cheer up! On your feet! He's calling you." Throwing his cloak aside, he jumped to his feet and came to Jesus. Jesus said to him, "What do you want me to do for you?" The blind man replied to him, "I want to see." Jesus told him, "Go your way, your faith has saved you." Immediately he received his sight and followed him on the way."

**Opening Prayer**: My Lord and my God, I am grateful for this opportunity to talk to you. I want to share with you all that is troubling me and listen to your words. Lord, I believe in you, I trust in you, I love you!

**Petition**: Lord, grant me the grace to walk this journey with hope and a desire to become a better person because of the experience. Help me to be convinced that, no matter how difficult things may get, there is never any reason to give up because you are by my side.

1. *Have mercy on me!*

   Bartimaeus' desperate cry for help from the Lord sounds much the way you sound sometimes. You want to be healed of your affliction. You want the pain to pass and to be able to move on to a better life. When you look at Bartimaeus, you see what an example of hope he is, even in the face of others trying to quiet him and being rude to him, he does not give up his appeal because he believes that Jesus can heal him. He believes, and his actions show Jesus how strong his faith is. When I look at my own situation, at my own prayers to God, do I sustain this same spirit of faith and do my actions reinforce that faith?

2. *What do you want me to do for you?*

   Bartimaeus wanted to see. What is it that you want? What are you praying for? God wants you to come to him with all your cares, worries, concerns, hopes, dreams and desires. It is not selfish to ask God for things that benefit you. He wants us to come and speak with him about these things. What is it that your heart most desires at this point in time?

3. *Your faith has saved you.*

   Jesus loved Bartimaeus and wanted him to be healed, yet he made him work for it to a certain degree. He did not answer him at first, but allowed Bartimaeus to work harder before Jesus turned his attention to him. When Bartimaeus showed Jesus the level of faith he had, Jesus blessed him with the miracle of restoring his sight. Jesus loves us the same way, with a passionate love that never holds us back from what is good for us. When you pray, do you feel you are praying with hope? Do you believe that Christ will give you all that is good for you?

**Closing Prayer:** Lord, hear my prayer and open my heart to your words. Grant me the grace of a greater sense of hope that you are taking care of me and will bring all things to good because I love you. I offer my suffering up for all those men, women and children who are also suffering the affects of divorce. In your name, I pray. Amen.

## Resolution

Make a visit to Christ in the tabernacle for thirty minutes and specifically ask him for peacefulness amid the turmoil. Ask him to increase your faith in him.

## Suggested Reading

Peter Kreeft, *Making Sense Out of Suffering*, Servant Ministries (May 1986)

Andre Frossard, *Forget Not Love*, Ignatius Press (October 1991)

Matt Pinto and Jeff Cavins, *Amazing Grace for Those Who Suffer*, Ascension Press (October 2002)

# Chapter Four:

# What Does the Church Really Teach About Divorce?

In this chapter, let's look at the facts regarding the Catholic Church's teachings about separation and divorce and shed some light on your own situation so you can get answers to the many questions you may have about where you stand with the Catholic Church.

There are about as many differing circumstances surrounding divorce today as there are divorces, and they range from basic situations such as lack of communication and selfishness to some very complicated and messy circumstances. Both wives and husbands are abandoning their families for the pursuit of selfish motives. When one spouse abandons the other, especially if there are children, this devastates the family and leaves a path of scandal and destruction. Many spouses are left in a state of shock and terrible suffering, trying to piece their lives back together and find some type of appropriate explanation to give to their children.

However, it's not simply about abandoned spouses these days, either. There are many men and women who are given little choice but to divorce and take their children with them in order to remove themselves from dangerous situations. Pornography, alcohol or substance abuse, physical, emotional or mental abuse... there are many situations that destroy families. So many spouses do everything they can to save their marriage from collapse due to addictive and/or abusive behavior, but in the end have no other option but to file for divorce and try to create some type of safe environment somewhere else.

Spouses who have been abandoned, as well as those whose last resort was filing for divorce, all suffer tremendously and on many levels. Many report that, in addition to the deep hurt and anger they feel, they experience an overwhelming sense of guilt, partly because even though they fought to save their marriage, it still failed, and partly because of their inability to reconcile the fact that they are both Catholic and divorced. If you ask them, they will tell you they married for life; in the beginning, divorce was never an option and they made their vows on their wedding day "till death do us part."

As a Catholic, especially if you are Catholic from birth, you were always taught that divorce was a mortal sin, and Catholics just don't get divorced. So, the fact that you are now facing your own divorce can be quite a disillusionment. Certainly, there are a myriad of questions beginning to surface, some so painful to think of you may feel you're not able to voice them. Many Catholics, confused and ashamed of their divorce, end up going to church less and less, eventually not at all, and many more of them just stop attending the Catholic Church completely. It is sad to know that so many people are hurting, need healing and become separated from the one thing that can provide true healing—their faith.

The goal of this chapter is to understand what the Church teaches regarding our situation and dispel many of the myths and misunderstandings that you may have heard are true. Are you still in good standing with the Church even though you are separated or divorced from your spouse? Can you still go to mass and receive the Sacraments? What if you were forced into a separation or divorce? What if you were the one who left your spouse behind? Many questions, some you never thought you would have to ask, are now begging answers.

In the pages ahead, you will be able to inform your conscience with the information you learn, contemplate your own circumstances in light of this information, and gain clarity about where you stand in your relationship with God and the Church.

## The Case

Catholics who are divorced or separated may typically feel confused about where they fit in with the Church. Many Catholics in this situation feel cut off or alienated from the rest of their parish and the Church in general. Why does this happen?

Of course, for the reason stated above—the inability to reconcile being divorced and Catholic. But also, it oftentimes is no one's deliberate fault. The reverberations of divorce have a tremendous impact on people, particularly emotionally and socially, that causes awkwardness and a desire to withdraw from others for both divorced and non-divorced people.

But the feeling of alienation is also due to the many misconceptions, misunderstandings and lack of proper knowledge of what the Church teaches that circulates throughout our society.

John tells us:

I really couldn't be sure if I could still receive the sacraments. I had initiated the separation between my wife and I and felt I had good reason to do so—primarily for my children's safety. My wife had an addiction to alcohol that was destroying the family. Even though I had not made a definite decision about our future, I believed a divorce was inevitable. I waited to act on this because I wanted to see if somehow we could all be a family again, but I knew that would not happen overnight and the likelihood was that it wouldn't happen at all. If the Catholic Church condemns divorce, where does this leave me?

Linda tells us:

My friends warned me that if I dated another man, even though my husband was the one that left and divorced me, I would be excommunicated from the Church. Why should I suffer the rest of my life because of the mistake my husband made?

David complains:

I feel like an outsider in the parish I've been attending for more than nine years! After my wife and I split up, it was suddenly as if some of my friends didn't even know me. They still talk to Julie, but won't give me the time of day. They have no clue what has happened between her and I, nor do they even consider that I, myself, am in a lot of pain over this. I am shocked and disappointed.

This is a lot to deal with! No wonder so many Catholics going through a divorce or separation end up staying away from the Church.

Now is the perfect opportunity to directly address these issues, and the remainder of this chapter will be spent exploring the answers. But, in order to fully understand the issue of divorce and the Catholic Church's stance on it, let's take a more in-depth look at what a marriage relationship is, or what it is meant to be. Here are some firm facts and practical knowledge about what the Church really teaches.

## What Does the Church Teach about Marriage?

Marriage is not just a legal contract, a piece of paper, a dress, a tuxedo and a party. It's more than a signed agreement between two parties and it even goes deeper than a life-long commitment. A true sacramental marriage is a covenant made between God, the bride and the groom, and for you, the one who is hurting so badly over the loss of your marriage you understand the pain and extreme sense of loss that occurs when a covenant is broken.

A covenant is a bond, a binding agreement; it binds together a man and a woman and they become one flesh, one heart, one mind.

> "This is why a man leaves his father and mother and the two become one flesh. They are no longer two, therefore, but one flesh. So then, what God has united, human beings must not divide" (Matthew 16:7 - 9)

Marriage is by all rights a covenant between the bride, the groom and God. In the words of Pope John Paul II:

> "The spouses participate in [marriage] as spouses, together, as a couple, so that the first and immediate effect of marriage (res *et sacramentum*) is not supernatural grace itself, but the Christian conjugal bond, a typically Christian communion of two persons because it represents the mystery of Christ's Incarnation and the mystery of his covenant. The content of participation in Christ's life is also specific: conjugal love involves a totality, in which all the elements of the person enter—appeal of the body and instinct, power of feeling and affectivity, aspiration of the spirit and of will. It aims at a deeply personal unity, the unity that, beyond union in one flesh, leads to forming one heart and soul; it demands indissolubility and faithfulness in definitive mutual giving; and is open to fertility (cf. *Humanae vitae*, 9).

Reading Pope John Paul II's words are like turning on a light in a dark room. His words bring a much deeper meaning to marriage than most of us think of. Through his words, he illustrates how the institution of marriage plays an integral, significant role in society; marriage and family are the fabric of a thriving society.

Here is a quote from Canon Law:

**Canon 1055**.1 The marriage covenant, by which a man and a woman establish between themselves a partnership of their whole life, and which of its own very nature is ordered to the well-being of the spouses and to the procreation and upbringing of children, has, between the baptized, been raised by Christ the Lord to the dignity of a sacrament.

Okay. So, marriage isn't simply "a natural next step in the relationship" as many couples in love conclude, but it is meant to be a lasting covenant that brings happiness to both spouses, brings forth new life, and is a reflection of God's love for each of us. That is what marriage is meant to be. It is not simply a piece of paper, a party with free food and wine, nor is it a contract that can be nullified. A marriage binds two people together for life and exists for the good of the spouses and the creation of new life; a beautiful, sacramental union meant to last until death.

## What Does the Church Teach about Divorce?

Now, let's begin to eliminate the confusion by looking at what the *Catechism of the Catholic Church* teaches:

Divorce is a grave offense against the natural law. It claims to break the contract, to which the spouses freely consented, to live with each other till death. Divorce does injury to the covenant of salvation, of which sacramental marriage is the sign. Contracting a new union, even if it is recognized by civil law, adds to the gravity of the rupture: the remarried spouse is then in a situation of public and permanent adultery (*CCC* 2384).

Divorce is immoral also because it introduces disorder into the family and into society. This disorder brings grave harm to the deserted spouse, to children traumatized by the separation of their parents and often torn between them, and because of its contagious effect which makes it truly a plague on society (*CCC* 2385).

If a husband, separated from his wife, approaches another woman, he is an adulterer because he makes that woman commit adultery; and the woman who lives with him is an adulteress, because she has drawn another's husband to herself (*CCC* #2384: cf. St. Basil, Moralia 73, 1:PG 31, 849 – 852).

There you have it, plainly put. The Catholic Church teaches that divorce is morally wrong and "a grave offense against the natural law." So if this is true, where does that leave all the spouses who were abandoned? Where does it leave the spouses who fought for their marriage, but in the end the only right decision was to divorce?

"It can happen that one of the spouses is the innocent victim of a divorce decreed by civil law; this spouse therefore has not contravened the moral law. There is considerable difference between a spouse who has sincerely tried to be faithful to the sacrament of marriage and is unjustly abandoned, and one who through his own grave fault destroys a canonically valid marriage (*CCC* 2386).

The separation of spouses while maintaining the marriage bond can be legitimate in certain cases provided for by canon law. If civil divorce remains the only possible way of ensuring certain legal rights, the care of the children, or the protection of inheritance, it can be tolerated and does not constitute a moral offense (*CCC* 2383).

So, you can see that if you were forced into a divorce against your will or if you personally initiated the divorce for protective issues, you have not committed any offense and are in full communion with the Church as long as you are maintaining a chaste lifestyle.

Overall, these words are strong, and they should be. It's critical to your ability to move forward in the healing process to recognize the seriousness of what has happened as a result of divorce, and the breakdown of the family. Jaded people everywhere simply shrug off their divorces and broken families with snide remarks and cold hearts. But for every person who takes that aloof attitude toward the loss of their marriage, there are many more who suffer tremendously for their callousness.

# What does Scripture Say?

Let's read from the book of Malachi:

"And here is something else you do: you cover the altar of Yahweh with tears, with weeping and wailing, because he now refuses to consider the offering or to accept it from you. And you ask, 'Why?' Because Yahweh stands as witness between you and the wife of your youth, with whom you have broken faith, even though she was your partner and your wife by covenant. Did he not create a single being, having flesh and the breath of life? And what does this single being seek? God-given offspring! Have respect for your own life, then, and do not break faith with the wife of your youth. For I hate divorce, says Yahweh, God of Israel, and people concealing their cruelty under a cloak, says Yahweh Sabaoth. Have respect for your own life, then, and do not break faith" (Mal 2:13 - 16).

Jesus, himself, had definite words regarding divorce:

Some Pharisees approached him and to put him to the test, they said, "Is it against the law for a man to divorce his wife on any pretext whatever?" He answered, "Have you not read that the Creator from the beginning 'made them male and female' and that he said, 'This is why a man leaves his father and mother becomes attached to his wife, and the two become one flesh'? They are no longer two, therefore, but one flesh. So then, what God has united, human beings must not divide." They said to him, "Then why did Moses command that a writ of dismissal should be given in cases of divorce?" He said to them, "It was because you were so hard-hearted that Moses allowed you to divorce your wives, but it was not like this from the beginning. Now I say to you: anyone who divorces his wife—I am not speaking of an illicit marriage—and marries another is guilty of adultery" (Matthew 19: 3 – 9).

The first point you can be certain of here is that through Jesus' words in the gospel and the teaching of the church, valid marriage vows cannot be broken.

What does the term "valid" mean in this instance? We will go further into this subject as we explore the issue of annulments in the next chapter, but for now we can state the term "valid" as used to describe a marriage that is truly sacramental, a covenant made on the day of the wedding in the eyes of God and the Church. If a marriage was not valid, the appearance of a marriage would be visible to everyone, but a sacramental marriage in the eyes of God would not exist.

The second and very important point is: someone who is separated or divorced and is maintaining a chaste lifestyle and not remarried without a declaration of nullity is considered to be in good standing with the Catholic Church. Someone in these circumstances is highly encouraged to attend mass and receive the sacraments as often as possible. Anyone who is not maintaining a chaste lifestyle, whether he or she is married, divorced, separated, annulled or never married, must receive the sacrament of reconciliation before receiving the sacrament of the Eucharist.

In essence, we are certain now of these two important facts:

1.  Valid marriage vows cannot be broken. Breaking them is considered adultery and a mortal sin.

2.  Being an innocent victim of divorce is not a moral offense in any way. Anyone (separated, divorced or not) who is in the state of grace is welcome to attend mass and receive the sacraments, and is considered an important member of the Church.

These facts provide some black-and-white answers to think about. Now, take these teachings of Christ and parallel them with your individual circumstances.

## So Where Does That Leave Us?

Well, let's begin clearing things up by stating that, despite your situation, you are always welcome in your parish and in the Church as the mystical body of Christ. You are an important part of the body of Christ and you need to remember this, especially if going to church is difficult for you.

Let's take a look at those initial questions posed earlier and answer them:

<u>John's question was</u>: "I really couldn't be sure if I could still receive the sacraments. I had initiated the separation between my wife and I and

felt I had good reason to do so—primarily for my children's safety . . . If the Catholic Church condemns divorce, where does this leave me?"

Answer: If your marriage relationship is a physically abusive situation or other harmful situation, a separation is obviously necessary for the safety of family members. God does not want you to remain in situations that are harmful. In addition to safety issues, staying in this type of situation "enables" the perpetrator of abuse to continue abusing, and no healing can take place then. Once a separation has taken place, it is possible for the abuser to be rehabilitated and the marriage repaired. Nothing is impossible for God. However, if the abuser refuses help or to change his or her behavior, it is likely that the spouses cannot live together under one roof. At this point, it should be discerned as to whether you should legally separate or divorce. The spouse filing for the divorce is not committing a moral offense.

Linda's question was: "My friends warned me that if I dated another man, even though my husband was the one that left and divorced me, I would be excommunicated from the Church."

Answer: This statement is false. There are nine grounds for ex-communication and spouses dating non-spouses after a divorce and without a decree of nullity is not one of them.

The nine grounds excommunication are as follows:

1. Procuring of abortion

2. Apostasy: The total rejection of the Christian faith

3. Heresy: The obstinate post-baptismal denial of some truth, which must be believed with divine and Catholic faith

4. Schism: The rejection of the authority and jurisdiction of the Pope as head of the church

5. Desecration of sacred species (Holy Communion)

6. Physical attack on the Pope

7. Sacramental absolution of an accomplice in sin against the Sixth Commandment (Thou shall not commit adultery) and the Ninth Commandment (You shall not covet your neighbor's house; you shall not covet your neighbor's wife, or his manservant, or his maidservant, or his ox, or his ass, or anything that is your neighbor's)

8. Unauthorized consecration of a bishop

9. Direct violation of the confessional seal by a confessor

However, this is an issue that should be discussed. We will address this issue at length in a later chapter, but for now it's important to understand that certainly during the first year after a divorce you should not date or entertain the idea of entering into other romantic relationships. This initial period should be spent working on yourself and doing what you need to do to heal. But more than that, it isn't a good idea to date until you have received a decree of nullity through the annulment process. The annulment process determines whether or not you are free to date and marry again in the Church. If you skip this important step, you may be setting yourself up for much greater pain and sorrow in the future. If you find out that you are not granted a decree of nullity for your previous marriage, this means you are still bound to your spouse you are divorced from until death. This would present tremendous problems and heartache if you were already involved with another person.

David's complaint was: "I feel like an outsider in the parish I've been attending for more than nine years! After my wife and I split up, it was suddenly as if some of my friends didn't even know me... I am shocked and disappointed.

Answer: It shouldn't be this way, but all too often it is, and primarily because of the widespread misunderstandings you have been discussing. People make judgements without knowing the full scope of the situation. But despite the actions of individual parishioners, the Catholic Church reaches out in compassion to those who are divorced and works to help them heal their lives. Pope John Paul II and Pope Benedict the

XVI have both stated that divorced men and women are an important part of the Church and should be treated with compassion:

> You all know that this [divorce] is a particularly painful situation. Given these people's situation of suffering, it must be studied . . . None of us has a ready-made solution because each person's situation is different . . . The Christian faith involves giving oneself to the community of the Church, a community that promises each believer that he or she will never be left alone in suffering and that calls each Catholic to reach out to others . . .

> - Pope Benedict XVI's Comments on Ministry to Divorced and Civilly-Remarried Catholics - Conference with priests, religious and deacons, July 25, 2005

> I earnestly call upon pastors and the whole community of the faithful to help the divorced and with solicitous care to make sure that they do not consider themselves as separated from the Church, for as baptized persons they can and indeed must, share in her life.

> - Pope John Paul II, *Familiaris consortio*

The fact of the matter is that Christ wants to heal you and he has specifically given you the sacraments as a source of healing. You cannot experience this healing unless you come to church.

In an instance where a parishioner, or anyone for that matter, judges you in a negative manner because of your divorce, a good response would be to pray for that person. Why? For the same reason that Christ, hanging from the bloody cross of his death, prayed to the Father and asked him to forgive us.

Being an innocent victim of divorce is not a moral offense in any way. Anyone (separated, divorced or other) who is in the state of grace is welcome to attend mass and receive the sacraments, and is considered an important member of the Church.

## Reconciliation

Now that you have seen what the teaching is on divorce, there is an important question to ask yourself: Have you considered reconciling with your spouse? Maybe you have already broached the subject with your spouse or maybe not because it may be a moot point depending on the circumstances. But why is it important to consider this option? For a number of reasons, but here are some good ones:

- You may have a difficult time imagining forgiving your spouse, but if your marriage is valid, this type of forgiveness and effort to make the relationship work could quite possibly result in a stronger marriage down the road.

- Nothing is impossible with God; you just have to be willing to be open and forgiving. Sometimes that means you have to swallow your pride, even if you know you have been unjustly hurt. What is most important is that we, as divorced Catholics, are able to move on in life with as much peace and understanding as possible.

> You are a fire that takes away the coldness, illuminates the mind with its light, and causes me to know your truth.
> - St. Catherine of Siena

## Concluding Thoughts

A philosopher once defined the conscience as "The place where man and God meet." This is because no one can truly judge us but God; no one knows our hearts the way God does. Only you, your spouse and God know the details of what happened in your marriage. Therefore, in your own mind you need to consider all the facts as honestly and sincerely as you can and ask for God's guidance while doing this.

But in addition to probing deeply into your conscience, you are obligated—as every Catholic is—to inform your conscience with the truth. If you do not have the answer to a question that troubles you, you need to seek out the answer as opposed to just letting the issue fall by the wayside. If you don't know or understand the Church's teaching on something, such as divorce issues or other moral matters, you must seek out the answers so you can understand and make informed decisions regarding your situation and your future. This is an aspect of dealing with divorce that only you can take care of—you can't blame someone else if you continue on in life without seeking answers to critical questions.

The next step is to find a priest and speak to him about what has happened. He will be able to provide even more insight and direction. If you are uncertain about whom to speak to, you can call the Office of the Tribunal in your own diocese and ask for a referral.

When you are able to describe your situation to a priest, based on the answers to his questions he would most likely be able to tell you if you have grounds for an annulment and where to go from there. He would not be able to give a definitive answer on whether or not an annulment would be declared.

If no reconciliation is possible between spouses and a civil divorce has been filed, many people choose to live as a chaste, single person in society, which is a state in life that has always been admirable. In other cases, the next logical step would be to apply for an annulment from the Catholic Tribunal, which is the legal branch of the Church. Those who want to remarry with the Church's blessings would be the most likely to apply for an annulment.

## Now What?

Unfortunately, society no longer emphasizes the beauty and importance of marriage. The high rate of divorce and the no-fault divorce laws only give the impression that marriage and family relationships are fragile and can break at any given moment. There is also extreme dysfunction that exists in many intact families because of harsh abuses—physical, emotional, and substance abuse—and so often, the children of these families never see what a real marriage is. They witness the abuse and form their ideas about marriage in that way. So many of us were not properly taught about the Church's teaching about marriage and the happiness it is meant to bring to the spouses. As a result, there is often misunderstanding about this topic. The permanence and exclusiveness of marriage tends to be just another set of rules to follow—or else. Yet, in reality the Church's teaching on marriage, its value to society and its role in leading us to happiness on earth and ultimately to heaven, would pleasantly surprise most people. Here are a few suggestions of things you can do to help yourself and others understand the beauty of marriage, the way God intended:

1. **Learn More**: In the Catechism of the Catholic Church you can find a very thorough and readable explanation of what marriage is. Read paragraphs 1601–1666 to learn more about the Church and marriage. The Catechism also provides a detailed description of its teaching on divorce in paragraphs 2382–2391. Read these sections at least once to better understand how marriage and divorce impact your faith.

2. **Talk to a Priest**: Everyone's situation is different. Talk to a priest about your particular situation. He will be able to guide you down the right path and answer any questions you might have. So many Catholics have suffered needlessly because they made incorrect assumptions or were misinformed.

3. **Teach the Truth**: Many Catholics are misinformed about their role in the Church as divorced Catholics and their ability to participate in the Sacraments. It is a tragedy that so many suffer needlessly—or worse still—leave the faith altogether. Share what you know with other divorced Catholics and help bring light to this darkness.

4. **Seek the Church**: The Catholic Church is the source of Christ's truth. While you may not always understand or agree with that truth, it is the truth nonetheless. Because it is of God, truth has by its very nature a healing and comforting aspect to it. Although sometimes difficult, the truth will always lead you to the right place—a place of peace. If you are feeling the desire to distance yourself from the Church, you are moving away from the very thing that will bring you the abundant peace and joy you are seeking. As you reflect and discern the impact of your divorce or separation on the rest of your life, it is best to remain engaged with the Church, her Sacraments, her teaching, and her community. So, go to mass, go to reconciliation, go to adoration in

front of the Blessed Sacrament (if available), seek out (or start) a divorce ministry, stay plugged into your faith and your Church. The Church needs you!

5.  **Pray for Hope**: It is easy to become disillusioned when facing the truth of your particular situation. All the reasons that caused you to find yourself divorced can pile up and make it hard to have hope for a future free from anxiety and pain. God can always make a way, even when it seems like there is no way. Give all those worries, uncertainties and doubts to God. Through prayer, you can develop a sense of hope that God really does have a plan for you, and that plan is greater then anything you can imagine.

# Meditation

## John 11: 1 - 44

There was a man named Lazarus of Bethany, the village of Mary, and her sister Martha, and he was ill. It was the same Mary, the sister of the sick man Lazarus, who anointed the Lord with ointment, and wiped His feet with her hair. The sisters sent this message to Jesus, "Lord, behold, the man You love is ill." On receiving this message, Jesus said, "This sickness will not end in death, but it is for God's glory so that through it, the Son of God may be glorified."

Jesus loved Martha and her sister and Lazarus, yet when He heard that he was ill He stayed where he was for two more days before saying to the disciples, "Let us go back to Judea." The disciples said, "Rabbi, it is not long since the Jews were trying to stone you; are you going back there again?" Jesus replied, "Are there not twelve hours in the day? No one who walks in the daytime stumbles, having the light of this world to see by; anyone walks around at night stumbles having no light as a guide." He said that and added, "Our friend Lazarus is at rest; I am going to wake him." The disciples said to Him, "Lord, if he is at rest, he will be saved." Jesus was speaking of the death of Lazarus, but they thought that by "rest" he meant sleep; so Jesus put it plainly, "Lazarus is dead; and for your sake I am glad that I was not there because now you will believe. But let us go to him." Then Thomas – known as the twin – said to the other disciples, "Let us also go to die with him."

On arriving, Jesus found that Lazarus had been in the tomb for four days already. Bethany is only about two miles from Jerusalem, and many Jews had come to Martha and Mary to comfort them about their brother. When Martha heard that Jesus was coming, she went to meet Him. Mary remained sitting in the house. Martha said to Jesus, "Lord, if You had been here, my brother would not have died, but even now I know that God will grant you whatever You ask of him." Jesus said to her, "Your brother will rise again." Martha said to Him, "I know that he will rise again in the resurrection on the last day." Jesus said, "I am the resurrection; anyone who believes in me, even though that person dies, will live, and whoever lives and believes in Me will never die. Do you believe this?" She said, "I believe that You are the Christ, the Son of God, the one who was to come into this world."

When she had said this, she went and called her sister Mary, saying in a low voice, "The Master is here and he wants to see you." Hearing this, Mary got up quickly and went to him. Jesus had not yet come into the village; he was still in the place where Martha met him. When the Jews who were in the house comforting Mary saw her get up so quickly and go out, they followed her, thinking that she was going to the tomb to weep there.

Mary went to Jesus, and as soon as she saw Him, she threw herself at his feet, saying, "Lord, if you had been here, my brother would not have died." At the sight of her tears, and those of the Jews who came with her, Jesus was greatly distressed, and with a profound sigh he said, "Where have you put him?" They said "Lord, come and see." Jesus wept and the Jews said, "See how he loved him!" But there were some who remarked, "He opened the eyes of the blind man, couldn't he have prevented this man's death?" Sighing again, Jesus reached the tomb; it was a cave with a stone to close the opening. Jesus said, "Take the stone away." Martha, the dead man's sister, said to him, "Lord, by now he will smell; this is the fourth day since he died." Jesus replied, "Have I not told you that if you believe, you will see the glory of God?" So they took the stone away. Then Jesus lifted up his eyes, and said, "Father,

I thank You for hearing my prayer. I, myself, knew that you hear me always; but speak for the sake of the people who are standing around me, so that they may believe it was you who sent me." When he had said this, he cried in a loud voice, "Lazarus, come out!" The dead man came out, his feet and hands bound with strips of material, and a cloth over his face. Jesus said to them, "Unbind him, and let him go free."

**Opening Prayer**: My Lord, and my God! I believe you are with me during these moments of prayer, listening and speaking to me. I come before you with a troubled heart, and I ask you for the gift of your grace and an increase in my faith in you. I believe you can restore my heart to its full capacity for love, and my life to complete peace. Help me to trust in you and give you control of all my cares, worries and pain.

**Petition**: Lord, give me the graces I need to go forward in peace, knowing that my situation is in your hands.

1. *This sickness will not end in death, but it is for God's glory so that through it, the Son of God may be glorified.*

   Divorce can feel like a sickness so terrible it makes you want to die. The pain is never-ending it seems. But God can take the most horrible situation and bring good out of it. In the same way he allowed Lazarus to die, he allowed your divorce to happen, and he is waiting for the opportunity to show us the good things he can bring about as a result of the bad. This is one way he brings us closer to himself; it is a way to show us how much he cares for you and how, if you let him, he will make you happy despite the terrible loss you are suffering. Are you open to giving him free reign in your life to accomplish good things?

2. *Jesus wept.*

   Certainly, in times of great distress you might feel as if God has forgotten you, as if he has left you alone to suffer. Yet this scripture illustrates how much he cares for you, how much it pains him to see you suffering. With each cross you carry, no matter how great or small, Christ carries you and is ready to show you a new path; a better way than the one you were on before. He wants you to experience growth, especially growing closer to him. You need to trust him that he will take care of you.

3. *Lazarus, come out!*

In the end, Jesus brought tremendous good out of the bad, for he raised Lazarus to life. The significance of this miracle brought about a strengthening of the people's faith. Christ is waiting to raise you from the dead, too; to raise you from the dead of pain and suffering into new life: "therefore if anyone is (A) in Christ, he is (B) a new creature; (C) the old things passed away; behold, new things have come (1 Corinthians 5:17). What great things can he accomplish out of divorce? Open your heart to him so you can witness his great work.

**Closing Prayer**: Thank you, Lord, for your light in my life. You are the way, the truth and the Life and I pray that you will continue to guide me and direct me through this time of my life. Help me to understand your plan for me.

# Resolution

A. Contemplate the issue of asking your spouse to reconcile. If there has been no attempt to reconcile, and you can see there might be a possibility of reconciling, seriously consider getting in touch with your spouse and proposing the idea.

B. If you have not discussed your situation with a priest, make an appointment to do so.

# Suggested Reading

G. K. Chesterton, *Brave New Family: Men and Women, Children, Sex, Divorce, Marriage and the Family*, Ignatius Press (October 24, 1990)

Christopher West, *The Love That Satisfies*, Ascension Press (July 31, 2007)

Patrick Madrid, *Does the Bible Really Say That?: Discovering Catholic Teaching in Scripture*, Servant Publications (July 30, 2006)

# Chapter Five:

# What is an Annulment?

In this chapter, we will look at the facts regarding the Catholic Church's teaching about the annulment process. Just as we discussed about marriage in the previous chapter, there are widespread misunderstandings and misconceptions throughout society about what a Catholic annulment is, what takes place during the process, how much it costs, what its implications are and whether or not it is a valid process. But despite all of the misinformation, there are reliable answers to everyone's questions and the assurance that the annulment process is one of hope and healing.

Some people have negative views toward the annulment process as a result of the misunderstandings that everyone talks about, but it's important to remember that the annulment process is a very sensitive matter, involving people who are also sensitive about very hurtful things because they have experienced a lot of hurt and anger. When emotions are high, it's easy to see how perceptions can become distorted over the details and processes.

However, the goal of the entire annulment process is very simple and clear cut—to determine whether or not a particular marriage was contracted as a sacrament, a covenant. That is all. The annulment process—and it is a process because of the different stages and steps—is one that promotes healing in the truest sense of the word. It provides the parties involved with the chance to honestly face and deal with the things that went wrong, not only in the marriage but in their dating relationship. Additionally, it helps close that chapter of life and lay it to rest. It provides answers to deep and troublesome questions. And it helps the divorced person know where he or she stands with God and the Church. Many people who have gone through the process from start to finish refer to it as "the eighth sacrament" because of its incredibly healing nature.

This chapter is broken into four parts that will help you clearly understand the following:

1) What the annulment process is;
2) What the annulment process is not;
3) What to expect if you decide to initiate the process yourself; and
4) What the most common grounds for annulment are.

## The Case

George says:

I don't believe the Catholic Church can annul a marriage. I don't believe it has the authority to do something like that. Jesus said in the bible that no man should separate what God has joined, and that's what I believe. I think the Church's probing questions are a violation of privacy. There is no need for them to know the intimate details of my marriage and divorce. Furthermore, I have no interest in digging up the dirt of my divorce. I buried all that years ago and dredging it up is pointless in my mind.

Bill complains:

I don't have three thousand dollars to pay for an annulment and I am angry that the Catholic Church, knowing how hard divorced people struggle, would be so bold as to charge us for this. I already have child support payments and legal bills to worry about. Why does the Church need to make money off of us?

Deana tells us:

I've heard so many people say that an annulment is just a "Catholic divorce." I must admit, I am really down on this. Why go through all that hassle twice, especially when I know that my marriage was real? My ex-husband and I have four children—sounds like a real marriage to me. If it really is just a Catholic divorce, it seems to me that a civil divorce is enough. Besides, if I want to get married again and the Church didn't grant me an annulment, I would get married anyway because I want to be happy. I don't want to spend the rest of my life alone.

Does any of this sound familiar? These are honest complaints, but they are all based on misinformation and a lack of understanding of how it all works.

## Where to Begin?

As we begin to look at the facts, we can identify a primary source of confusion up front, and that is some of the confusion is created from the language that is typically used in reference to the annulment process. The phrase "to get an annulment" can be confusing because it sounds as if you are trying to obtain permission to dissolve a marriage contract. As previously noted, a sacramental marriage that has been consummated can only be dissolved by the death of one or both of the spouses. So, a more concise term for what happens as a result of the "annulment process" is a "declaration of nullity," or "declaration of validity"; the first being a formal declaration that despite the fact that a marriage relationship was present, a marriage was never valid in the eyes of God; the second, the declaration that a sacramental marriage indeed exists between the two spouses.

As you read through the following pages, you will find some concrete information that will answer many questions.

## What an Annulment Is

Let us immediately begin to dispel the myths and misinformation surrounding this very important issue.

An annulment, or more appropriately termed "the annulment process," is the formal process of investigation into a marriage, petitioned by a spouse, with the intention of determining whether or not a sacramental, life-long bond was entered into by both spouses on the day of the wedding.

A valid marriage requires the proper intention of both the bride and the groom at the time the vows are exchanged. Both parties must intend to make a marriage, which by definition is a life-long communion open to new human life. These are called the unitive and procreative meanings of marriage. If either of the two meanings of marriage (an indissoluble union and procreation) are excluded by the will of either the man or the woman no marriage is made on the wedding day (canon 1096).

Simply stated, if a man or woman stand at the altar on the day of their wedding and do not fully intend to 1) make a life-long commitment to the other, and 2) have children together during their marriage, there is no sacramental marriage in the eyes of God, despite the fact that the bride and groom kiss, have a reception, go on a honeymoon and live their lives as a married couple. It is the sole purpose of the annulment process to gather information about the couple's relationship and make a determination as to whether or not a sacramental marriage exists. However, it is assumed by the Church that all marriages are valid unless proven otherwise by the annulment process.

> A valid marriage requires the proper intention
> of both the bride and the groom
> at the time the vows are exchanged.

# What an Annulment Isn't

- **The annulment process is not a "Catholic divorce."**

A divorce is the dissolution of a marriage contract by the state government; the state declares the marital contract legally void. However, an annulment is a determination by the Church that the elements required for a valid marriage to take place were not present when the parties exchanged their consent. The Catholic Church is loyal to the teaching of Christ on marriage.

- **The annulment process is not an attempt to make money for the Church.**

Real people work full-time in the Tribunal and many of them are not priests or deacons, but lay people and they are paid a salary just as in any other job. Any funds collected as a fee for the annulment process go toward the payment of the administrative costs incurred. Most of the time, the tribunal does not collect the full amount of the cost for each case.

Although each diocese across the country has its own process, the cost of annulment is typically about $1000 for an average case, sometimes less. A tribunal will most likely offer to make payment arrangements for the petitioner if finances are tight, and at times if a person is absolutely unable to pay, the fee will be waived. In my own experience, I was able to make a payment arrangement of $10 per month because my budget was so tight and my total cost was only $600. The truth is that the Church is not trying to exploit or take advantage of divorced men and women, but help them in the best way they can while recouping some of their costs.

- **The annulment process is not a violation of privacy.**

The Church, in its desire to bring all souls to Christ, seeks only to make this determination of whether or not a sacramental bond existed between two spouses, and with the process bring hope and healing to the parties involved. But the Church is only acting on the request of the petitioner. The spouse filing for divorce has essentially invited the Church to make a determination one way or another; therefore, it is necessary for the Tribunal to be able to gain the appropriate information to make an informed determination. The more detailed the information, the better picture a tribunal can have, but what is terribly important also is that the more detailed the information is, the deeper the petitioner can go into the problems that destroyed their marriage to begin with, and with this kind of depth comes understanding followed by deep healing. It is for this very reason that so many people walk away from their annulment process with closure, a great release of anger, and wisdom to face the future.

## What to Expect From the Process

If the couple gets a civil divorce, one of the spouses is eligible to petition the tribunal for the annulment process and this is where the investigation commences. The process is similar to putting a puzzle together. When an applicant initiates this process, he or she will also be providing the pieces of the puzzle to the Tribunal so they can put the pieces together and see the whole picture in order to make the most accurate determination.

So, what are the pieces of the puzzle?

1. It begins with the petitioner being assigned an "advocate" by the parish. An advocate is a layperson trained and appointed by the parish to assist petitioners of the annulment process, answer questions and provide support. The petitioner fills out the initial paperwork and submits it to the Tribunal. The petitioner and the Advocate will meet frequently during the process.

2. From that point, the petitioner fills out the initial paperwork that provides valuable information to the Tribunal to get the process going.

3. Witnesses are provided by the petitioner, and the witnesses should be people who have been present in the couples' lives and have observed the things that went on, even if they were unaware a divorce was impending. These witnesses will be sent their own set of questions to answer by the tribunal and it is up to the petitioner to make sure the questionnaires are sent back to the tribunal.

4. One of the most important pieces of the puzzle is the comprehensive questionnaire that is mailed to and filled out by the petitioner. This can be anywhere from 75 to 110 or so questions, and they focus on what happened from the time the couple met each other, through their dating relationship and engagement, and finally the day of the marriage. There is focus on what happened after the wedding day and throughout the length of the marriage, but the previous stages are more important to the determination of the case. The questions are meant to be a tool, not only in helping the Tribunal gain a clear picture of what happened with the couple, but also to help the petitioner begin to directly face the issues and problems surrounding the demise of his or her marriage.

5.  Another piece of the puzzle is the personal interview with the petitioner, which normally takes place after the comprehensive questionnaire has been submitted and reviewed by the tribunal (this may not take place in every diocese).

6.  After the pieces have been gathered, the Tribunal's case lawyers (typically three priests and/or deacons) review the case and all the information that has been gathered. It is their job to put it all together and make a determination about whether or not a sacramental marriage was made on the day of the wedding.

7.  The next step involves the defender of the bond, who is a canon lawyer, who reviews the case and defends the matrimonial bond in front of the Tribunal as to the likelihood of validity—kind of a devil's advocate.

8.  After this process, the final step is to make a determination and issue a decree in the first instance. This is a letter sent to the petitioner stating the determination; either the marriage was a sacramental marriage or it wasn't. However, the case must still go to the local archdiocese for the archbishop's final approval on the case. After this has been received, a decree in the second instance is issued and this is typically what is referred to as "an annulment." A petitioner is not free to marry or make plans to marry before this decree of nullity is received.

*Note: Each diocese's process might differ in procedural ways from other dioceses, but the process in general is the same wherever you go.*

## Petrine and Pauline Privileges

The explanation above is the average procedure that takes place for reviewing a marriage in which both spouses are baptized Catholics. If one of the spouses is not a baptized Catholic, the process is somewhat different and is called the Petrine Privilege. It is called the Petrine privilege because it is the authority of the pope, the successor of St. Peter that is involved in dissolving the natural marriage bond.

If neither of the spouses were baptized, the process is referred to as the Pauline Privilege, which is based on the 7th chapter of the first book of Corinthians. In this part of scripture, the apostle, Paul, allowed a married person who had been baptized into Christianity to remarry another person because the original spouse refused to remain married due to baptism.

It is easy to see, after reviewing the steps involved in the process, that it takes time for this all to happen. Many people complain about the length of time an annulment takes, but very often the process is delayed because the petitioner does not follow through with all the paperwork. If everyone does their part and if there is not a huge back-log of cases, on average, the annulment process can take as little as nine months. However, if the petitioner or witnesses delay the paperwork, if there is a back-log of cases, or if the case is a particularly difficult one, it can take longer than one year.

## What are the Grounds for Annulment?

When the tribunal is assessing the petitioner's case, the following grounds are the most commonly used to make their determination about whether or not a marriage is null:

- **Lack of Use of Reason: Canon 1095.1** -- The following are incapable of contracting marriage: those who lack sufficient use of reason.

   Those persons are considered to lack sufficient use of reason who are affected by mental illness (irrespective of whether it is congenital or acquired, endogenous or exogenous, or whether it is of general relevance or relevant only in relation to marriage) and lack, at the moment of consent, the effective use of their intellectual and volitional faculties. The expression sufficient use of reason refers to the degree of effective possession of the faculties of comprehension and will which is normally acquired from the age of seven years and which is absolutely necessary for a person to be the subject of human acts and to be morally responsible (Caparros, E.; Thorn, Thériault, J., eds. Code of Canon Law Annotated. Montreal: Wilson and Lafleur Limitée, 1993).

- **Lack of Due Discretion**: Canon 1095.2 -- The following are incapable of contracting marriage: those who suffer from a grave lack of discretion of judgment concerning the essential matrimonial rights and obligations to be mutually given and accepted.

   The object of matrimonial consent -- the very persons as man and woman give themselves to each other as an obligation and as man or as woman accept the other as a right to be claimed -- require on the part of the contracting parties a degree of maturity that is not only greater than simple use of reason, but also than one necessary for many affairs. There is a grave lack when it is proven that a contracting party lacks intellectual and volitional maturity necessary to discern, in view of binding oneself in an irrevocable manner the essential rights and duties of marriage which are the object of mutual surrender and acceptance. The discretion of judgment refers to that degree of maturity of comprehension and of will of the contracting parties which enables them to give and receive each other, through a juridical bond, in a unique community of life and love (Caparros, E.; Thorn, Thériault, J., eds. Code of Canon Law Annotated. Montreal: Wilson and Lafleur Limitée, 1993).

- **Inability to Assume**: Canon 1095.3 -- The following are incapable of contracting marriage: those who, because of a psychological nature, are unable to assume the essential obligations of marriage.

The legislator acknowledges, as consensual incapacity and cause of nullity of marriage, a complex series of psychic anomalies (among which psychosexual disorders are prominent although these are not the only conditions) which affect the personality structure of the subjects, and may deprive them of sufficient use of reason, or impede directly and clearly their discretion of judgment or discernment of the object of consent, nevertheless produce in them a psychological incapacity to assume, in undertaking the task in a truly committed and responsible manner, the essential obligations of marriage. It is important to remember that these essential obligations must be mutual, permanent, continuous, exclusive, and irrevocable so that there would be incapacity of one of the contracting parties should be, due to psychological cause, incapable of assuming these obligations with these essential characteristics (Caparros, E.; Thorn, Thériault, J., eds. Code of Canon Law Annotated. Montreal: Wilson and Lafleur Limi.

- **Partial and Total Simulation**: Canon 1101 -- §1. The internal consent of the mind is presumed to conform to the words or signs used in the celebration of a marriage. § 2. If, however, either or both of the parties should by a positive act of will exclude marriage itself or any essential element of marriage or any essential property, such a party contracts invalidly.

A marriage comes into being when two juridically capable persons express, in a legally recognized fashion, their consent to be married (c. 1057, 1). By means of this consent, a man and a woman irrevocably give and receive each other (c. 1057, 2) so as to establish a relationship embracing the whole of their lives; a relationship that intrinsically tends towards the good of the spouses and the procreation and education of children (c. 1055, 1). Because marital consent is an internal act not subject to direct inspection, church law presumes that two people who undergo a ceremony of marriage elicit it (c. 1101, 1). This presumption does yield to contrary proof. "If, however, either or both of the parties by a positive act of the will exclude marriage itself, some essential element of marriage, or some essential property of marriage, the party contracts invalidly" (c. 1101, 2). Jurisprudence terms the act of excluding marriage itself total simulation and calls the exclusion of some essential element or property of marriage partial simulation (coram De Lanversin, 18 February 1984, *Sacrae Romanae Decisiones*, Dec. 76 (1984), 100). Total or partial simulation invalidates the marriage because either form of simulation describes the discrepancy between the words or signs used in the marriage ceremony and the internal attitude.

•   **Fraud: Canon 1098** -- A person contracts invalidly who enters marriage inveigled by deceit, perpetrated in order to secure consent, concerning some quality of the other party, which of its very nature can seriously disrupt the partnership of conjugal life.

Even though any person who is deceived errs, error and deceit are not to be confused. While in error the subject makes a false judgment concerning the object and is the author of the lack of correspondence between his or her idea and reality, in deceit it is a third person who, through fraud, fabricates a false reality which gives rise in the subject to an apparently "true" perception of an object that is in itself false. Consequently, there is, in deceit, an inappropriate manipulation by a hired person of the formulation of the act of comprehension in the subject who is its victim. This act of comprehension is absolutely necessary to consent which of its very nature must correspond to the self-determination of the contracting parties themselves. The attempt at controlling a person's process of comprehension as a prerequisite of the act of the will, and also deceitfulness incompatible with the dignity of marriage, in our opinion, are more than sufficient reasons for deceit to be grave in itself, and for the legislator to determine it as a cause of nullity.

- **Force and Fear: Canon 1103** -- A marriage is invalid which is entered into by reason of force or of grave fear imposed from without, even if not purposely, from which the person has no escape other than by choosing marriage.

Grave fear proceeding from an external cause and inflicted unjustly to extort matrimonial consent renders marriage null and void, as indicated in Canon 1103, §1. The reasons for this norm of law are given by St. Thomas to be the following: the matrimonial bond is perpetual; wherefore, whatever is in opposition to this perpetuity does away with marriage. Unjustly inflicted fear of such a nature as to overcome a steady and firm character destroys the perpetuity of the contract, as *restitutio in integrum* can be invoked against this according to the principle that those things done by force and fear must be revoked as null and ought to be devoid of the binding force of validity. Furthermore, marriage signifies the union of Christ and his Church, which has been effected according to the liberty of love. Fear as described above is absolutely and unalterably opposed to such liberty. Therefore, the sacrament cannot proceed from such a source. In view of this, Pope Alexander stated that since consent could not be present where fear and constraint interfered, it is necessary that where one's consent is required the force of constraint be excluded. If such constraint were employed, the marriage would be null.

- **Error: Canon 1099** -- Provided it does not determine the will, error concerning the unity or the indissolubility or the sacramental dignity of marriage does not vitiate matrimonial consent.

Provost describes error as "the false apprehension of a thing, or false judgment of the mind. Over and above ignorance, error adds a fallacious judgment about the object that is willed. People who are in error know something, and know that they know something; but what they know is not correct, objectively speaking ("Error as a Ground in

Nullity Cases," James H. Provost, CLSA Proceeding, 57 (1995) 306-324, p.308). The Thomistic philosophy teaches us that the two faculties of intellect and will harmoniously cooperate to allow a person to function in a truly human way. Before a person makes a decision the intellect provided a practico-practico [sic] judgment which then moves the will to act. Such judgments are formed on the basis of the information provided to the intellect and if this information or knowledge should be erroneous and the will would be directed toward a mistaken end ("Deceit and Induced Error About a Personal Quality," Kenneth E. Boccafola, Monitor Ecclesiasticus, Vol. CXXIV, Series XXXIX (a. 114), Oct.-Dec. 1999, 692-710, p. 695). Error of law, then, is present when the false apprehension or judgment is so pernicious (pervicax) that the person cannot desire or act otherwise than how he or she thinks. Error of law regarding unity or indissolubility or sacramental dignity (c. 1099), is error about something which amounts to a condition sine qua non (c. 126). Other elements of marriage have also been identified as conditions sine qua non, for instance, the procreation and education of offspring, or the good of the spouses (c. 1055 §1).

## Concluding Thoughts

People are different, marriages are different and annulment cases are different. Some people are not interested in the annulment process and that is fine. The annulment process is not mandatory for divorced Catholics unless he or she wishes to remarry with the blessing of the Catholic Church. But the process is not meant to be intrusive or unreasonably daunting. It is here to help you understand what happened in the past, bring healing to your life, and most importantly provide you with a practical means to make better decisions in the future. Get in touch with your pastor and discuss the whole issue in light of your situation if you feel you will want to remarry sometime in the future.

# Now What?

The annulment process can be one of the Church's greatest gifts, if you allow it to be so. This means that much of it depends on your attitude toward the process and the people helping you though it, as well as your openness to the truth about yourself, your spouse and all that happened. The annulment process plays an essential role in showing you where you may have made mistakes in your marriage, and even more important it helps you to avoid making the same mistakes again. The process can also be very difficult because of the focus on these things, but as the saying goes, no pain, no gain. Here are some good ways to determine if going through the annulment process is right for you and if you are ready:

1.  **Reflect**: While the annulment process can be very healing, it is also usually not without pain. Being totally honest with yourself and digging back into the past is required to complete the process. Are you ready for this step at this point in your life? Is this what God is calling you to do right now? Are there other motivations you may have for doing this now?

2.  **Investigate**: Talk to someone at your local parish about the annulment process. Typically, a layperson or a deacon is the main contact and can answer all your questions about annulments and how to begin the process.

3.  **Prepare**: Gather the facts pertinent to your situation. Remember, the tribunal is primarily concerned with what the relationship between you and your ex-spouse was like before you were married and on the day of the wedding. Review the section "What are the Grounds for Annulment?" again and try to narrow down what your grounds might be. Try and identify who would be good witness in your case who can speak to the issues that would support your grounds. Do you know where these people are and are you able to contact them? Would they be cooperative? If you have decided to move forward with the annulment process, it is a good idea to contact your ex-spouse and let them know. They will have the opportunity to respond, and it is always better if they are fully aware of how the process works. This will avoid them being surprised by any correspondence from the Tribunal. It is also very important that they understand that this is not a "witch hunt" and the Church is not trying to assign blame. On page 52 of the Workbook companion, you will find

an "Annulment Preparation Worksheet," which is a great tool to help gather all the important information when preparing for an annulment.

4.  **Pray**: The annulment process can be quite detailed and lengthy. Prayer can be very helpful in preparing for and completing the process. Pray the rosary with the following intentions before each decade:

    1<u>st</u> Decade: Pray for the courage to accept the truths about your marriage relationship as they are brought to light, as well as to tell the truth when stating your case and answering the questionnaire.

    2<u>nd</u> Decade: Pray for humility to assume appropriate responsibility for the failure of the marriage.

    3<u>rd</u> Decade: Pray for forgiveness for your ex-spouse.

    4<u>th</u> Decade: Pray for wisdom to know the right time to begin the process.

    5<u>th</u> Decade: Pray for openness to the Tribunal's decision.

## Meditation

### Matthew 9: 27 - 31

As Jesus went on his way two blind men followed him shouting, "Take pity on us, son of David." And when Jesus reached the house the blind men came up with him and he said to them, "Do you believe I can do this?" They said, "Lord, we do." Then he touched their eyes saying, "According to your faith, let it be done to you." And their sight returned. Then Jesus sternly warned them, Take care that no one learns about this." But when they had gone away, they talked about him all over the countryside.

**Opening Prayer**: Dear Jesus, I want to spend these moments with you to learn from you and experience your love for me. Help me to be attentive use this time wisely. I pray for your guidance in the midst of these difficult decisions I must make.

**Petition**: Dear Lord, grant me the grace of a greater faith in you.

1. *Do you believe I can do this?*

   It is interesting to see how the blind men asked Jesus to cure them, and Jesus didn't just wave his hand and give them their eyesight—he tested their faith. He wasn't testing them to be cruel; he wanted them to recognize that faith was the key, faith in him. Jesus healed them because of their faith. How much faith do you have in God at this time? As you reflect on all that has happened to you in your divorce and all that is ahead of you, what would your answer be to his question, "Do you believe I can do this?" It is easy to say the words and ask God to help you in whatever you need, but how much do you really believe that he will take care of you? Are you prone to complaining? Whining? Bouts of self-pity? This is doubt in action and does not help you. In going through a divorce, it can be particularly hard to trust again, and God knows your reservations. Yet, he continually calls you to come closer to him because he wants you to put your trust in him alone. Sometimes, the trust issue is rooted in the fact that you just don't want to let go of the relationship with your ex-spouse. Sometimes, the issue is regretting the mistakes you have made and the pain that has resulted; therefore, you may want to control everything yourself. You need to ask God for his help—to forgive, to heal and to move on. But you also need to trust him and believe that he will help you.

2. *According to your faith, let it be done to you.*

   How can you increase your ability to trust in such a difficult time? First, ask God for the grace to grow in your faith and ability to trust in him. He will give you what you need. Second, proceed in your life as if he has already taken care of the things you need. For Jesus told us, "Have faith in God. In truth I tell you, if anyone says to this mountain, 'Be pulled up and thrown into the sea,' with no doubt in his heart, but believing that what he says will happen, it will be done for him. I tell you, therefore, everything you ask and pray for, believe that you have it already, and it will be yours. And when you stand in prayer, forgive whatever you have against anybody, so that your Father in heaven may forgive your failings, too." God can heal you. God can make your life happier than you can ever imagine. Believe in his love for you and trust that he will take care of you.

**Closing Prayer**: Dear Lord, I believe that you will heal me and I pray for the grace to never doubt you. Thank you for all you have done for me.

## Resolution

Spend one hour in Adoration. During that time, bring this situation to God and talk to him about it, especially if you are feeling confused or uncertain about it. Offer your hour of Adoration for others who are suffering in troubled marriages.

## Suggested Reading

Michael Smith Foster, *Annulment: The Wedding That Was: How the Church Can Declare a Marriage Null*, Paulist Press (April 1999)

Edward N. Peters, *Annulments And The Catholic Church: Straight Answers To Tough Questions*, Ascension Press (May 31, 2004)

# Chapter Six:

# Stay Close to the Sacraments

We have wonderful gifts, the sacraments, at our disposal. They contain the graces necessary to heal us and make us whole again. They are the sure-fire way to gracefully and peacefully get through rough times.

As we discussed in the third chapter, "What Does the Church Really Teach About Divorce," separated and divorced Catholics are welcome and encouraged to attend mass and also to receive the sacraments as long as they are chaste and have not remarried without a declaration of nullity.

Those issues aside, you are encouraged to attend mass and receive the sacraments as often as possible, even daily if you choose. But some people may still have a difficult time just coming to mass on Sunday because of their intense feelings surrounding their divorce and their relationship with God. Many people feel awkward and ashamed about their divorce and don't want to be in the presence of others at church; many are angry with God and feel their attendance at mass is hypocritical; some just can't sit through a mass while they are surrounded by happy families. They find it difficult to get through five minutes without becoming emotional.

Also, many people find it quite daunting to go to confession during a divorce because they don't want to be judged or criticized about their situation. Some have complained that they are not ready to let go of their anger toward their spouses and only want to see them fail and to confess this would be wrong in itself because they cannot be sorry for the way they are feeling.

Knowing all this, why, then, would anyone want to go to mass daily or to the sacrament of confession more than once a year, which is what is required to be a Catholic?

The goal of this chapter is to understand what the sacraments are and how they will help you. You want to realize the great source of strength and stability that you will receive by staying close to the sacraments.

# The Case

Cathy shares her story:

It had been several years since my husband and I had divorced. I had hoped that by that time I would have found some peace about it all and moved on with my life, but things just seemed to remain very difficult. In one sense, I had moved on by taking a job in a completely different state. Our kids were in college and didn't need me around constantly, so I found a nice house in a good area and tried to begin a new life. I devoted myself to my work. I had a few friends, but kept to myself mostly, doing all the things I said I never had time for when I was married. I made good money and believed I was doing everything I needed to be happy.

During our marriage, we went to church on Sundays as a family, but I really didn't put forth much effort after that. I was pretty busy. Oddly enough, our sons were more Catholic than my husband and I. They didn't get that from me and they certainly didn't get it from their father. But after he moved out, I began spending a lot of time in the adoration chapel at church, just sitting in front of the Blessed Sacrament. I felt peaceful when I was there and spent the time trying to sort everything out. I began to go to mass a few times during the week and felt I had been changing for the better. But then I began to get depressed and I couldn't seem to bring myself back to normal.

One day I was on the phone with my older son, Brad, who called me almost every day. He mentioned that the parish priest in our hometown was being sent to a parish close to where I was now living. I knew my son well, and recognized that in his subtle way was hinting that I should go talk to this priest. As soon as he said this, I had two thoughts . . . first, that it would be great to see a familiar face, but the next thought was not pleasant. That was the thought of sharing with him all that had happened to our family. It had been a devastating experience. If I saw him, I knew I couldn't avoid talking about all that. In the end, I decided I wouldn't go out of my way to see him. I was feeling bad enough without having to go through it all again with Fr. Joe.

But a few days later, as I tossed and turned in bed I thought more about the fact that I had been so depressed. The loss of my marriage was something I didn't speak about with anyone. I had been through some initial counseling at first and it was helpful. But now, I felt I just wanted to move on. As I lay there wide awake in the middle of the night, I began to ache for a change in my life. Anything! Something! I knew I could not continue this way. There had to be a change. And then I realized what it was I needed to do.

A few weeks after he arrived at his new parish, I made an appointment with Fr. Joe. The day before the appointment, I had just about talked myself out of going because I knew I would feel humiliated by admitting what had happened and I was heavy with the weight of the things that had been bothering me. But I told myself it would be a quick visit—I would welcome him to the area and chat about his new parish for a bit.

As I sat in Fr. Joe's office, I did tell him a little about what had happened. I tried to keep it as basic as possible. Fr. Joe listened intently to my words, his arms folded across his chest. Then he said to me suddenly, "Cathy, would you like to go to confession?" His words surprised me and I didn't know what to say. "Has it been a long time?" He smiled gently as he reached into his drawer and grabbed a purple stole, putting it around his neck.

"I guess, it has been," I said, looking down. Somehow, the thought of going to confession seemed like a good idea. "And yes," I admitted to myself, "it's got to be at least ten years since my last one. How did he know?"

Fr. Joe listened without interruption as I told him everything. I cried a lot, but surprisingly was not embarrassed. When I was finished, I felt as if a tremendous weight had been lifted from me. I walked away from that meeting with Fr. Joe experiencing the peace I had been looking for all along. I realized that through my faith, my happiness in life would gradually be restored.

## The Trouble with Divorce

Enduring a traumatic situation, such as a divorce or separation, has harsh effects on people's emotional well being. The extreme sense of loss that accompanies divorce really shakes us up inside. It rattles our belief system and can cause us to rethink almost everything we know because now there is a great sense of doubt. Without someone to support us, to help us keep our feet on the ground, this shakiness will affect just about every aspect of our psyche, especially our spiritual well being. It is so easy to question our faith at a time like this.

There is also the issue of the scarlet "D." Being divorced places a person in a unique situation, one that is misunderstood by many who have never had to walk a mile in your shoes. It is easy to feel as if you are wearing a huge scarlet "D" on your chest that everyone can see and judge you for. Just as Hester Prynne, the protagonist in Nathanial Hawthorne's *The Scarlet Letter* suffers condemnation by the community she lives in, it is easy to feel similar emotions such as shame, despair, and solitude when attending church, visiting family or just going about your daily life. It is because of these things, assuming that others are making judgments, as well as not understanding the teachings of the faith, that causes so many Catholics to leave their faith altogether. This is such a tragedy because the Church is the one place where broken life can receive true healing. How can you ever experience this healing if you separate yourself from your faith?

Let's look more closely at the sacraments of confession and the Eucharist so we can appreciate these gifts that are ours, free for our taking.

## The Sacrament of Confession

One day, my five-year-old daughter and three-year-old son were playing quietly in the play room as I was folding laundry and putting it away. As I walked past the hall closet, I noticed a beautiful rendition of a snowman drawn on the wall with purple crayon. I knew this was likely not the actions of my daughter who had long since learned the lesson of coloring on the walls. No, it had to be my three-year-old son, but I didn't want to confront the situation with an accusation; I wanted them to tell me what had happened and give them an opportunity to exercise their honesty. So I went into the playroom and asked them both, "Who drew the snowman on the wall out there?" They both looked at me like deer in headlights and my daughter pointed to my son and said, "Ryan did it." In great protest, Ryan immediately replied, "No, I didn't. Christina did it!"

"Mmm hmm." I knew there might be some resistance, but I was not going to give in just like that. I said to them again, "Children, you need to tell me the truth. Who drew the snowman on the wall?" I only got the same response; both of them pointing at each other saying the other was to blame.

I brought the children out to the hallway where we have a picture of Jesus and His Sacred Heart with Mary and her Immaculate Heart hanging on the wall. I sat them down in front of the picture and said, "I want you both to look at that picture and think about what Jesus and Mary would say about this right now. I'm going to give you a few minutes and I will be back to talk to you about it."

After a few minutes of finishing the laundry, I returned to the hallway and stood the kids up. Looking into their eyes I said, "Okay. Now, Ryan, did you think about what Jesus would say about this?" Ryan nodded affirmatively. "Alright then, why don't you tell me what he said?"

Ryan looked at me with his big beautiful brown eyes and said, "Jesus said Christina did it."

Now, that is a cute and simple story, but oddly enough many grown men and women take the same approach toward going to confession as Ryan did toward owning up to his graffiti; they are afraid to own up to their sins.

These days, the idea that people actually "sin" is fading into the background in shades of very light gray. There are the obvious sins, such as robbing a bank, committing a murder, etc., and many people believe that since they are not committing those big crimes, they are basically good people who have no sins to confess. We're all basically good people, right? True, but we are all sinners, too. All of us.

When you experience a divorce, you begin to see much more sinfulness than robbing a bank or murder; you see very serious sins, such as adultery, pornography, addictive behavior that destroys families, extreme selfishness, abandonment of spouses and children. All of these situations are gravely serious. Now, if your spouse has taken part in any of these types of behavior and you have not, you may feel justified in thinking you don't need to go to confession. But that is not true—we all need to go. Even so, you would still benefit greatly from going. Why?

One good reason is if you are angry. As we discussed previously, anger in and of itself is not sinful, it is a natural reaction to circumstances. However, if you perpetuate your anger, it does become sinful, and if left unchecked you could easily be dealing with rage issues in the future.

Christ told us, "But I say this to you, anyone who is angry with a brother will answer for it before the court; anyone who calls a brother, 'fool' will answer for it before the Sanhedrin; and anyone who calls him 'Traitor' will answer for it in hell fire. So, if you are bringing your offering to the altar and there remember that your brother has something against you, leave your offering there before the altar, go and be reconciled with your brother first, and then come back and present your offering" (Matthew 5: 22 - 25).

Going to confession reconciles us with God and "our brother" even in respect to venial sins, which all of us are guilty of. It brings us back into God's grace and cleanses our soul.

Practically speaking, when you go to confession and speak to the priest, you have the opportunity to "get things off your chest" and really get to the root of your problems. In turn, you receive counseling from the priest, who is in persona Christi, or representing Christ.

Why isn't it enough to ask God's forgiveness through our private prayer? Well, it is always enough in one sense because God wants you to ask for his forgiveness, and this can be done any time, anywhere. But going to receive the sacrament fortifies you with a special grace that you cannot get from just asking for forgiveness through private prayer. You need to make the effort to go and that is a sign of a penitent heart.

Let's read from the gospel of Luke:

Now it happened that on the way to Jerusalem he was traveling in the borderlands of Samaria and Galilee. As he entered one of the villages, ten men suffering from a virulent skin-disease came to meet him. They stood some way off and called to him, "Jesus! Master! Take pity on us." When he saw them he said, "Go and show yourselves to the priests. Now as they were going away, they were cleansed" (Luke 17: 11 - 14).

It is in this scripture that we see an illustration of our answer, an actual parallel to the sacrament of confession. In the days of Jesus, lepers were considered to be sick because of sins they had committed. When these lepers saw Jesus, they knew He could heal them of their affliction and so they called out to him and asked him to heal them, much the same way you go to Jesus and ask him to forgive us our sins. Jesus healed the lepers, but still sent them to the priests: "Go and show yourselves to the priests." This was because the priests were the ones that could officially declare a person "clean." And this is the same when you go to confession—you confess your sins to the priest who is in persona Christi, and in turn the priest absolves us of our sins—he declares us clean.

The Catholic Church states that any Catholic must go to confession at least once a year to remain an active member, but recommends that everyone receive the sacrament every two weeks. This may seem extreme, but the graces you receive in doing so are tremendous. It also helps your conscience to become sensitive to sin and helps you to develop virtuous habits. Anyone going through a divorce, regardless of how it happened, could benefit from some grace every few weeks. Confession is a beautiful gift to you. All you need to do is partake.

> Going to confession reconciles us with God
> and "our brother" even in respect to venial sins,
> which all of us are guilty of.
> It brings us back into God's grace and cleanses our soul.

And so you see the importance of receiving the sacrament of reconciliation, but what about the sacrament of the Holy Eucharist?

## The Sacrament of the Holy Eucharist

There are countless writings, books and teachings about the Eucharist that can enrich our knowledge and understanding of this most holy sacrament. We could spend weeks discussing this sacrament. But for the sake of this chapter, let us talk about the most basic elements, which in and of themselves are points for reflection for the rest of our lives:

With great truth is the Holy Eucharist called the fountain of all grace . . . the source of all gifts and graces.

. . . consider attentively the nature of bread and wine, the symbols of this sacrament: what the bread and wine are to the body, the Eucharist is in a superior order to the health and joy of the soul (*CCC*).

The effects of receiving the Eucharist include the following:

1. It imparts grace to the worthy recipient.
2. It remits venial sin.
3. It is an antidote against future sin.
4. It increases strength over the unhealthy desires of the flesh.
5. It facilitates to an extraordinary degree the attainment of eternal life;

> "Anyone who does eat my flesh and drink my blood
> has eternal life and I shall raise that person up on the last day."
> John 6:54

If you consider the great gifts that are yours, just waiting for you to come and receive them, your life would change considerably. Especially in times of personal difficulty and sorrow, you need the strength and grace that comes from the sacrament of confession and the sacrament of the Eucharist. Christ waits for you, patiently but anxiously, for he has so much to give you. He wants to heal your heart and set it on fire with love.

It is also important to note that, for a divorced person, there are great temptations that lay around every corner. The devil has laid traps especially for you because he knows you have a weak spot caused by the pain of your divorce. He uses your circumstances to make you vulnerable to these pitfalls.

Christ knows the trials you will be sent (and have been sent). That's why he has given you the sacraments—to strengthen you, enlighten you, and sustain you through your difficulties. He suffered, died on the cross and went to heaven to prepare a place for us, yet he is still with us here through the sacraments.

## What Does Scripture Say?

"I am the living bread which has come down from heaven. Anyone who eats this bread will live for ever; and the bread that I shall give is my flesh, for the life of the world . . . for my flesh is real food and my blood is real drink. Whoever eats my flesh and drinks my blood lives in me and I live in that person" (John 6: 51, 55-56).

Jesus makes no bones about it—his flesh is real food, his blood is real drink, and he is giving himself in this way to you to give you eternal life. Just as a husband gives himself to his wife and they become one, so does Christ give himself to you under the appearance of bread and wine, that you may be one with him.

## Concluding Thoughts

The *Catechism of the Catholic Church* teaches:

"Sacramental grace" is the grace of the Holy Spirit, given by Christ and proper to each sacrament. The Spirit heals and transforms those who receive him by conforming them to the Son of God (*CCC* #1129).

Take advantage of these wonderful gifts, that you may become strong and hopeful in your times of trial.

> What material food produces in our bodily life,
> Holy Communion wonderfully achieves in our spiritual life.
> Communion with the flesh of the risen Christ . . .
> preserves, increases, and renews the life of grace
> received at Baptism.
> - St. Ambrose

## Now What?

When you are seriously ill, you go to the hospital because hospitals contain those things that will heal you: experts with deep knowledge of medical issues, pharmaceuticals, medical devices, and therapies to make you well. One of the key components of healing is hope—hoping that the treatments will work and you will recover.

What hospitals and medicines do for your physical health, the Church and the sacraments do for your spiritual health: they heal you and make you stronger. As with health care, it is essential for you to participate in the sacraments to realize their powerful benefits. Here are some practical ways to do that:

1. **Read**: Learn more from scripture about the Eucharist and how Christ gave us himself in the Blessed Sacrament by reading John 6:26-58. Really study this scripture passage and see how strongly Christ conveyed the importance of eating His body and drinking His blood.

2. **Believe**: Many Catholics struggle with the doctrine that during the mass, the bread and wine is actually transformed into the Body and Blood of Christ. If you have some reservations about this too, you are not alone. The disciples themselves found Christ's words hard to believe, yet these same disciples witnessed many incredible miracles. But scripture is forthright in declaring this real presence. Take 30 minutes or so and read 1 Cor. 10:16–17, 11:23–29; and, most importantly, John 6:32–71.

3. **Pray for Your Unbelief**: Believing is a conscious decision, not a feeling or emotion. Just because you don't feel it "in your gut" or have a negative emotion about some truth, does not make it any less true. For example, if you are hiking in the mountains and come across a precarious rope bridge and on it is posted a sign by the National Forestry Service stating that the bridge has been recently tested and approved as completely safe, would you not be inclined to believe the authority that made that declaration? Sure you would! Why? Because you trust the authority that said it even though you did not test it yourself. You believed it without seeing proof. If you are like most people, you would walk across the bridge, maybe a little apprehensive, but trusting in the Forestry Service that you will make to the other side. That is how you are to approach the Church and its sacraments, with trust that they contain God's truth. Read Mark 9:20-24 and pray that your unbelief may be turned into a deeper trust and belief in the truth the Church proclaims.

4. **Go to Mass**: Exposure to the sacraments will have an impact no matter what you believe. If you can't receive the Eucharist, don't let that

prevent you from going to mass. Just being in the presence of Christ in the Blessed Sacrament is going to have a positive and healing impact on you. Go every Sunday. If you can, go during the week at least once. Mass is available from early in the morning, at noon, and even in the evening at different parishes. Check with your local parishes and find out their daily mass schedules. One is bound to celebrate mass at a time that works for you. Commit to going weekly (or more) for a month. You will be amazed at the positive impact it will have on your life.

5.  **Listen**:  Listen to Fr. Larry Richards' talk titled "The Mass Explained" and to his talk entitled "Confession." These are available at www.thereasonforourhope.org.

6.  **Go to Adoration**: Christ promised to be with us to the end of time (Matthew 28:20). Christ fulfills that promise in the Blessed Sacrament, the Eucharist. Fortunately for us, the Blessed Sacrament is present in every Catholic Church. Many churches now have perpetual adoration where the Blessed Sacrament is exposed in a monstrance 24 hours a day. This is an even more powerful way to experience Christ as you can actually see Him exposed in the Eucharist. Simply being in the same room close to Christ will have a significant healing and uplifting effect. Try it for 30 minutes at first and build up to an hour per visit. This is your time to be with Christ and experience His love and mercy in a very powerful way. You can pray, read, reflect, meditate, even rest. Like listening to soothing music, watching a sunset, or walking down the beach, spending time in adoration will not only rejuvenate you, it will draw you closer to Christ—the key to a life full of peace and joy.

# Meditation

### Matthew 26: 26 - 29

Now as they were eating, Jesus took bread, and when he had said the blessing he broke it and gave it to the disciples. "Take and eat," he said, "this is my body." Then he took a cup, and when he had given thanks he handed it to them saying, drink from this, all of you, for this is my blood, the blood of the covenant poured out for many for the forgiveness of sins. From now on, I tell you, I shall never again drink wine until the day I drink the new wine with you in the kingdom of my Father.

**Opening Prayer**:  Dear Lord, I thank you for all you have done for me. You have chosen to suffer as you did, die on the cross and still remain present on earth in the sacrament of the Holy Eucharist so I may be one with you. What a great miracle you have given me and I pray for the grace to appreciate your gift even more as I contemplate this mystery in my heart right now. Please help me to hear your voice.

**Petition**: Grant me the grace, O Lord, to love you more and come closer to you through the sacraments.

1.  *This is My Body.*

    In the sacrament of marriage, spouses give themselves totally to each other and become one heart, one mind, one flesh. This is a beautiful reflection of what Christ does for us in the Eucharist…he gives himself totally to us so we can be one with him; one heart, one mind, one flesh. What an incredible sign of love for you, that even though your spouse is gone, he or she will never leave you. Unlike the imperfect love of your spouse, Christ gives you his passionate, unconditional love because his greatest desire is for you to spend eternity with him in heaven. The gift of himself that he gives to you will strengthen you for the long haul and gives you the graces you need during this terribly difficult time you are experiencing.

2.  *This is My Blood.*

    When you receive the precious blood during communion, it is under the appearance of wine, yet it is the same blood that covered the whips and chains that were used to scourge Jesus as he was so unjustly punished. It is the same blood as that which ran down the cross and dripped onto the ground as Jesus hung there, suffering for us. It is the same blood that burst forth from his side when the soldier's arrow pierced his chest. And you are able to receive it! The blood of the new and everlasting covenant, as it is declared during the celebration of the mass. May you receive the grace to understand how precious his blood is. Even though you are not worthy to receive this gift—none of us are—Jesus still gives you the opportunity to come and be one with him.

**Closing Prayer**: Heavenly Father, you have given your Son to the world as a sign of your love for us. Grant that, through participating in the sacraments, I may increase in the virtues of faith, hope and love, and never underestimate the healing power of the sacraments. In Jesus' name I pray. Amen.

## Resolution

Make time this week to go to confession at a time when you won't feel rushed; when you have the time to make a good examination of conscience and can speak with the priest in a relaxed manner. A general confession is always a good idea if you're able to make an appointment, especially after a milestone in life like the one you have just experienced. On Sunday, as you receive communion, make a special act of thanksgiving to God for his gifts.

## Suggested Reading

Scott Hahn, *The Lamb's Supper: The Mass as Heaven on Earth*, Doubleday (November 9, 1999)

Scott Hahn, *Lord, Have Mercy: The Healing Power of Confession*, Doubleday; 1st edition (March 18, 2003)

John H. Hampsch, *The Healing Power of the Eucharist*, Charis Books (August 1999)

# Chapter Seven:

# Dealing With Your Ex-Spouse

Quite possibly, you may find this chapter to be the hardest chapter of all. Dealing with your ex-spouse can be extremely difficult, and having to encounter him or her continuously helps to perpetuate many of the feelings you are trying to rid yourself of: anger, resentment, frustration, anxiety, and at times, the feelings of love you had for your ex and your desire to hold on to the marriage relationship that used to be.

You may have to deal with your ex-spouse for the rest of your life for your children's sake and you will constantly be sharing custody of them. Maybe you'll have to deal with your ex-spouse because of businesses, possessions or other issues. Sometimes the ex-spouse just keeps coming back into your life even though there is no real reason for you to be in contact with them. Whatever the reasons are, it isn't always easy to confront your ex-spouse. Do these incidents spark arguments and fights? Do you find it difficult to control the tone of your voice and keep your conversations civil? Is it all you can do to maintain some patience and not blow up?

Many people have described having feelings of insanity during and after their dealings with their ex-spouses. Insanity, or emotions that are totally out of control, are a result of the volatile situations that keep this range of extreme emotions always fresh—never being able to make any progress in gaining control over them. Well, according to the wisdom of Benjamin Franklin, the definition of insanity is doing the same thing over and over and expecting different results. Very wise, indeed. Maybe it's time to try something different?

The goal of this chapter is to identify the triggers of a bad encounter with your ex-spouse and find some simple, practical ways to counteract those triggers. You want to get your hands on tools that allow you to gain control and make some good progress in this area, turning your explosive encounters with your ex into benign events.

# The Case

Jill has this to say about dealing with her ex-spouse:

It was a terribly difficult time for us. I was just about ready to take my kids and leave town for good because I was so angry and frustrated with my ex. He had initiated the divorce because he had begun a relationship with someone else. The kids and I were left high and dry with nothing. After we settled everything in court, he got the kids one night a week and every other weekend. He was also ordered to pay 32 percent of his income to me for child support.

But now, he never arrives on time to pick up the kids. Sometimes, he's late by an hour or two and sometimes he comes an hour early, complaining that I am doing a terrible job making sure the kids are ready to go with him. He never calls to say he's late or early, he just shows up when he wants to. He makes promises to the kids that he never fulfills and it kills me to see them so upset when they get home from staying with him. I believe he's doing these things to upset me, not even thinking about what it does to the kids. I am doing my best not to share my negative feelings with the kids and keep them focused on the fact that he is their dad and he loves them, but doing so is getting harder and harder. His support payments are almost 30 days late each month and I can't manage my budget with his sporadic contributions.

Each time I have to talk with him, I hang up crying and upset because he is so hostile toward me. I still don't know what I did to make him hate me so much. I know I have my faults and was not a perfect wife, but I tried to be good to him. I don't understand why he is so angry. Why does he want to see me suffer like this? I don't think I'll ever understand. The best thing I can do, I guess, is learn to deal with him and try to move on somehow. I just don't know how.

# Stop the Insanity!

It may seem like the frustration will never end! If you can't control your ex-spouse's behavior and you must continue communicating with him or her at least some of the time, how in the world will you ever survive with your sanity intact? How will you ever gain peace of mind?

You simply need to put this simple rule into practice—figure out what you can and cannot control and then focus on what you can control. Separating things in this manner and learning how to work with it all can become an art: the more you practice it, the better you become and the more naturally it integrates into your personality and temperament.

When ex-spouses engage in volatile confrontations, there are some typical reasons why—you call them "hot buttons" and here are some of those:

- Jealousy over the "other woman" or the "other man."
- An overwhelmingly guilty conscience that has no way to express itself other than mistreating others.
- Extreme hurt and anger over the divorce itself.
- Victimization - an unwillingness to take any positive steps toward moving on and simply blaming others for your pit of misery.

## Gaining Some Control

Gaining control over the situation is not difficult when the keys to success in this area are identified and utilized. When you know what these keys are and how and when to use them, they will help you in almost every situation. Jill explains how one of these key points helped her:

It actually first began one day when I got off the phone with Robert. He had me so upset I was shaking. He had screamed at me, used foul language and I got so angry that I joined in the screaming. When I hung up, I felt horrible because I had given in to my anger and frustration and stooped to his level of communication. I felt miserable and out of control. All I knew was that I didn't want to live this way. For days I was a wreck, trying to figure out how I was ever going to make it through life with this going on. Then one night as I was praying the rosary alone in my room, I had an epiphany and it was as simple as it was true... I couldn't control him, but I could control myself and all I had to do was make the decision not to join him in his barbaric behavior. He was the one who left, he got what he wanted, and I didn't have to accept this type of treatment anymore! He made his decision, now I would make mine. I would not be a part of his madness and I would not accept his obnoxious treatment any longer.

He called again a few days later, and within a few short seconds he was swearing at me and telling me what a terrible mother I was. I held the phone away from my ear until he was done and then I told him very plainly and calmly: I'm tired of your insulting behavior and if you can't speak to me calmly and without swearing, then you can't speak to me at all. You will have to speak to my attorney for everything. The choice is yours, Robert. I was shaking because I was trying hard to not let my nervousness show! And after a few moments of silence on the other end of the phone, it worked! Robert still sounded put out, but agreed that he would not continue in that mode of communication. After I hung up, I began to feel a great sense of relief that maybe, just maybe, I could actually move beyond this ugly stage of our lives into something better. I began to feel a strength in me that reminded me I am a good person and I deserve to be treated with dignity, just as everyone does.

Jill made tremendous strides for herself by simply recognizing the fact that she had a choice in the matter. She did not have to be intimidated by her ex-husband, nor live with his treatment of her. She made the decision and she took the stand and held on to her principles. Jill had no need to be rude, angry, or spiteful. In fact, she used a great deal of charity.

You are never completely without choices unless you are entirely without your ability to communicate. You just need to step back, analyze the situation, pray, and discover the choices you do have. Then you need to put those decisions into use. It is amazing how well this works in just about any situation.

What are some other ways you can gain control over situations that are out of control? There is another good way and it requires some deeper thought and a willingness to forgive. Yes, I know that word keeps coming up.

You need to recognize that these explosive situations you engage in with your ex-spouse are games. They are games because either one or both parties are unwilling to address the root of the problem.

For example, let's look at a wife, Tracy, who can barely tolerate speaking to her husband, Tim, and engages in the same behavior that Robert did with Jill. Each time Tracy comes in contact with Tim, whether in person or on the phone, she is angry and spiteful in the way she speaks to him. Tim does not engage in this behavior, but simply tries to make the encounter as brief as possible, sticking strictly to business. Tracy left Tim because she had fallen in love with a co-worker. Tracy's leaving the marriage fulfilled her desire to love and be with another man, yet deep inside she knew she was wrong in what she had done. She had betrayed her husband. She knew she had thrown away her marriage and was well aware that she had devastated Tim in the process. The guilt she felt over the months of having an affair without Tim's knowledge, and then witnessing how the divorce had hurt Tim so badly weighed on her to the point she could barely stand it. Her conscience was like a roaring lion that was starving for food and attention. Tracy knew she either had to completely silence her conscience in order to continue on with the decisions she had made, and as long as she was with her new man she could accomplish that. But each time she encountered Tim, the guilt would rear its ugly head again and all she felt was misery. Her immediate reaction was to unleash the roaring lion that was her guilt and attack Tim.

Tim, on the other hand, still loved his wife and although he was truly devastated by her choice to leave him for another man, he did not allow his anger and hurt to control him. At first, he was bewildered that Tracy was so vicious each time they encountered each other, but he was soon able to come to terms with the fact that now they were leading separate lives and he did not want to remain stuck in pain. He wanted to be able to move on and find a new life. And so with each encounter with Tracy, Tim remained calm and reasonable. Each morning before work, Tim took the time to read the gospel and reflect upon it. He found this gave him much peace and a good foundation for the day. Through his prayers and reflection, he realized how sorry he felt for his ex-wife. He couldn't change her or make her do what he wanted, but he still felt sorry for her and he prayed for her. He prayed that she would some day find the happiness she was looking for. Tim, as did Jill, acted upon their ability to choose, and they both found peace in doing so.

## Our Temperaments

Another great thing that can help you in this area would be to understand your temperament and that of your ex-spouse. Knowing as much about yourself as you can—knowing how you react to situations, understanding your temperament, recognizing what your primary defects are as well as the gifts and talents you possess—can help you learn to deal with your divorce, ex-spouse and related challenges on a much more effective level. The more you understand your tendencies, attitudes, etc., the better you know how to find ways to overcome your weaknesses. Each one of us has a unique temperament, which, when identifying your own, helps you to better understand the reasons why you might lose your temper quickly, fall into depression more easily than someone else, or any of the other ways you react to different situations.

The four basic temperaments are Choleric, Melancholic, Phlegmatic, and Sanguine. Although there is much to know about these temperaments, they are briefly described as follows:

- **Choleric** - Cholerics have intense reactions to things. They are entrepreneurs and leaders but do not require the approval of others for their beliefs and actions; they base their conduct on their own convictions. A Choleric is headstrong and impatient, but when something needs to get done, a Choleric is the person for the job.

- **Melancholic** - A Melancholic also has high ideals and extreme highs and lows, but is often steeped in perfectionism; tends to be more emotional than logical and sees the glass as half empty because of his or her desire for perfection.

- **Phlegmatic** - He or she is not easily upset, even when things are upsetting. He or she has a relaxed attitude and will avoid conflict at all costs. A Phlegmatic can be mistaken at times for not being sensitive to a person or situation because little to no emotion is displayed. But most often, a Phlegmatic is classified as level-headed and is very often the one that people look to for guidance in difficult situations.

- **Sanguine** - A Sanguine loves to be loved and craves attention and acceptance; he or she has a happy-go-lucky personality; the class clown. People love a Sanguine because of his or her ability to enjoy the moment. A Sanguine also reacts quickly to situations and people, and those reactions are often short-lived.

Most likely, you have a combination of elements from all of these temperaments, but you will find as you investigate that there is one temperament that is more dominant than the others. If you investigate these temperament descriptions and then reflect upon yourself and the way you react to people and situations, you can identify your dominant temperament. Then, you can identify your typical reactions to situations and understand the pitfalls you typically encounter when dealing with a challenging situation. From there, you can teach yourself better ways to deal with the difficult situations that arise because of your divorce.

Let's take an example that is fairly common to divorce situations and apply it to this issue. John has to meet his ex-wife, Sherry, at the parking lot of the local grocery store where he will pick up his children and keep them for the week while Sherry goes on vacation. John arrives on time to the appointed place of exchange and ends up waiting for 40 minutes for Sherry to arrive with the children. She does not call to tell him she's late, she simply arrives late. When she arrives and the kids get out of the car, Sherry gives John a list of directions for the week and mentions she will be picking the kids up a day early. She did not discuss any of this prior to the meeting; she simply announces that these directives are now in place. Let's look at how John would react to the different situations based on different temperaments:

- **Choleric**: John begins to argue with Sherry about being late with an "in-your-face" attitude. He's upset that she did not address the other issues with him before the drop-off. For John, it isn't that much of a problem that she will pick them up early or that he has to take care of the other things, he's more upset because she does not operate in a forthright manner. John will stew over this incident for the next two weeks, and it will probably play a role in the next argument that occurs between him and Sherry.

- **Melancholic**: John is somewhat disturbed by the fact that Sherry is late, and asks her why she's late. Didn't she leave her house on time? Hadn't she prepared for this the night before? All-in-all, he feels he can let go of the stunt his ex-wife is pulling, but over the next few days he will become more angry about it and by the time they exchange the kids at the end of the week, he will be very upset about it.

- **Phlegmatic**: John will be angry about what Sherry is doing, but he won't say much at all during the child exchange. He won't mention her being late, he will respond to her demands with, "Fine" and he will remind himself that he is happy he doesn't have to deal with her on a daily basis. There will be very little conflict during the meeting, if any. John will drive away angry and will stay that way until the next morning when he's simply let go of it all so he can enjoy the week with his kids.

- **Sanguine**: John is upset by his ex-wife's tardiness, and as she pulls up and starts talking he feels the pain of his divorce as if it were just happening. He doesn't want to argue because the last time that happened, Sherry would only communicate with him by e-mail. He gets his kids in the car and wonders if she is dating anyone. Their divorce was very painful, but he still believes that after a while she will come back to him. He is angry, but he's not willing to rock the boat. He would rather keep the small bit of relationship they have in tact.

You might be able to identify yourself or your ex-spouse in these scenarios, and it's good to be able to recognize your patterns of reactions to things because this becomes fertile ground for profound change to take place. You may not be able to change your temperament, but you can certainly pinpoint ways to avoid the weaknesses that come with them. By finding ways to counteract negative reactions to situations and putting them into practice, you provide yourself with the opportunities for significant personal growth. When you identify the positive aspects of your temperaments, not simply the negative, you can temper your reactions to situations. Let's look at what may help.

- **Choleric**: The great thing about a Choleric's temperament is that he's a born leader and self-starter. These are great strengths that, despite adversity, never fail. As a leader, John could be the first person in the relationship to address the points of contention with his wife in a calm and level-headed manner, putting a stop to the frustrating behavior.

- **Melancholic**: A Melancholic is self-disciplined and self-sacrificing, to name a few of his or her gifts. In the situation with his wife, instead of being focused on the details of why she was late and allow the stress level to increase, John could detach himself from the need to know why and let it go. They are, after all, divorced and learning to live new lives. Clinging to the frustration of the situation and constantly trying to figure out why it happened does no good. If he can detach, he can also go about his week without anyone ever knowing what happened because it would not be important to him either.

- **Phlegmatic**: One of the gifts of a Phlegmatic's temperament is his or her ability to remain calm in practically every situation. In this case, John already brings calm to the situation because he doesn't react and quickly let's go of the anger he feels. Something else that can help greatly in this situation is to make use of the diplomacy that he naturally has and find a way to get his wife to agree to stick to the schedule or plan that is laid out for their good, but especially for the good of the children.

- **Sanguine**: A great strength of a Sanguine temperament is their ability to be compassionate toward others. John could easily turn his frustration into compassion for his wife, taking note that she is the one resorting to playing games and being the one to take the high road and not join in.

Understanding your inner workings will help you determine what is holding you back from letting go, forgiving, moving on, etc., and allow you to adopt new behaviors. The more information you have about yourself, the better you can guide yourself on the road to healing.

> You simply need to figure out what you can and cannot control and then focus on what you can control.

## Out of the Mouths of Babes

Another important consideration is how your behavior and the way you and your ex-spouse treat each other affects your children.

Children do not understand divorce on an adult level. They do not think like adults, nor do they speak in adult terms. In her book, *The Unexpected Legacy of Divorce*, Dr. Judith Wallerstein reports that 85 percent of children are shocked when their parents divorce, even when there has been violence in the house. Few children are relieved that their parents have split up. It is clear that their view of what is happening is much different than an adult's, and far more confusing. Their world has been turned upside down and they are desperate to find some stability.

Sadly, many spouses use their children as shields or pawns in their divorce. Parents manipulate their children into siding with them and not the other spouse for whatever gratification it is they are looking for. Sandy, a very angry ex-spouse, only gives her children a negative image of their father. She never reserves time to let out her anger and frustration for when the kids are not around; she openly fights with her ex and speaks about him with angry words in front of and directly to them.

It's not that the truth should be hidden and children lied to; it's more that children should be given every opportunity to love their parents as if they were the only thing that mattered in the world. To a child, their parents are heroes; the smartest and wisest people alive. You are their examples of what people should be. The things you say and do will directly impact them in the near future and as they enter adulthood. They will look to your example as they begin their adult life. If you truly love your children and want them to lead happy lives, how can you help them gain confidence in you if you constantly berate and belittle your ex-spouse?

# What Does Scripture Say?

In the gospel of Matthew, Christ tells us:

You have heard how it was said, *You will love your neighbor and hate your enemy.* But I say this to you, love your enemies and pray for those who persecute you; so that you may be children of your Father in heaven, for he causes his sun to rise on the bad as well as the good, and sends down rain to fall on the upright and the wicked alike. For if you love those who love you, what reward will you get? Do not even the tax collectors do as much? And if you save your greetings for your brothers, are you doing anything exceptional? Do not even the gentiles do as much? You must therefore set no bounds to your love, just as your heavenly Father sets none to his (Matthew 5: 43 - 48).

## Being Charitable without Being a Doormat

How in the world can God expect me to pray for my spouse after what has happened? You might be thinking. How could it ever be possible for me to love my (spouse) enemy? It may not be easy to envision, but it is possible for this to happen.

What Christ is telling you in these passages is simple: let love be ruler of your heart. First, let's define love. St. Paul tells us:

Love is always patient and kind; love is never jealous; love is not boastful or conceited, it is never rude and never seeks its own advantage; it does not take offense or store up grievances. Love does not rejoice at wrongdoing, but finds its joy in the truth. It is always ready to make allowances, to trust, to hope and to endure whatever comes (1 Corinthians 13:4 – 7).

Yes, this description of love is a beautiful truth, and can seem rather lofty in the midst of a divorce. So let's put it in simple terms: love is desiring good for others. No retaliation, no desire for revenge, no desire to see things go wrong for that person.

Both Jill and Tim dealt with their ex-spouses in a very loving manner. If you go back and read their stories, you can see that A) they were firm and stood up for themselves in an appropriate manner; B) they both brought their ex's abusive behavior to an almost instant halt instead of enabling them to continue their pattern of angry abuse; and C) they did this without any malice or mistreatment of their ex's themselves. Both Jill and Tim were examples of how Christians can love, even in stressful situations.

Christ does not want you to lay down and be a doormat. No, you need to stand up for justice and do what you know is right. But in dealing with your ex-spouse, you must be charitable. Who knows, your attitude of love might even have an affect on them.

## Concluding Thoughts

Loving is simple, it just takes your decision to put it into action. Treating your ex-spouse in a loving way does not mean you put yourself at risk in any way whatsoever; in fact, it means you will be the one to make a difference. When you treat your ex in a loving manner, you change the dynamic of the broken relationship. You diffuse the explosive nature of your encounters. You bring a sense of dignity and respect into the broken relationship, even though there may have been very damaging words and actions. Love has a calming effect and speaks louder than a bullhorn. Love is all that Christ asks of you—you don't have to like them, you don't have to subject yourselves to their mistreatment; you simply need to recognize the fact that Christ loves them as much as He loves you, and for that reason alone you should be able to find it within yourself to treat them in a fair and decent manner.

> **Love is desiring good for others.**
> **No retaliation, no desire for revenge,**
> **no desire to see things go wrong for that person.**

## Now What?

While it may be unrealistic to think that you and your ex-spouse would ever become good friends, it is not unrealistic to expect that you can have a cooperative and respectful relationship, especially if you have children. You might have to take the lead in helping shape the relationship, but in the end it will be well worth it for everyone involved. Believe it or not, if you work at it your relationship with your ex-spouse can be one based on cooperation, consideration and mutual respect. Here are some ways you can make that a reality:

1. **Communicate Better**: So many of the on-going problems between ex-spouses are perpetuated by poor communication. The first thing to remember here is what we have discussed in this chapter – that you have a choice in the matter; you always have control over if and how you will respond. Confusion, verbal confrontations, or misunderstandings do nothing but create opportunities for tension and disagreement. Therefore, if tensions are high, it is best to keep verbal communications to a minimum. E-mail is one of the best ways to communicate day-to-day information like schedules, plans, and requests. It also creates enough

"space" between ex-spouses that it is less likely to trigger a confrontation. One precaution with e-mail is to remember the recipient cannot hear the "tone" you intend, so sometimes the written word can be misunderstood. It is always best to stick to factual information and steer clear of opinions or emotional comments when sending e-mail.

2.  **Plan Ahead**: You can minimize the possibility of triggering arguments and confrontations by planning ahead. When both of you are on the same page and have plenty of time to know what is going on, there is less chance of aggravation. With the help of e-mail, electronic calendars, and multifunction phones, it is easier than ever to keep track of today's hectic schedules. Use them to your advantage.

3.  **Forgive**: Problems dealing with ex-spouses are invariably caused by simmering anger and resentment. Forgiving your ex-spouse is the best way to end the cycle of bitterness and retaliation. It is easier said than done, for sure, but certainly possible—with God's help. Remember, forgiveness is not a one-time event; it is a process. Prayer helps begin and sustain that process. Pray daily for the grace to forgive. Many have found that praying the "Our Father" before having to communicate or interact with an ex-spouse, or any spontaneous prayer, helps put them in a better frame of mind to deal with their ex-spouse cooperatively and peaceably. Try it and see for yourself!

4.  **Do Nothing**: Rarely is a response or action taken when you are angry or upset going to lead to a positive result. Try doing nothing about your frustration for 24 hours after having a confrontation with your ex-spouse. Not only will this allow you to calm down, it will create a sense of "space" between you and your ex. This will give you time to more carefully think things through and, more importantly, to pray about the situation and to ask for God's grace to take the proper next step.

5.  **End the War**: So often problems between ex-spouses are caused by a never-ending cycle of retaliation. Retribution becomes the name of the game. However, this type of behavior creates a toxic environment for everyone—especially the kids. Have the courage to take the first step at breaking this cycle. Let your ex-spouse know that you will no longer participate in the arguments and destructive behavior. Tell him or her that you will respect him or her and you will expect the same

in return. Let them know that you will not tolerate anything less and you hope you can both find a common ground for a working relationship. It may take some time for your ex-spouse to realize you have truly changed your approach and you were serious about what you said, but stick to your guns. It will pay off in the long run.

6. **Don't Use the Kids**: Nothing will cause more problems then involving children in disputes with ex-spouses. Tell your ex-spouse you want both of you to commit to leaving discussions about issues that affect the children to a time when they aren't around—never in front of them. Another important point to apply here—never say anything derogatory about your ex-spouse in front of your children. Ask your ex-spouse to do the same. Many times, it will take a tremendous amount of prudence to bite your tongue, but in the long run you and the kids will be better off. Once your ex sees that you are taking the high road, he or she will be more likely to do so as well.

7. **Pray**: You can't control what you ex-spouse does, but you can always pray for them and for a better relationship with them. Pray for your ex-spouse that their heart may be open to being more respectful, more cooperative, and more rational. Prayer invites God into what may seem like an impossible situation and give him the opportunity to work. Remember, nothing is impossible with God!

> Ah, Lord Yahweh, you made the heavens and the earth
> by your great power and your outstretched arm.
> To you, nothing is impossible (Jeremiah 32:17).

8. **Pray the Rosary**: Pray for the Blessed Mother to intercede as you deal with your ex-spouse by praying the following intentions before each decade:
   1st Decade: Pray for the grace to forgive your ex-spouse.
   2nd Decade: Pray for the grace to be charitable to your ex-spouse, especially when you don't feel like it.
   3rd Decade: Pray for peace and cooperation in your dealings with your ex-spouse.
   4th Decade: Pray for patience when interacting with your ex-spouse.
   5th Decade: Pray for the fortitude to endure the difficult or negative times when dealing with your ex-spouse.

# Meditation

## Mark 14: 32 - 37

They came to a plot of land called Gethsemane, and he said to his disciples, "Stay here while I pray." Then he took Peter and James and John with him. And he began to feel terror and anguish. And he said to them, "My soul is sorrowful to the point of death. Wait here, and stay awake." And going on a little further he threw himself on the ground and prayed that, if it were possible, this hour might pass him by. "Abba, Father!" he said, "For you everything is possible. Take this cup away from me. But let it be as you, not I, would have it."

**Opening Prayer**: Dear Lord, I am here to spend these moments with you. I long to hear your words of consolation, to feel your presence and peace. I look to you in the misery of your passion and wish to unite my suffering to yours. Stay with me, Lord, for I am weak and I need you.

**Petition**: I pray, Lord, for an increase in the virtue of love, and a firm desire to treat others with love.

1. *My soul is sorrowful to the point of death.*

   Christ suffered more than you will ever know. He was the true, innocent victim, convicted and punished unjustly, but suffered out of love for us. If there is anyone who can understand our anger, our outrage at what has happened to you, it is Christ. Not only did he suffer every injustice as a completely innocent and loving human being, but he knows all that you have been through better than anyone. He knows the pain, the frustration, the insanity. Go to meet him in the garden and kneel down with him at the rock and talk to him about your situation. Unite your pain to his and embrace your cross with his help.

2. *But let it be as you, not I, would have it.*

   God's ways are not ours. He has a completely different perspective on what is happening because he sees everything, knows everything. The suffering you bear will bring about good things somewhere else, and this is one reason why God allows us to suffer. What good things will God bring out of your situation? What good things have already happened? As you kneel with Jesus in the garden and see his sweat turn into drops of blood, knowing he suffers for your sake, ask him to help you suffer as he did; out of love for others and the desire for good.

**Closing Prayer**: Dear Jesus, I am in awe of what you have done for me as I contemplate all that you suffered. Help me to imitate you in your suffering and take care of those I love. In your name, I pray. Amen.

## Resolution

1. Reflect upon any re-occurring, problematic situation you encounter with your spouse and try to come up with a way to bring peace to the situation so that next time it arises, you will know how to react and likely defuse a volatile situation.
2. Offer your next mass for your ex-spouse.

## Suggested Reading

Art Bennett, Laraine Bennett, *The Temperament God Gave You: The Classic Key to Knowing Yourself, Getting Along with Others, and Growing Closer to the Lord*, Sophia Institute Press (June 15, 2005)

Thomas D. Williams, *Spiritual Progress: Becoming the Christian You Want to Be*, FaithWords (February 13, 2007)

Lawrence G. Lovasik, *The Hidden Power of Kindness: A Practical Handbook for Souls, Who Dare to Transform the World, One Deed at a Time*, Sophia Institute Press (October 1999)

# Chapter Eight:

## How Are the Children?

In this chapter, let's take a good look at how you can help your children get through the serious changes that have taken place in the family. You know how the events of the separation or divorce have affected them, so what can you do to help them now? What do they need from you? Are there things you can do for them that will help them gain some peace, some stability, some understanding?

After a divorce has occurred, many adults assume that their kids will simply bounce back from the shock of their family unit being destroyed. This is the case, but only for a small percentage of children, even when children seem to be fine. The truth of the matter is that children are not capable of expressing their feelings in an adult manner. Even adults find it difficult to speak their mind openly and honestly—how much harder it is for children who do not understand the adult world, nor possess the vocabulary to convey the type and depth of their feelings! So many children bury their deep hurt, anger and feelings of instability and simply go back to their normal routine because they don't know how to communicate their grief over their situation. But it is still there and this kind of pain is capable of producing disastrous results later in life if it is not addressed.

In her exceptional book, *The Unexpected Legacy of Divorce*, Dr. Judith Wallerstein writes about her 25-year landmark study of children both from divorced families and intact families. Her findings are eye-opening and heartbreaking:

From the viewpoint of the children, and counter to what happens to their parents, divorce is a cumulative experience. Its impact increases over time and rises to a crescendo in adulthood. At each developmental stage divorce is experienced anew in different ways. In adulthood it affects personality, the ability to trust, expectations about relationships, and ability to cope with change.

The first upheaval occurs at the break up. Children are frightened and angry, terrified of being abandoned by both parents, and they feel they are responsible for the divorce. Most children are taken by surprise; few are relieved. As adults, they remember with sorrow and anger how little support they got from their parents when it happened. They recall how little support they got from their parents when it happened. They recall how they were expected to adjust overnight to a terrifying number of changes that confounded them. Even children who had seen or heard violence at home made no connection between that violence and the decision to divorce. The children concluded early on, silently and sadly, that family relationships are fragile and that the tie between a man and woman can break capriciously, without warning. They worried ever after that parent-child relationships are also unreliable and can break at any time. These early experiences colored their later expectations.

It is difficult to expect a child to be able to describe this wide range of emotions. Especially if there is great distrust in the stability of the relationship with their parents, it is not reasonable to expect that children will approach their parents to discuss these painful feelings. They will, in fact, bury those feelings. When they do this, their behavior often is tell-tale; fighting, grades dropping, distancing themselves from others. But a great majority of children do nothing different. They simply go back to their daily routines of school and sports or other activities where they feel safe and can appear normal even though they don't feel normal. They don't know how else to deal with it. Thus, we adults get the impression they have simply "bounced back." But those feelings that remain buried and are never dealt with will resurface at some point.

With all that you have to deal with in your divorce, this aspect of it may seem completely overwhelming. You are trying to deal with your own brokenness and distress, so how can you be a pillar of strength for your children and give them what they need?

The goal of this chapter is to identify practical and positive ways to provide stability for your children and give them the loving support they need to make their way through these important years in their lives. You will look at ways to reinforce the positives in your children keeping them, as much as possible, in a loving and healthy environment.

# The Case

Tanya tells us about her kids, Sarah, 15, Daniel, 8 and Bruce, 4:

My children had always been happy-go-lucky kids, for the most part. My husband, Derek, and I knew that even though we hadn't agreed on a divorce yet, the separation would be difficult for them and that we might have to take them to counseling. We stayed together in the house as long as we could for their sake without telling them our plans. I thought this was the right thing to do, but they knew something was wrong. Daniel was always asking me if I was mad at him and Bruce wanted to know if I thought he was a bad boy. Sarah just stayed quiet all the time. So Derek and I decided the best thing to do was to move forward with the separation. I knew it would be difficult, but I could never have prepared myself for the pain I now see in their eyes. Bruce is always upset and nothing I do comforts him. He never smiles, even when he has the things that used to make him happy. Daniel wakes up every night with bad dreams and crawls in bed with me.

My kids fight with each other all the time now! They used to be good buddies but I have to separate them often and send them to their rooms. Daniel's grades are beginning to drop and he just doesn't seem to take an interest in things anymore. Sarah is distant and won't talk to me. I know the teenage years are difficult, but I get the distinct feeling she blames me for the breakup and doesn't trust me even though she won't say that. At this point, I'd be happy if she said that to me because then she'd at least be talking to me. She is very angry.

Perhaps the most difficult thing for me is trying to explain to them why their dad doesn't live with us anymore. How much do they really need to know? None of them want to go to counseling and all of this on top of everything else makes me feel like I'm fighting a losing battle. But I can't lose my kids! My children are my whole world and I will do anything to bring them back some happiness, to make them feel safe and secure again. But I fear that my own hurt and sadness over this situation, along with the stress of making sure they have all that they need now and in the future, is going to take its toll on me sooner than later.

I need help. My kids need help.

## Silence is Loud

Grief and sorrow are powerful emotions in children, just as they are in adults. Perhaps they are more hurtful in children because of the loss of innocence that accompanies a fuller understanding that life is not all happiness. Teenagers, although older, still experience a "rude awakening" to the sufferings of life. Adult children may seem further removed from the situation if a divorce occurs after they have left the house and have families of their own, but they still suffer immensely, and some psychologists report that adult children suffer the most. However, what's really important is that irreversible changes have taken place in these lives that can have a tremendously negative effect. This is why it is so important to ground yourself as a parent in the belief that God brings good things out of bad. You need to cling to this and start the process of helping your children now.

The first point in helping your children cope, regardless of their age, is to recognize one of the gifts God gave us as parents. Fathers are protectors and of their tremendous gifts, this is probably the greatest gift they give to their families. Children know that when there is trouble, Dad is the one they turn to. Dad has the answers; Dad knows the right way to go. Dad—he's the pillar of strength and safety.

The French poet Charles Peguy is quoted as having written:

There is only one adventurer in the world, as can be seen very clearly in the modern world, the father of a family. Even the most desperate adventurers are nothing compared with him. Everything in the modern world . . . is organized against that fool, that imprudent, daring fool, . . . against the unruly, audacious man who is daring enough to have a wife and family, against the man who dares to found a family (Clio I (Cahiers), in Temporal and Eternal, New York 1958), p. 108.

These words could not be more true, for being a father and founder of a family these days takes great courage, anyone would agree.

As a mother, you have a wonderful and special gift from God—a mother's heart. He made your hearts particularly sensitive to the emotional and physical well being of your children. He gave you the gift of being nurturers; caretakers in the most intimate sense. Your children's welfare on all levels is naturally your biggest concern and your heart breaks when you cannot comfort them and make them feel better right away. You are creatures made for healing hurt and this disposition sets the tone for how you deal with your children in a loving and positive way. A mother's role is paramount to a child's well-being.

What else can you do for them in such a difficult situation? How can you take a child whose world has been shaken and become full of reasons to mistrust and provide him or her once more with a sturdy and dependable foundation where he or she feels safe again?

Well, there are many things that can be done. Let's take a look at some of the most important ones:

- Do the best you can to provide a sense of security for them that you can, primarily through establishing a routine. When there is a routine or some type of schedule in place, parents and children alike know what to expect from day-to-day, week-to-week, and this can be comforting in itself. School, homework, playtime, dinner, bath time, bedtime. Each day, always the same, and it's very helpful.

  But this must also be taken into consideration when the child is moving from one parent's location to the others. When a child is shuffled from place to place, his or her social life gets put on hold, and this is not helpful in providing security. Many times, a child has to spend a week or so with the non-custodial parent, and when they arrive he has to fit into the parent's schedule, which often can leave much time for boredom and getting into trouble. During this time, the child might be missing events that he considers to be very important—baseball practice or some other sporting event—piano practice or other similar regularly scheduled events. These things are of extreme importance to most children because the regularity is what gives them security in addition to seeing their regular friends. It is important to take into consideration their schedules when custody and visitation is being worked out.

- Because what has happened will not be fixed overnight, you as a parent must fortify yourself for the long haul. Therefore, strengthen yourself with the sacraments and prayer so you will have more to give them and more wisdom in dealing with them.

Just as the human body is endowed with organs capable of "providing for the life, health, and development of each of its members, so the Savior of the human race . . . has provided in a marvelous way for His Mystical Body, endowing it with the Sacraments, so that by so many consecutive, graduated graces, as it were, its members should be supported from the cradle to life's last breath" (*Mystici corporis*).

> If I am distracted, Holy Communion helps me to become recollected. If opportunities are offered each day to offend my God, I arm myself anew each day for the combat by the reception of the Eucharist. If I am in special need of light and prudence in order to discharge my burdensome duties, I draw nigh to my Savior and seek counsel and light from him.
>
> –St. Thomas More

Your children also need to see a firm example in their parent. They will take heart and find stability as they observe you finding strength and consolation in your faith. Christ is with you at all times. All you need to do is turn to him.

For your adult children, being a good example remains very important, but communication is also key. Not so much in divulging to them the super-personal details, but more in being open about answering the basic questions they may have about the situation. Many adult children side with one parent or another, but the big ways to help them get through this (and yourself as well) is to: a) not get bogged down with spouse-bashing or wallowing in all the negativity and self-pity; and b) to help them look forward—this moment and each future moment. What can be learned from the situation? Can their marriages be strengthened as a result of what's happened?

It is imperative for your non-adult children to know, really know and understand that they are good and that you love them. You should continually tell them they are loved and make certain that your lifestyle reinforces this. The most troublesome aspect for children at this stage is insecurity: "If Dad is gone, will Mom leave, too? Will I ever see Dad again? Will I always feel this lonely and hurt?" You know that actions speak louder than words and that is why it is so important to be very close to them now.

It is also important to allow them time to ask you the questions they have about what has happened in the family and give age-appropriate answers. Just as it is important for adults to discuss their feelings, so it is with children, and this is a very healthy aspect of helping your child to be happy. Bad feelings resulting from what has happened tend to take root when they are kept inside and cause greater problems later in life. So an open and loving discussion with your child will bring the issues to light and bring you closer to each other in the process.

It is also healthy for children to see a family counselor or psychologist. If this option is utilized, it is extremely important to find a good Catholic family counselor with a solid faith in God. There are many excellent therapists available to us today, but finding a solid Catholic therapist is key because many theories and philosophies are harmful to people who are vulnerable and hurt. Choosing someone who holds the same values you teach your children is critical to their mental, emotional and spiritual welfare.

Another very important thing you can do is to keep them involved in their faith. The positive reinforcement that comes with giving your child the gift of their faith is invaluable, not to mention the graces they receive from the sacraments if they are old enough to partake. When a child learns to have faith and trust in God, his or her foundation is strengthened for life. It is a priceless gift. Christ, himself, told us (adults) that we must become like little children in order to get to our final destination in life—heaven.

## What Does Scripture Say?

Then people brought little children to him, for him to lay his hands on them and pray. The disciples scolded them, but Jesus said, "Let the children alone, and do not stop them from coming to me; for it is to such as these that the kingdom of heaven belongs. Then he laid his hands on them and went on his way (Matthew 19: 13 – 15).

Not only is Christ showing us here how to deal with our children, but also that we need to learn from them! We need to become just like them! What a valuable lesson for us adults to learn in the midst of such anger and back biting in a divorce; the innocence, trust, honesty and humility of a child is the key. It is the key that will open the gates of heaven to you, and while you are still here struggling on earth, you will find great peace and confidence in all that you are undertaking if you practice these simple virtues you find in your children.

## Concluding Thoughts

You might now have to work, whereas before you didn't, and that may make things quite difficult. But if it is at all possible, you should make sure you can be home when your kids get home from school. More importantly though, you should be present at their sporting events and parent-child outings whenever it is possible. You need to spend good, quality time with them, reading to them, talking to them about their day and their thoughts, letting them help with making dinner, renting a movie they'd like to see and popping the popcorn. The point is that little to nothing is more important now than giving them assurance that they can count on you.

You also need to make sure that your children see you as trustworthy and someone they respect. For this reason, if it has been less than one year since your divorce, it is a good idea to refrain from dating. Aside from the fact that you, yourself, have a lot of healing to do, you might do more damage to the children and their ability to trust you if you begin introducing other people as friends, boyfriends or girlfriends, or even potential parent-figures. Even if the children do not meet your date, staying out late in the evening with, who in their eyes are strange people, does not help them feel more comfortable.

Another excellent way to help them get through this is to help them understand what was pointed out earlier—that God brings good things out of bad. It is true that when there is pain, things change. Let us help them make these changes into something positive. Keep them focused on their future and point them in the direction of hope. They need to know there is still so much promise for their lives in the weeks ahead as well as the years to come.

By being available for your children and reinforcing their lives and your love for them with a solid faith and the grace from the sacraments, you can be certain they have a great advantage in life, despite the situation at hand.

In the words of Mother Teresa:

Bring prayer to your family, bring it to your little children. Teach them to pray. For a child that prays is a happy child. A family that prays is a united family. You hear of so many broken families. And then you examine them: Why are they broken? I think because they never pray together. They are never in prayer before the Lord. . . .

You are here to be witnesses of love and to celebrate life, because life has been created in the image of God. Life is to love and to be loved. That is why you all have to take a strong stand so that no child, boy or girl, will be rejected or unloved. Every child is a sign of God's love that has to be extended over all the earth (No Greater Love).

## Now What?

There is no doubt that divorce is extremely difficult for children. Worse still is that children can suffer the greatest consequences for the longest period of time. However, there is hope. With an abundance of love and sacrifice, children of divorce can endure these consequences and go on to live a normal life filled with peace, love and joy. Here is what you can do for your children to help ensure that happens:

For the Custodial Parent

1. **Create Routine**: Divorce crashes into a child's world and creates an intense feeling of insecurity. Suddenly, everything they took for granted is shattered: mom and dad loving each other for life, living in the same home with mom and dad, having the security of a predictable life— things they should always be able to count on. Divorce ushers in a time of real uncertainty and stressful changes. One of the best ways you can restore security and certainty into your children's lives is to make sure that they have a routine. Make every day look and feel like the last as much as possible. This means the same time out of bed each day, same daily routine, same dinner time, same bed time, etc. The more consistency there is in your children's lives—the more each day is like the last—the more your children will begin to rebound and adjust to the reality of your divorce. Children of divorce go through so many major changes that, the sooner you can make things predictable for them again, the better.

2. **Be Available**: You are the center of your children's world and they need you now more than ever. You should make a conscious effort to reduce any activities or demands that pull you away from your children

and work hard to reserve your time for your children. Custodial parents are often doubly burdened because they must struggle with their own emotional pain as well as helping their children cope. In an effort to relieve some of the stress and heartache, there is a tendency to seek a dating relationship or take part in other activities away from the home and children. This is a temptation that needs to be resisted and tempered by the understanding that your children need as much of you as they can get. Typical custodial agreements provide the custodial parent alternating weekends without the children, and those weekends are the best time to do things for yourself.

3. **Simplify**: There always seems to be a never-ending supply of activities for your children to get involved in. If you allow it, you'll be slaves to the hectic schedules too many activities can create. Try and simplify your lives as much as possible. As the custodial parent, the responsibility rests mainly on you to get your children to and from their various activities. If there are too many of them, that will sap you of the time and energy you really need for your kids. No sport or extra curricular activity can take the place of time spent with you. Simplify yours and your kids' lives to make sure that there are enough opportunities for one-on-one time and family activities. This may mean one extracurricular activity during the week instead of two, or it may mean only committing to those activities that they can do on the weekend. However that plays out for you and your kids, the time together is something you all will benefit tremendously from.

For the Non-custodial Parent:

1. **Be Available**: Not being able to live in the same house or having open access to your children can seem like the greatest injustice ever. Many non-custodial parents feel helpless and fail to realize there is so much they can do to make sure they are readily available to their children. First and foremost is being as close to where they live as possible—the closer the better. This allows you to participate in their school and extracurricular activities as much as possible. Do your absolute best to be at every school function, coach their sports team, teach their PSR/CCD class, be their Scout leader, have lunch with them at school, often. The key is making sure you are taking as active a role in their lives as

possible. Yes, this will take some real sacrifice and reprioritizing your time, but your children are not only worth it, they want so much for you to be in their lives. Give them the gift of you.

2. **Reprioritize**: Your children are important. The greatest gift you can give them is not your money, but your time. So many non-custodial parents hide behind the excuse of having a job that limits their ability to be present in their kids' lives. Sadly, the children are the ones who suffer from this poor decision. Technology and increasing flexibility as to work hours and work locations make working from home a real possibility in many cases. Many jobs can be done from home at least part of the time and you might consider taking advantage of that, if at all possible. If your job doesn't give you the flexibility you need to live near your children or have the time you need to be present to them, get a different job. Also, look closely at your calendar. Do you really need to go on so many business trips? Is that golf game really important? Do you really need to take your clients to every home sports game? Many times the answer is no. Have the courage to put your kids first. Most people, your boss included, will admire your courage and your character.

3. **Pray for Courage**: Making significant life changes such as moving, changing jobs, standing up to inconsiderate bosses, etc. is difficult and takes a lot of courage. Pray for the courage to make these changes. A great way to do this is to offer up an entire rosary or Divine Mercy for the virtue of courage. You can also offer up each decade for a specific act that you need more courage for. God will hear your prayers, see your true intention and not abandon you.

"So I say to you: Ask, and it will be given to you;
search, and you will find; knock, and the door will be opened to you.
For everyone who asks receives; everyone who searches, finds;
everyone who knocks will have the door opened.
What father among you, if his son asked for a fish,
would hand him a snake? Or if he asked for an egg,
hand him a scorpion? If you then, evil as you are,
know how to give your children what is good,
how much more will the heavenly Father give the Holy Spirit
to those who ask him!"
Luke 11:9-13

4. **Friday Night Visitation**: Most visitation schedules provide for the non-custodial parent to see the kids for three to four hours during the middle of the week and then every other weekend. The mid-week visit can be very hectic for you and the kids as there is often homework, sports, and other extracurricular activities vying for their time. See if you can't get your ex-spouse to agree to overnight visitation on Friday night instead of the mid-week visit. This will be less hectic for you and the kids because it will allow you to have more quality time with them as there is no homework to worry about, typically no work the next day, and the kids won't miss you as much because they get to see you longer in between weekend visits. It also gives the custodial parent an overnight break as well. This may be one of the best things you can do to minimize the impact of the divorce on you and your kids.

For Both Parents:

1. **Get Along with Your Ex**: One of the best things you can do for your children is to get along with your ex-spouse. Your children can sense when you and your ex are fighting and that will do nothing but increase the tension and anxiety in their lives. Remember, that person is your child's mother or father. Respect that fact by working hard to cooperate and compromise with your ex-spouse. Pray for the grace to be able to do this as often it will take supernatural help.

2.  **Be Real**: Your children are going to look to you for the answers to their questions—the most burning question, of course, is why? They want to know why this tragedy happened. They do not need all the details of why the divorce happened. And it's okay to say "I don't know" when you really don't know the motives of your ex-spouse's behavior. What can be helpful is talking to them in terms of how marriage is a promise to stay together for life and how the divorce resulted from that promise no longer being kept. It is also perfectly okay to let your children know you are sad, or missing their other parent, too. This helps them relate to you and gain a sense of comfort and peace.

3.  **Take Your Kids to Mass**: There is no better place for you and your kids to be during a time of extreme turmoil than in Mass. They may not understand it now, but over time they will come to realize how receiving the Eucharist and participating in the Mass helped strengthen them during what is most likely going to be the most difficult time of their lives. Tap into the healing grace and unlimited mercy that is available to all of us in the Eucharist and the celebration of the Mass.

4.  **Pray**: Did you know that all of heaven is waiting for you to ask them to help you? The communion of saints, or the blessed who have gone before us to heaven – they can pray for us, petition God for us . . . all you need to do is ask them for their help. When you become overwhelmed, pray and seek help from the saints; they are one of the greatest spiritual resources you have. Many mothers can relate to the Blessed Mother, Mary. She is the most powerful intercessor you have. Many fathers can relate to St. Joseph. His prayers are particularly powerful for fathers and families as he was the head of the Holy Family. Go on-line and search for prayers to these and other saints. There are many great prayers, litanies, and memorares to the saints.

# Meditation

## Luke 1:57-66, 80

When the time arrived for Elizabeth to have her child she gave birth to a son. Her neighbors and relatives heard that the Lord had shown his great mercy toward her, and they rejoiced with her. When they came on the eighth day to circumcise the child, they were going to call him Zechariah after his father, but his mother said in reply, "No. He will be called John." But they answered her, "There is no one among your relatives who has this name." So they made signs, asking his father what he wished him to be called. He asked for a tablet and wrote, "John is his name," and all were amazed. Immediately his mouth was opened, his tongue freed, and he spoke blessing God. Then fear came upon all their neighbors, and all these matters were discussed throughout the hill country of Judea. All who heard these things took them to heart, saying, "What, then, will this child be?" For surely the hand of the Lord was with him.

**Opening Prayer**: Dear Lord, I thank you for this time with you. I know you are listening to me and I pray that you will help me to leave my worries and distractions aside for a few minutes so that I may truly be in your presence and hear your words in my heart.

**Petition**: Good and gentle Jesus, I pray for the grace to be a strong, patient and wise parent for my children and for a greater appreciation of the gift of my children.

1. *The Lord had shown his great mercy toward her, and they rejoiced with her.*

   Elizabeth had been blessed with a bundle of joy, despite her history of barrenness. God had given her and Zechariah the unique joy of being parents. In times of distress and worry, how easy it is to forget what a gift our children are to us. Children are a sign from God that life goes on and should flourish with hope. When your family is suffering through a divorce, it is easy to lose sight of your blessings, but don't forget that, as painful as things are, you need to go on. Life needs to be lived and if we, as parents, remain rooted in Christ, then despite all the suffering, you can show your children how to be strong and find the path to a happier life.

2. *John is his name.*

   No one in the family was named John and everyone knew this and protested. Yet, Elizabeth and Zechariah were obedient to God's plan and trusted him, and so as soon as Zechariah insisted the child be named John, God immediately loosened his tongue and he was free to speak again. You are no different in that God will bless you for trusting in him and following his plan. It may be difficult to do what your conscience tells you is right, especially when family members or friends are giving you advice that is different. But you can only win when you follow Christ, for he knows what will truly make you happy, even though you may not be able to see it right away. As a parent, you have a difficult task, but there is much joy that comes with parenting, especially if you follow God's plan for families.

**Closing Prayer**: Thank you, Lord, for the priceless gift of my children. I believe that you can heal all of our hurts and bring us to the fullness of happiness once again. Please help me to bear my trials with patience and love. I ask this in Jesus' name. Amen.

## Resolution

Spend some time in Adoration and place your family and all your own concerns at Christ's feet.

## Suggested Reading

Ross Campbell, *How to Really Love Your Child (How to Really Love)*, Cook Communications (March 25, 2004)

Ross Campbell, *How to Really Love Your Angry Child*, Life Journey (March 25, 2004)

Ross Campbell, *How to Really Parent Your Teenager: Raising Balanced Teens in an Unbalanced World*, Thomas Nelson (March 14, 2006)

Linda Bird Francke, *Growing Up Divorced*, Fawcett; Reprint edition (May 12, 1984)

# Chapter Nine:

# The Healing Begins

In this chapter, let's contemplate what it means to begin the healing process. You have already discussed some basic elements of repairing your life, such as the need to deal effectively with your anger so it doesn't control you, the need to practice forgiveness and understand that God can bring good things out of bad things if you are patient, and trust that he has a plan for your life. Now, let's focus on the healing power of God's love.

After any traumatic event, you need to give yourself time to heal. After a divorce, the healing can seem to take forever! During a time such as this, it's important to take an objective look at your behavior so you can first recognize the ways that you are suffering so you know how to address them, and second to see if your actions are helping you, or are obstacles to the healing process.

How is your suffering manifesting itself in your life? It could be in a number of ways, but one very common manifestation of suffering after a divorce is memory flashbacks. Constantly reliving the stressful, hurtful moments of your marriage as it was ending, or encounters with your ex-spouse that were quite painful. Many people report painful feelings that, even years later, are almost as painful as the moment they were first lived. Flashbacks, if you entertain them as often as they present themselves, keep you steeped in pain and anchored in the past, unable to forgive or really move forward.

Sometimes, flashbacks become "shields" for a hurting heart; almost as if a person clings tightly enough to the pain, they will never allow themselves to be hurt again. Some people, without even realizing it, feel that keeping pain fresh in their minds is a sure-fire way to avoid getting into other painful situations in the future, but doing so only prevents us from really experiencing healing.

Your life will never be without pain of some sort, until you die of course and go to heaven. Holding on to pain does not make you wiser, it only perpetuates the pain. You need to learn how to let go of it.

The goal of this chapter is to understand that no matter what stage you are at in your separation or divorce, you need to give Christ permission to enter your heart and heal it. You need to determine what this means to you personally and how you will put this into action.

## The Case

After a tragedy strikes, many people wander through their lives without ever being healed of their hurt. A personal crisis can shake us to our foundation, rob us of our willingness to trust and encourage us to become sour about things in life that are good, particularly love and hope.

John gives us an example through his story:

I'd never felt such deep pain as when my wife and I divorced. I've lost both my parents in an accident and a close friend to cancer, and although these losses were painful, neither of them was as devastating as my divorce.

Luckily, I was able to throw myself into my work. Now that I was not expected home at night, I could stay at the office as long as I wanted. And staying late paid off because within six months, I had received two promotions and a raise in pay. Soon, my career became my life. The harder I worked, the better my standard of living was and the better I felt about myself.

I didn't have much time to think about the things I used to do before my career took over my life. Basically, if I wasn't working in the office, I was working out in the gym or indulging in my new-found passion: travel. Since my promotions, I had begun traveling for work and I had also acquired the means to go pretty much wherever I wanted. Without the attachment to my ex-wife, I had no need to ask anyone's permission. So when I had the time off, I just went wherever I wanted.

The first real trip I had taken that was strictly for pleasure and not business was to Italy. It was somewhere I had always wanted to go and now I could enjoy it at my own pace. I traveled with a group, but didn't mingle much. I was still experiencing a lot of pain from my divorce and really didn't feel like answering strangers' questions about "family." But what an experience! Florence, Tuscany, Assisi and Rome . . . it was better than I expected. The food was unbelievable and the time I had to just sit by myself and take in the scenery was good for my soul. But my favorite was Rome. Even though I didn't pray much, I believed in God. During this time in Rome, I began to feel a closeness with God that I had not experienced before. In a way, it was almost as if I could hear him calling me. But then I reasoned it was probably just the wine. I left for home feeling more like my old self than ever.

Shortly after I returned home and dove back into the intensity of my work, my ex-wife called to tell me she was getting remarried. It was as if everything around me froze. I thought I had been making good progress in moving on and accepting the divorce, especially after my trip to Italy, but I couldn't believe how instantly her announcement made me feel as if I were back at square one. I believed I was strong and capable, and yet all it took was this one call from her and I felt as bad as the day she first walked out.

The day of her wedding was a very bad day for me. I was not present—not invited—but just knowing what was taking place brought such intense pain. I spent that day in my dark home, letting the answering machine pick up the calls. After that, it was all I could do to motivate myself to get out to the gym. I didn't understand how this could be happening to me. I thought I had made more progress toward healing, but maybe I was wrong. The months passed and my I grew severely depressed.

Not long after that weekend, I was on my way home from work and I drove over to my church. I decided to stop and see if the doors were unlocked so I could go in and clear my head. The doors were open and I walked through, finding myself enveloped in silence. Suddenly, strikingly, I felt God was there, just the way I had felt his presence in Rome. I walked up the dark, empty aisle and sat in the first row. After a moment, I hung my head and wept. I could not contain my hurt any longer. I wanted to be heard and I begged God to help me.

I felt a hand on my shoulder, and I turned around to see a priest behind me. "Let me help you, my friend," he said. He sat down in the seats behind me and listened to everything I had to say. I told him all that had happened and how I felt now, even things I was afraid to admit to myself. In response, his words to me were surprising. He did not judge me for being divorced. He was understanding. When I finally left, hours later, I felt as though the weight of the world had been lifted from my shoulders. I didn't know how I would heal from all this, but still I had a sense of peace. I knew God was with me and would give me the help I needed.

## No Man is an Island

As humans, we need to realize that grief and sadness are completely natural reactions to traumatic situations. Sometimes, the difference that's made in a difficult situation is simply a matter of recognizing that you can't do it all yourself; more importantly, you don't need to do it all yourself! If healing were left entirely up to us, we'd never make it because healing is hard work. You need to let God be a part of the process.

Pain brings about change, and this change can be for the good, or for the bad, depending on what you do with it. And so a very good habit to form is learning how to recognize what you can and cannot control. For example, you cannot control your ex-spouse or his or her words or actions. Nor can you control anyone else who has hurt you—your in-laws, other family members, various people who may have played a part in your divorce. No matter how hard you try to control them, you can't and you will only end up with serious frustration in trying to do so. It is better to acknowledge this fact of not having control and leave these people and their thoughts, words and actions in God's hands.

In sorting through it all and setting aside the things you have no control over, you will begin to uncover many things you can control. For instance, at the beginning of this chapter we discussed one of the most common roadblocks to healing—flashbacks, or an inability to move out of the past and focus on the things at hand and the future. Flashbacks are something you can control. But each individual has various and different reactions, all which are normal and also controllable. Here are a few recommendations for learning how to relieve the stress and anxiety of your divorce:

1. **Talking**. You need to talk about your hurts with people you trust; parents or family members, friends, therapists, priests or spiritual directors. The most important aspect of this is making sure whomever it is you talk with is someone you trust and believe that any advice they may dispense to you is trustworthy and will not lead you in a direction that is counter-productive.

2. **Slowing down**. You need to slow down and take time for yourself. If you are used to going at a fast pace all day, set aside a weekend or evening when you can be alone and rest in some fashion. Read a book, take a hot bath or take a walk at sunset.

3. **Taking time to reflect**. Are you learning anything about yourself through this process? Are you gaining insight about what happened as time goes on? Despite all the terrible hurt, have there been positive things that have happened as a result of all of this?

There are many things you can do to help yourself heal. But suffering manifests itself in many other ways such as loss of appetite and rapid weight loss, inability to focus or feeling as if you are walking around in a fog, anxiety attacks, insomnia, overreacting to situations and people, depression, aggressive behavior, uncontrollable tears, and the list goes on. These are not things that you can necessarily control.

## What Does Scripture Say?

When you are faced with the things you cannot control, call on our Lord for help for healing. Let's listen to the gospel of Luke for a moment:

But the man was anxious to justify himself, and said to Jesus, "And who is my neighbor?" In answer, Jesus said, "A man was once on his way down from Jerusalem to Jericho and fell into the hands of bandits; they stripped him, beat him and then made off leaving him half-dead. Now a priest happened to be traveling down the same road, but when he saw the man, he passed by on the other side. In the same way a Levite who came to the place saw him and passed by on the opposite side. But a Samaritan traveler who came on him was moved with compassion when he saw him. He went up to him and bandaged his wounds, pouring oil and wine over them. He lifted him onto his own mount and took him to an inn and looked after him. Next day, he took out two denarii and handed them to the innkeeper and said, 'Look after him, and on my way back I will make good any extra expense you have.' Which of these three, do you think, proved himself a neighbor to the man who fell into the bandits' hands?" He replied, "The one who showed pity towards him." Jesus said to him, "Go and do the same yourself" (Luke 10: 25 - 37).

We've probably heard this story a million times, it must seem. And it carries a strong message, which is that we must love our neighbor. You already understand this message, so in light of your personal situation let's look at the parable from a different angle...

Consider the story as if the man who was brutally beaten and taken advantage of by robbers is you. In many instances, what has happened to you and your dream of a good marriage and family life might make you feel the same way—like you've been beaten and left by the side of the road to die. The Samaritan, the one who stops and takes the time to care for the dying man is Jesus. Let's read again how Scripture describes the Samaritan's actions:

But a Samaritan traveler who came on him was moved with compassion when he saw him. He went up to him and bandaged his wounds, pouring oil and wine over them. He lifted him onto his own mount and took him to an inn and looked after him. Next day, he took out two denarii and handed them to the innkeeper and said, 'Look after him, and on my way back I will make good any extra expense you have.'

It is beautiful to see how the Samaritan—someone who, in those days would be the first to ignore a non-Samaritan because of social prejudices and never would have considered stopping to help—compassionately cared for this broken human being. And he cared for him with the best that he had, pouring oil and wine on the wounds, laid him on his own animal to be carried while he walked, took him to an inn where he would be able to rest and heal, and finally paid for it all out of his own wallet. Isn't this so much like the way Christ cares for us? He would never leave you alone to die, and it's not just a matter of him accidentally passing on the same road that you are on—Christ goes in search of you. He tends to all your wounds, great and small, and wants to heal all of them so you can be whole again. He carries you as you journey through your difficulties and pain and brings you to a place where you can rest. And finally, he has paid the price for you through his own suffering, his cross and resurrection. It is also beautiful to contemplate what could be the significance of the inn, the place of rest . . . the Church.

## Concluding Thoughts

Christ came to earth to save us, and when he left he gave us the Church to continue to be our safeguard, our haven of truth and solace. It is interesting to note that the Good Samaritan cleansed the man's wounds and began the healing of them with oil and wine—two important attributes in the sacraments of the Church.

Allow yourself to be carried and cared for by the supreme example of the Good Samaritan, Christ himself. Open your heart to him and allow him to see every detail; the good, the bad, the indifferent. He will treat you with loving care and will make you a new creature in him.

Hail, saving Victim, who was offered on the gibbet of the cross for me and for all mankind, when you washed away the sins of the whole world. O Lord, be mindful of your creature, whom you redeemed with your blood. I am sorry for having sinned; I wish to amend what I have done. Therefore, most merciful Father, take away all my sin and wickedness, so that, purified in soul and body, I may merit to partake worthily of the Holy of Holies. Lord, grant that this offering of your body and blood, which, although unworthy, I intend to receive, may be for the remission of my sins, the perfect cleansing of my faults, the banishing of bad thoughts, the rebirth of good intentions, the salutary performance of works pleasing to you, and the firmest defense of body and soul against the snares of my enemies. Amen.

From "My Prayer Book", Fr. Lasance, 1908, p 370. Ref. Pope Leo XIII, June 30, 1893.

# Now What?

The healing process is not like an exercise plan. You can't expect a specific result in a given period of time. A better analogy may be that healing from a divorce is like healing from a major illness. The process is slow and many times painful. Like healing from any ailment whether physical or emotional, there are going to be good days and bad days, forward progress and setbacks. The key is to create an environment and a daily approach that will keep you moving down the road to healing and getting stronger. Here are some ways you can do this:

- **Take Time**: Try to see the free time that you now have as a gift. For most people, especially if you have children, days are typically hectic and filled with many obligations and distractions. Embrace the time alone that you have, typically on weekends, as an opportunity for rest and relaxation as well as an opportunity to really reconnect with yourself. Take this time to do the things you have always wanted to do, or the things you used to really enjoy doing, but could not find the time. Pick up an old hobby, read those books you never got around to reading, pray and meditate, hike that mountain, clean out your closets, remodel your house, or volunteer at church or charity, to offer a few suggestions. Try not to use this time to just hang out at home by yourself and watch TV. If used well, your free time will not only rejuvenate your body and soul, you will also come to a clearer understanding of what is really important to you and what God's plan is for you.

- **Create Peace**: Adjusting to life after divorce can be very difficult and painful. It may seem that you can't escape the shadow that the reality of divorce creates. It can permeate your life. Try and create peace in the midst of this turmoil by identifying the one thing that you do that brings you even a moment's peace. This is very different for each person. For some people it is prayer, for some it is listening to music, for others it is exercising, for others it is a long walk. Identify what it is for you and do it—every day. What you will find is that at first you may only have one minute of true peace, but over time that sense of peace will grow longer and longer each day. That is a sign that you are healing.

- **Seek Christ First**: Divorce is so painful that it tends to sensitize you to further pain. This is compounded by the fact that divorce typically results in loneliness, making life even more painful. As a result, many people will avoid pain at all costs just to cope with the realities of life after divorce. This is a very human thing to do. However, avoiding pain can cause real barriers to the healing process. So many times this type of behavior manifests itself in unhealthy life patterns such as excessive drinking and taking illegal or prescription drugs to mask their pain, overworking, overeating, and unwise relationships. People are very vulnerable after a divorce and as a result try to sooth their pain by jumping into some other relationship. While this may validate their need to prove they are still lovable in the short-term, it is certainly a formula for an unhealthy, unsuccessful, long-term relationship. Your perspective, your decision making, and your view of the future are not lucid or stable in the first year after a divorce. The best serious relationship you can pursue is one with Christ. He is the true healer. His guidance is always perfect. The key is to orient your life around Him and His teachings and open your mind and heart to the guidance of the Holy Spirit. This is done through daily prayer and participation in the Sacraments. Turn those alone times into opportunities to really embrace Christ and your faith. Reading scripture, extended prayer time, time in front of the Blessed Sacrament, participating in Mass, and socializing with people of strong Catholic faith are great ways to deepen your relationship with Christ. This will help sensitize you to the promptings of the Holy Spirit and result in living a life more fully aligned with God's will. When you do that, not only will you heal, you will become a living testament to God's love and mercy and an inspiration to others. Your life will actually draw others closer to Christ. You will become a gift to all you meet. When this happens, you will have a deeper understanding of Romans 8:28: You know that all things work for good for those who love God, who are called according to his purpose.

- **Pray for Hope**: After a divorce, it is so easy to lose hope. While most people have a general understanding of the concept of hope as it relates to everyday things—you may hope for a raise, hope for good weather, or hope your team will win—you often don't understand how critical hope is in our personal life's journey. Without hope you tend to become negative or bitter, make poor decisions, and actually make life worse, not better. But what is hope, really? Pope Benedict XVI defines hope very clearly in his masterful Encyclical, God is Love, like this:

> Hope is practiced through the virtue of patience, which continues to do good even in the face of apparent failure, and through the virtue of humility, which accepts God's mystery and trusts him even at times of darkness.
>
> - Pope Benedict XVI

Along with faith and love, hope is one of the theological virtues from God that is given freely as a gift; all you need to do is ask. When you live in hope, you are able to endure even the darkest of time with a sense of patience because you believe that God has a plan for us and He will lead us through this time of darkness to a life of peace and joy. When you live in hope, you make better decisions, are less apt to take matters into our own hands, are able to face challenges head-on, and are more apt to live a life of joyful anticipation of what God has in store for us, despite our current circumstances.

## Meditation

### John 15: 1 - 4, 16

I am the true vine, and my Father is the vine dresser. Every branch in me that bears no fruit he cuts away, and every branch that does bear fruit he prunes to make it bear even more. You are clean already, by means of the word that I have spoken to you. Remain in me, as I in you. As a branch cannot bear fruit all by itself, unless it remains part of the vine, neither can you unless you remain in me. You did not choose me, no, I chose you; and I commissioned you to go out and to bear fruit, fruit that will last; so that the Father will give you anything you ask him in my name.

**Opening Prayer**: Father in heaven, I believe that you love me like no other can. Please help me spend these moments with you with as few distractions as possible so that I may hear your words.

**Petition**: Lord, grant me the grace of a deeper faith—one that trusts in you no matter how difficult life may be.

1. *The Divine Pruner.*

During the winter season, you prune the branches of the tree. You cut off the dead limbs and areas where disease may have infected the tree. To the casual observer, the tree looks barren and bald—almost void of life. But when the spring comes, the tree bears beautiful blossoms in abundance and much more than if it hadn't been pruned. You may feel that you are experiencing this sort of wintertime in your life because of your divorce. What has God pruned from your life? Relationships, homes, possessions? You may even feel like Job, as if you have lost everything—everything important to you. But it is important to remember that spring will come. This part of your life will not last forever and the pruning that has taken place will allow you to change and grow and become better people because of the experience. As you journey through the wintertime of your life, you should seek to remain as close as possible to your faith and the Church so that when the springtime arrives, you will be renewed and joyful.

2. *You are God's chosen ones.*

It is awesome to think that you are the one chosen by God—chosen to be his instrument of love here on earth and chosen by Him to live in eternal happiness with Him in heaven. Especially during this difficult time, when very little seems to make sense, try to remain as close to him as possible; cling to him as a branch to the vine so that you will bear fruit and that your life will have meaning and purpose amidst the turmoil.

**Closing Prayer**: My Lord and my Father, grant me the grace of a deeper faith that I may trust in you with all my heart and bear the fruit of your love in my life. Amen.

## Resolution

Spend time in front of the Blessed Sacrament and make a list of the areas in your life right now where you need the most healing. Ask God for healing of these hurts and ask for the grace to be patient and hopeful.

## Suggested Reading

Mother Teresa and Thomas Moore, *No Greater Love*, New World Library (March 5, 2002)

Fulton J. Sheen, *Life Is Worth Living: First and Second Series,* Ignatius Press; New Ed edition (March 1999)

Conrad W. Baars, *Born Only Once: The Miracle of Affirmation*, Franciscan Press (2001)

## Chapter Ten:

# Your Own Self -Worth

In this chapter, it's time to take a look at your own self-worth. Often-times, when going through a separation or divorce, this is one aspect of your life that goes unchecked for a long time. Particularly if you are the spouse who has been abandoned for another relationship or was completely surprised by the announcement that your spouse wanted a divorce, the rejection felt is on so many levels, and self-doubt creeps in and tries to wreak havoc on your opinion of yourself. Do you spend inordinate amounts of time trying to figure out why your spouse's love didn't last? Do you wonder if it was something about your physical appearance? Was it your personality? Did it have to do with sex or maybe a lack thereof? Do you wonder if your spouse fell out of love at some point or if he or she was ever really in love with you to begin with? If you ponder these questions long enough, the mind games begin to take over and your self-esteem can plummet to rock-bottom levels.

It is at this point that you need to take a look at yourself through the eyes of Jesus. To him, you are everything, his treasure. His greatest desire is for you to spend eternity with him in heaven. And because of Christ and his love for us, you are worthy of being loved with a strong and lasting love.

But do you believe this? Do you feel worthy? Imagine being able to step outside of yourself and observe yourself through the loving eyes of Christ. Would you see yourself differently?

Many painful words have been exchanged between you and your spouse, and most likely there have been many attempts to hurt each other. These are not the actions of people who profess to love each other with real love. Christ wants to show what real love is—a perfect and lasting love. He will heal you. Christ is the one who can transform the pain and make your life good again.

The goal of this chapter is to understand that, regardless of what has happened with your spouse, you are truly loved by God and lovable to others.

## The Case

Carl speaks plainly about this particular viewpoint now that he is divorced:

My wife and I were married for twenty-seven years. We have five grown children and two grandchildren so far. All our kids are still practicing Catholics. I believe this is an accomplishment to be proud of.

But I can't be proud. I am ashamed. Ashamed because my wife and I are now divorced. Despite all that I did to please her, she was never really happy in our marriage. We talked about the reasons why she was unhappy many times, and now that she's gone I still don't understand what was wrong. I gave her everything – a good life, vacations, flowers, the chance to stay home and raise our family. I don't know what more I could have given her.

Now that I am alone, I am dealing with feelings I never believed I would have to address. For one thing, I am embarrassed to see anyone, whether I know them or not. Everywhere I go, I feel as if they all know I'm divorced; as if they see me as a failure, especially going to mass. I had to switch parishes because I couldn't bring myself to go to the parish we attended as a family for so many years. There were people—friends, I thought—who suddenly avoided me like the plague and then others who asked questions with feigned sincerity, as if they were just wanting information so they could discuss my personal business with their friends.

I have two brothers and a sister who call from time to time to check up on me, but I sense their awkwardness and I know they don't really know what to say to me. They don't even know what to tell their own children about what's happened. But I believe they view me as someone who is not a good example anymore. I'm sure part of it is my own feelings of humiliation, but many times I feel as if I'm wearing a scarlet "D," as if I am now someone who is scandalizing others, and the scarlet "D" is something everyone sees and speaks quietly about behind my back.

The odd thing here is, when I was married, I probably would have acted the same way these people do. I hate to admit it, but before my own divorce happened, I always believed that a divorced person, especially a Catholic, was a complete failure. I judged those people without even knowing what their circumstances were. Well, I'll never do that again. I have a lot more understanding and sympathy for them now. I just wish others would have some for me.

## All You Need is Love

Love is a necessity for all humans—without it we will die. But true love, real love, the kind we all crave is more than a wonderful feeling or powerful attraction. Love is a decision; a desire to seek the constant good of the person we love. Love is a desire to make the object of our affection happy. "To love is to will the good of another" (St. Thomas Aquinas, STh I-II, 26, 4, corp. art.). Now, no human love is perfect, but the goal of a loving relationship is to seek each other's good and be ready to forgive each other's failings along the way.

You are experiencing a breakdown that was caused by imperfect love; a relationship that was not focused on seeking the good of each of the spouses. But despite the fact that this love relationship is no longer something you can rely on, you can still experience love, and in it's perfection because Christ is the one who will accept you as you are and show you this love.

Let's read one more time what St. Paul tells us about real love:

Love is always patient and kind; love is never jealous; love is not boastful or conceited, it is never rude and never seeks its own advantage; it does not take offense or store up grievances. Love does not rejoice at wrongdoing, but finds its joy in the truth. It is always ready to make allowances, to trust, to hope and to endure whatever comes (1 Corinthians 13:4 - 7).

It is powerful to realize that true love will, "endure whatever comes"; to realize that real love is still there when times are tough or when things look hopeless; to realize that love is what inspires us and sustains the hope in us.

# What Does Scripture Say?

"Can a woman forget her baby at the breast, feel no pity for the child she has borne? Even if these were to forget, I shall not forget you. Look, I have engraved you on the palms of my hands, your ramparts are ever before me" (Isaiah 49: 15 – 16).

Christ loves you with this love. And because he knows you intimately and the secrets of your heart, you are especially dear to him in this time of loneliness and struggle. Jesus is the Good Shepherd and when you wander away because of self-doubt, he comes after you and calls you to him. He waits for you to give him the chance to show you how much you are worth to him.

Christ is not ashamed of you. He is there for you, especially during this time of difficulty. He never forgets you, and moreover he is trying to get your attention! He wants you to come closer, always closer. He has seen every fight, heard all the painful words that were spoken; he knows when you fought valiantly to save your marriage, and when you grew tired of trying; he knows your heart and the hurt and disappointment you are struggling with. He wants you to come to him and let him take your burden.

Another important point is that God gave each of us a distinct purpose in life; a mission. Only you can fulfill the mission God gave you—no one can do it for you. God also gave you gifts and talents that would help you accomplish that mission. Divorce has such a harsh, negative effect that it is easy to lose sight of all the good things. The negativity can almost completely derail us from fulfilling our mission.

If you allow the devil and all his lies to conquer your spirit and lead you to believe you are not worthy, you will not accomplish what you need to. Many souls that you will come in contact with will not see the wonderful person God created you to be, but instead a broken and completely uninspiring individual. Don't allow this to happen to you! If you persevere and stay close to Christ, you will be able to rise above it all and find your comfort and strength in God, our Savior.

# Closing Comments

Imagine two people who are just falling in love. They can't wait to spend time together and make plans for the future. This image is quite the same way that God loves us. When you spend time with God in prayer, you will realize his great love for you. Just like the couple in love, you will begin to see your future and the plans he has for you. It's certain that your future with Christ will be a happy one, provided you give him access to your heart. There has never been a better time to come closer to Christ.

> Let us understand the tenderness of God's love.
> For he speaks in the Scripture,
> "Even if a mother could forget her child, I will not forget you.
> I have carved you on the palm of my hand" (see Isaiah 49: 15 – 16).
> When you feel lonely, when you feel unwanted,
> when you feel sick and forgotten,
> remember you are precious to Him. He loves you.
> - Mother Teresa

# Now What?

The fights, the rejection, the insults—being told you are not loved—all of this is extremely painful and damaging. This pain can be so intense that it distorts your perspective of who you really are and all that you have to offer to others. The truth is that God made you, he loves you, and to him you are a priceless treasure. Here are some ways you can reclaim that truth:

1. **Take Inventory**: When you've been told over and over that you are no good or unlovable, you have a tendency to believe it. Don't fall into that trap. It is not the truth! Try this exercise: find a quiet place and turn to page 102 in your Workbook. There you will find three columns labeled Family, Work, and Community. Now think about the accomplishments in your life, the skills and talents that you have, and how you have improved other people's lives. Write down all the ways you were not only personally successful (e.g. got the big promotion), but more importantly how you made a difference in someone else's life (e.g.

helped your mother when she was sick, tutored a child, etc.). If you are a parent, think of all the ways you have enriched your children's lives. Certainly, your value to your children is immeasurable. The same is most likely true for your extended family and community. When you step back and look at your list, you will see that you have made a real difference in so many people's lives. Doing this exercise will begin to help you to see yourself as God sees you: someone who is precious, who loves, and someone who has made a positive difference with their life.

2. **Go On a Silent Retreat**: Today we have so many distractions – cell phones, iPods, Blackberry's, Tivo, email, and the Internet, to name a few, and they are constantly filling our minds with information. It's difficult to find God amidst so much noise. A silent retreat is an excellent opportunity to get away from the distractions for an entire weekend and find yourself and God within the quiet. While silence must be observed by retreatants during the retreat, they are typically facilitated by a priest or religious figure. The series of meditations would assist you in recognizing the truth about yourself and what God's will is for you. Many silent retreats follow the spiritual exercises of St. Ignatius of Loyola, founder of the Jesuit religious order. Check with your local parish or diocesan newspaper for information on silent retreats in year area.

3. **Avoid Serious Relationships**: Whether you believe or not, you are a gift to this world. God has made you with unique talents and gifts. It is easy to lose sight of that during a crisis like a divorce. As a result, many people seek validation of themselves in a dating relationship. They may not even be conscious of doing it, but often their motives for seeking out these relationships is to restore their sense of self worth. It can be exciting and invigorating to be in a relationship with someone who praises you for your many gifts and talents. It can be a big boost to your sense of self worth to have someone who not only praises you, but actually wants to be with you, who seeks you out. This often is a very refreshing change from the relationship you had with you ex-spouse. However, the problem lies in the risk—it is risky to base your sense of self-worth on the opinion of someone else. After all, that person's opinion can change and there is no guarantee that the relationship will last. However, your true value is lasting. Your value comes from God and is nurtured inside of you, not from another person.

Ask yourself these questions and be completely honest with yourself: Am I in a dating relationship because it makes me feel good about myself? Does it make me forget my past? Keep me from being lonely? None of these are very good reasons for being in a relationship. In fact, jumping into a dating relationship too soon after your divorce can actually make life worse for you, not better. Healthy relationships are based on being willing to sacrifice for the good of another, not on self-serving reasons like validation, escapism, or avoiding loneliness. If any of this is ringing true for you, then it is best for you to strongly reconsider your current relationship. Focus on your relationship with Christ first through prayer, the sacraments, and involvement in your faith community. That is where you will find an infinite source of validation and love.

4. **Be Social**: Being socially active in the right ways are excellent opportunities to help you regain your self-worth. A good social mirror will reflect your importance and value to other people and your community. There are a variety of options within the Church for you to reach out socially. In the past, many Catholic churches offered little if anything for divorced Catholics. That is changing—slowly—but it is changing. Seek out the organizations or ministries at your local parish that either cater to divorced Catholics or tend to attract people of your age and similar life experiences. You can find a great example of this by visiting www.embracedbythechurch.com. While singles ministries, or ministries for families may not be a perfect fit, in the absence of a divorce ministry they may be worth trying. You should also consider ministries that are centered on doing charitable work or sharing your faith. Ministries like St. Vincent de Paul and Habitat for Humanity are great ways to meet people and give of your time. Doing works of charity helps you see how valuable you are through the value you bring to others. There are often faith-sharing ministries that focus on prayer, scripture study, and praise and worship. This is another great way to not only build your faith, but it is a "safe" way to meet people and be social. Being involved socially is so important in nurturing your self-worth because it allows you to bring the gift of yourself to others.

5. **Seek the Truth**: Similar to the Take Inventory exercise above, another useful way to get a true picture of you and your self-worth is to seek the input of someone who will give you straight answers. Therapists are

great for this. They are not biased and their only agenda is to help you. This is not always true with family or friends. While counseling can be expensive, check with your church or diocese; often there are counselors who offer their services for a reduced fee that fits your budget. You can also locate a good Catholic therapist in your area by visiting www. catholictherapist.com. If counseling is not an option, seek out someone you can really trust and is unbiased. A priest, a close relative, or one of your parents are good options.

6.  **Pray**: Since after a divorce you can be very vulnerable, it is important to gird yourself with prayer so that the Holy Spirit will guide you to places and people that will reflect the tremendous value you have because you are God's creation. Pray the rosary (or Divine Mercy) with these intentions:

    - 1st Decade: Pray for God to reveal your infinite self worth to you through your family, work and community.
    - 2nd Decade: Pray for the openness to see yourself as God sees you: infinitely valuable and lovable.
    - 3rd Decade: Pray for the prudence to make sound judgments about dating and relationships.
    - 4th Decade: Pray for the courage to reach out socially in your church and community.
    - 5th Decade: Pray for the fortitude to endure the times of self-doubt.

# Meditation

### Matthew 5: 13 - 16

You are salt for the earth. But if salt loses its taste, what can make it salty again? It is good for nothing, and can only be thrown out to be trampled under people's feet.

You are light for the world. A city built on a hill-top cannot be hidden. No one lights a lamp to put it under a tub; they put it on the lampstand where it shines for everyone in the house. In the same way your light must shine in people's sight, so that, seeing your good works, they may give praise to your Father in heaven.

**Opening Prayer**: My Lord and my God, I come to you now desiring to hear your voice and understand the things you want to teach me. My heart is heavy with the weight of my situation, but I trust in Your goodness and love for me. Please help me as I spend this time with you to be attentive to you.

**Petition**: Lord, grant me the grace to trust you more fully and be wise in the decisions I must make.

1. *You are salt for the earth.*

   It is not by accident that you are who you are. God created each one of us for himself. Your divorce places such heavy burdens on you that in your time of difficulty you may be tempted to give up hope and become discouraged. But you are precious to him and he loves you, he loves everything about you because he created you. Through your pain and suffering, you can be an example of love to others simply by drawing on the strengths Christ has given you to help you get through this difficult time.

2. *You are a light for the world.*

   Christ gives himself to you each time you receive the Eucharist. Through this most holy Sacrament, you receive the Father, Son, and Holy Spirit within you. Don't close yourself off from others because of your divorce, but allow Christ and his holy Light to work through you for the good of others.

**Closing Prayer**: Dear Lord, I thank you for creating me and for all that you have given me. Please help me during this time to recognize my self-worth and to experience your love for me in a more profound way. Amen.

## Resolution

Spend at least fifteen minutes this week contemplating the gospel account of Jesus' passion and crucifixion as told by St. John (John 19: 1 - 30). As you read, bear in mind how far Christ went to prove his love to us, despite the hatred and ridicule he encountered.

## Suggested Reading

Robert Spitzer S.J., *Healing the Culture: A Commonsense Philosophy of Happiness, Freedom and the Life Issues*, Ignatius Press (October 2000)

Rick Sarkisian, *Life Work: Finding Your Purpose in Life*, Ignatius Press (October 1997)

Peter Kreeft, *The God Who Loves You: Love Divine, All Loves Excelling*, Ignatius Press (November 30, 2004)

Thomas Dubay, *Happy Are You Poor: The Simple Life and Spiritual Freedom*, Ignatius Press; New Ed edition (December 2002)

# Chapter Eleven:

## The Value of Suffering

In this chapter, direct your attention to the suffering you are experiencing. Suffering is a disdainful word in today's society. The word suffering carries with it a feeling of discomfort, unhappiness, senselessness; a feeling that you are wasting your time when you could be doing other fun or important things.

With our busy lives filled with fast-paced work environments and deadlines, information and entertainment on demand, the ability for the average individual to travel around the world and even into space, suffering serves only as a roadblock to the immediate gratification that we can access in our technologically advanced environment. Suffering becomes an albatross around our necks and our first reaction is to get rid of it.

The goal of this chapter is to realize that, although suffering is not a pleasurable experience and in your circumstance is normally quite difficult, it can be worth more than anything money can ever buy. Suffering, endured with an attitude of acceptance and love, can be a gift that you can offer for others—a powerful contribution that God uses to work miracles for ourselves and for others.

## The Case

Grace describes for us how challenging the fight to recover can be:

Some of the most difficult periods of my life were several years after my divorce when I was living on my own, far away from my ex-husband and the things that brought about bad memories. I would drive home from work each evening with a growing ache in my heart. I could barely bring myself to walk through the front door again because I knew there would be no one there to greet me; it would be another night all by myself. I never ate dinner... what was the point in cooking when I had no one to cook for? I would stay up very late, and most often fall asleep on the couch because I couldn't bear going upstairs and getting into bed by myself again.

I would lie awake with a deep sadness and think, "Will it ever get better? Lord, will you help me to see this through your eyes because I can't see anything good through my own?"

I knew God heard me and I believed that he had a plan for me, but waiting for something to happen or for something to change – that was the hardest part. I was lonely. I hated being alone, but despite this cross I had to bear, I knew I couldn't allow it to consume me or drag me down completely.

I knew I needed to focus on something other than my loneliness, so I tried to do different things to direct my attitude in a good way. I tried to identify and focus on the positives in my life. Sometimes, the positive focus was as simple as acknowledging the fact that I was a healthy person. I could breathe, I could see, I could walk and I could go anywhere I wanted. This helped, but something helped even more...

I thought seriously about how years before all this had happened, I had watched my grandmother suffer and die from ovarian cancer. It was a horrible disease that settled and spread quickly. I saw her go through the various stages of this terrible disease . . . losing her hair, losing her independence and having to live in a wheelchair, losing control over her bodily functions—everything from having to have someone bathe her to not even being able to feed herself. She suffered through the intense physical pain and sickening side effects of her treatment. I watched her drift in and out of dementia until she was no longer able to recognize her adult children. They, themselves, were suffering tremendously as they cared for their dying mother.

My grandmother always had a tremendous faith and I remembered how, at the beginning of her illness, she, of all people, was the one who comforted me and those who came to visit her. She told me not to be afraid and to understand the value of suffering. She said she would offer it all up for others—for the salvation of souls, for a friend she knew who had been depressed over losing her son in a car accident, for her own children and grandchildren; the list was endless. There was always someone out there suffering or in trouble who could benefit from her offering. I was in awe of her, wondering how a woman who was in such intense pain could be thinking of others and not be completely focused on herself. And as I contemplated these memories of my grandmother, I realized that now, in my suffering, I had the chance to follow her example. I didn't know if I could actually do this nearly as well as my grandmother, but I did know that as I tried to think of people who needed my offering, I actually had to sit down and make a list of their names because there were so many people I knew who needed help. I began to offer any suffering I may have had for people I knew, or even for more general intentions, such as for the souls in purgatory or peace in the world. I knew these people I prayed for would benefit whether I could see it happen or not, but the most amazing thing about this was that I benefited tremendously. In a very subtle way I began to change. My heart grew more patient and more compassionate, and I began to realize how much I complained about things, even little things. I began to make peace with life and with others and the love I felt for God grew.

My troubles did not disappear overnight, and I still had a lot of work to do on myself. But, I found a great sense of gratitude toward God for all that he allowed me to learn. And during these lonely years of my life, I remembered the example my grandmother gave to me. A priceless gift that made my cross bearable.

I could not be more thankful to my grandmother for her example, and I could not be more grateful to Christ, the One who best understands what it is to suffer, for through his suffering he gave my life light and hope.

## The Essence of Pain

Sometimes, the toughest thing in life to deal with is suffering. Suffering is not a pleasurable experience and of course, our immediate reaction is to stop the pain. For so many people who don't understand that suffering can have value, pain is pointless and a waste of time. But this perspective prevents us from recognizing the great opportunities for good that are being missed, and that is truly where the waste of time lies.

When the loss of a marriage occurs, suffering and grief is experienced on many levels—physical, mental, emotional and moral—and it can seem impossible to heal from such a deep, deep hurt. But the healing you seek lies in the pain that generates from the very root of your problem. Why? Because when you dig up that root, remove it, examine it, it changes and then you change. You face the painful incidents and memories—the things that have damaged you so. This pain is like a cancer that spreads its disease, infecting your heart. When you cut deep and remove the tumor, it can no longer cause you pain or spread its disease. Taking the knife and cutting deep will hurt and it's not something anyone would really enjoy. Yet, it is necessary to be well and heal.

This is the same with the pain you suffer from because of your divorce. When you face it, really look at it; accept that it has happened and you can make peace with it. Even if screaming at the tops of your lungs or crying for hours is necessary first, you can make peace with it. For some, this may seem impossible and insulting. Why would we choose to make peace with such an injustice? Why should I accept the fact that my spouse cheated on me and left me? Why should I simply be okay with having cancer? Why should I make peace with being wrongly accused of a crime and being punished for it? Because we cannot change what has happened.

When a person is diagnosed with cancer, it is not something that can be reversed. It can only be removed and treated. It is the same with your pain. There is nothing you can do to change the fact that it happened. You can only dig in and cut it out, allowing the chance for healing to take place. The digging you do is confronting the details of what happened with honesty and resignation and putting it all in God's hands. When you face the issues of your divorce head-on the pain may flare at first, but if you truly want to heal you will stay strong and little-by-little the pain will begin to fade. The healing begins as you allow it to change from within. And this is where great things can happen.

## Our Loving God Allows Us to Suffer

It is good to revisit the points made in earlier chapters about suffering. Of course you need to remember that God will never force you to do things his way; therefore, suffering arises as a result of all of us making poor decisions or deliberately hurting each other.

It is also important to remember the question: "Why do good things happen to bad people?" We all are essentially good people, made good by God, but our free will ensures that we will commit sin. We are not perfect and we all have our faults and failings. Yet, God continues to bless us with many good things. And here is the best part of that point: even the crosses we bear are blessings because when we suffer, we learn, we grow, we change, we become wiser and more loving. We become more like Christ. Suffering can be the door to new life. We become gold purified by the fire.

It is precisely at this time that we can see the beautiful way God involves us in his redemptive work. Christ died for us and paid the price completely, yet he still involves us in bringing souls to him. We pray for each other and ask for help for each other. Offering our suffering for others who are in need is no different. Offering up our suffering to God for the benefit of someone else brings meaning and value to our suffering and helps to bring us peace.

Here is an analogy that helps to understand how suffering has value or meaning:

Imagine a busy city street and suddenly a man throws himself into the path of an oncoming bus. The bus hits him and kills him. The people who witness the incident are shocked and horrified, and the man's family suffers tremendously at the loss and the nature of the incident. This would be classified as needless, senseless suffering—there is no value in it. The man who jumped in front of the bus committed suicide and caused tremendous suffering for no good reason.

Now, imagine the same scenario – a busy city street, and another man who throws himself into the path of an oncoming bus . . . but this time, he pushes someone else out of the way. The person he pushed out of the path of the oncoming bus lives and he dies. People are still shocked and horrified at the incident and the man's family still suffers a great loss, but their sentiments are not of hopeless sorrow and senseless suffering. The man who jumped in front of the bus is hailed as a hero because his actions saved the life of another. Many people have their belief in the goodness of humanity refreshed and reinforced because of this man's death.

This is exactly what "offering it up" means. You need to carry your cross with love in your heart and offer your suffering for the good of others. Mother Teresa compassionately spoke:

Suffering will never be completely absent from our lives. So don't be afraid of suffering. Your suffering is a great means of love, if you make use of it, especially if you offer it for peace in the world. Suffering in and of itself is useless, but suffering that is shared with the passion of Christ is a wonderful gift and a sign of love. Christ's suffering proved to be a gift, the greatest gift of love, because through the suffering our sins were atoned for. Suffering, pain, sorrow, humiliation, feelings of loneliness, are nothing but the kiss of Jesus, a sign that you have come so close that he can kiss you (*No Greater Love*).

## What Does Scripture Say?

You see, there is merit if, in awareness of God, you put up with the pains of undeserved punishment; but what glory is there in putting up with a beating after you have done something wrong? The merit in the sight of God is in putting up with it patiently when you are punished for doing your duty.

This, in fact is what you were called to do, because Christ suffered for you and left an example for you to follow in his steps. He had done nothing wrong, and had spoken no deceit. He was insulted and did not retaliate with insults; when he was suffering he made no threats but put his trust in the upright judge. He was bearing our sins in his own body on the cross, so that we might die to our sins and live for uprightness; through his bruises you have been healed (1 Peter 2: 19 - 24).

Suffering changes us. It is up to you to decide how it will change you. You can become a victim, blaming God, society, your spouse, or anything and everything for your situation and let yourself become a product of your environment—bitter, prideful, and mistrusting. The world is full of this type of person: the victim. Why not be someone who can say "no" to the world and it's attitudes of selfishness? Why not be someone whom others can look to and feel inspired? This is the type of person the world is waiting to see. Instead of giving in to bitterness and anger, you can face up to the pain and come closer to Christ through prayer, offering up your suffering, and mostly through admitting to yourself that you need God to help you, to heal you. And by doing so, you will find all the consolation and peace your heart can handle.

> If we are to rise above this depression, dejection, and despondency of soul
> and turn it to use in God's service, we must face it, accept it,
> and realize the worth of holy self-abasement.
> In this way you will transmute the lead of your heaviness into gold –
> a gold far purer than any of your happiest, most light-hearted days.
> The past must be abandoned to God's mercy, the present to our fidelity,
> and the future to divine providence.
> – St. Francis de Sales

## Concluding Thoughts

It is human nature to harden our shell in the face of pain and suffering. It is a natural reaction to be angry and want to fight. Yet, however normal the reaction may be, you should not allow your emotions to dictate your behavior.

You need to rely on God for strength and the graces to get through this difficult time. There are many virtues that will help you now, but hope is the key virtue that will sustain you. Hope enables you to offer up your suffering for others. In doing this, you are saying, "I know my suffering is not a waste of time, nor an end to my happiness. God can bring good things out of my suffering." And this is where offering your suffering for others plays an important role.

Let us contemplate Christ, beaten and mocked, crowned with thorns and placed in front of Pontius Pilate and the crowd that wanted to crucify him (cf. John 19: 1 – 16). For all that he had endured and as innocent as he was, he had every right to be angry and to fight for his life. Yet, because he loved us all and was obedient to his Father's plan, he remained humble, patient and collected. Because he knew that the plan of salvation was greater than any retribution that could take place, and his love for each one of us was far greater than his human nature, he had no need to seek an eye for an eye. Christ and his love for us in embracing his cross is the example we should follow in our times of difficulty.

## Now What?

Suffering is like a fog that envelopes you. No matter where you go or what you do, you can't get away from it—nor should you. To avoid suffering is to avoid the healing that will ultimately result. You know the (overused) saying: "No pain, no gain." Much easier said then done, for sure. Here are some ways you can actually use suffering to bring about good for you and for others.

1. **Prepare Yourself**: Suffering has both an emotional and physical impact. During a time of intense emotional suffering, your subconscious equates that to a "fight or flight" situation. The intense pain is not something you or your subconscious wants any part of. As a result, your stress level increases significantly when you suffer. It is not uncommon for you to be exhausted at the end of the day even though you have had minimum physical activity. This is because your subconscious has revved up your body to handle the suffering. It is important that you take care of yourself physically during this time. This includes eating well, taking vitamins, exercising routinely, and getting enough sleep. Suffering is more like a marathon than a sprint. Prepare yourself emotionally and physically for the long haul.

2. **Seek Help**: Christ knew that our lives here on earth would be difficult. He speaks to us very lovingly in scripture:

"Come to me, all you who labor and are overburdened, and I will give you rest" (Matthew 11:28).

In his infinite wisdom and love, he gave us himself to help us endure our sufferings. First and foremost, we find Christ most powerfully in the Eucharist. During your period of suffering, seek Christ by going to mass and receiving him in the Eucharist. Pray daily for him to help you endure your suffering, to give you some rest from its daily struggle. Be with Christ physically by going as often as possible to visit him in adoration. Use that time to talk to Christ intimately and let him know of your pain. He loves you more than you can ever imagine and wants to give you strength. Praying the Divine Mercy Chaplet is an excellent devotion during times of intense suffering. Christ gave us that Chaplet as a gift to remind us of His infinite mercy and love for us. Prayer is like the physical therapy we go through after a bad injury or illness. It makes us stronger and reduces our pain. Tap into Christ's promise to give you rest from your suffering by seeking Him daily through prayer and the sacraments.

3. **Shift Your Paradigm**: There is some real truth to the cliché: "Let your attitude determine your altitude." Interestingly, Scott Peck in his landmark book, *The Road Less Traveled*, begins the book by talking about this very point. He describes the difficulty of life as one of the great truths. He states that, if we recognize the truth, we can transcend it, accept it, and thereby we process it until it no longer is difficult, but totally integrated into our reality.

While it is very true that these words are easy to comprehend in the mind, they are difficult to accept in the heart. Just saying that something is no longer difficult does not make it so. However, accepting the reality that life has forever changed and those changes are demanding a response from you is a first step toward not only enduring the suffering, but allowing something good to come from it. Take that first step by praying for the openness to accept your divorce and all the suffering that has resulted from it. Take real comfort in these words from St. Paul and trust that God will give you the strength and perseverance to endure your suffering:

None of the trials which have come upon you is more than a human being can stand. You can trust that God will not let you be put to the test beyond your strength, but with any trial will also provide a way out by enabling you to put up with it (1 Corinthians 10:13).

4. **Unite Your Suffering**: Suffering just to suffer has no value. That may be where you are right now: struggling to understand how suffering has value. Your suffering has value when you unite it to someone else's

suffering. Do you have a loved one who is sick? Do you know someone who is suffering the loss of a loved one? Do you know of another marriage destroyed by infidelity or abuse? Maybe someone struggling from the loss of a job? These are all opportunities for you to tie your suffering to someone else's. By doing this, the act of bearing your suffering is actually making someone else's burden more bearable. Doing this is truly an act of love. It is how you can directly fulfill Christ's command to: Love one another (John 13:34). Try this: each morning and again every time you feel the weight of your suffering bearing down on you, say this short prayer:

> Dear Lord, I am really struggling. I offer my suffering up for: (specify for whom you are uniting your suffering).

You will begin to feel a sense of peace in spite of your pain because you are helping someone else to endure their suffering.

5. **Help Others**: Another way to unite your suffering to someone else's is to actually reach out and help someone. You can do this in a number of ways. If you personally know someone who is going through a difficult time, send them an e-mail letting them know you are thinking about/praying for them, make them dinner and bring it over, invite them to go out socially, mow their lawn, watch their kids, or wash their car. It can be anything. The point is to help yourself endure your suffering by helping someone else endure theirs. Another way is to get involved in a charity through your church or community. There are many outreach ministries that focus on helping those in need. St. Vincent de Paul, Habitat for Humanity, and MUST Ministries are just a few charities that are always looking for volunteers.

6. **Stations of the Cross**: Praying the Stations of the Cross is a great way to unite your suffering to Christ's. The Stations of the Cross depict fourteen ways Christ suffered as he carried his cross up to Golgotha and was crucified. Every Catholic Church has these 14 scenes of Christ's suffering displayed on the walls of the church. They are always available to help us mediate and pray. Christ suffered so much pain and agony for us because he loves us so deeply. Praying the Stations allows us to understand how love can be reflected in suffering. This will allow us to gain

strength to endure our own suffering with a sense of love for others. On page 175 of the Workbook companion, you will find that the Stations of the Cross were written just for someone suffering the pain of divorce or separation in their marriage. Pray these as often as possible.

# Meditation

## Matthew 8: 23 - 27

Then he got into the boat followed by his disciples. Suddenly a storm broke over the lake, so violent that the boat was being swamped by the waves. But he was asleep. So they went to him and woke him saying, "Save us, Lord, we are lost!" And he said to them, "Why are you so frightened, you who have so little faith?" And then he stood up and rebuked the winds and the sea; and there was a great calm. They were astounded and said, "Whatever kind of man is this, that even the winds and the sea obey him?"

**Opening Prayer**: Dear Jesus, I long to be with you now to hear your words of wisdom in my heart. I have many worries and concerns and I want to leave them aside for a few minutes and sit at your feet, listening.

**Petition**: God, grant me the grace to know you better through this meditation.

1. *Save us, Lord!*

Save me! Sometimes the frustration, the anger and the disappointment are so overwhelming we can hardly stand it. The fear of the unknown future and the implications of things continuing to turn out badly can weigh heavily upon us. We can easily see ourselves in the shoes of the apostles in the boat, with the storm beating at them and the waves seeming to overtake them. But Christ was there. He was sleeping and many mistake his sleeping for ignoring the apostles in their time of need. But Christ was setting the example for us. Be at peace in the midst of your storm. Do not worry. Do not fear. Have faith, have hope, be peaceful, for I am your Lord. I will take care of you.

2. *They were astounded*!

The apostles were astounded because, although they loved Jesus and believed in him, their faith was still weak. They had much to learn about Christ and to realize that their peace would only come through their faith in Christ. And so this time their fear ruled their souls and dictated their behavior. But oh, how different it was when the Holy Spirit came to them at Pentecost and filled them with a holy boldness! How their fear changed to inspiration and zeal! Let us imagine ourselves in the boat with Jesus asleep. Let us imagine our fears, worries and hurts as the waves, crashing upon us as if to destroy our boat. Let us look at Jesus asleep and imagine—what would we do?

**Closing Prayer**: Gentle Jesus, hear my prayer. There is so much I am concerned about. I have been hurt so badly and I feel as if I have nowhere to rest and heal. Help me, Lord, to contemplate you asleep in the boat while the storm rages. Help me to come closer to you and find the graces that will help me find peace amidst my own troubles. I ask this in your name. Amen.

# Resolution

1. Make a list of intentions that you can offer up your crosses and suffering for. This can be for everything from world peace and the conversion of all souls to something as personal as asking for strength for yourself in a particular trial or the safe trip of a friend. Put this list in a place where you will see it and be reminded of it when you pray.

2. Pray or attend the Stations of the Cross and walk beside Christ on his way to Calvary.

# Suggested Reading

Fulton J. Sheen, *Life Worth Living - Pain and Suffering* (VHS), Ignatius Press

Regis Martin, *The Suffering of Love: Christ's Descent into the Hell of Human Hopelessness*, Ignatius Press

Fr. Alfred Delp, SJC, *Advent of the Heart - Seasonal Sermons and Prison Writings - 1941-1944*, Ignatius Press

# Chapter Twelve:

# Letting Go

In this session, let's look at the difficult subject of letting go of your marriage. You may be too new into the separation or divorce to be ready for this stage, or maybe you are ready for it; but regardless of where you stand, you probably already know you will have to let go at some point if you want to move on in life. Take this time, now, to discuss this important step in relation to your own situation.

Initially, the issue of letting go might seem to be the same as forgiving, and in a sense it is. But letting go is really practicing the virtue of detachment, or as the *American Heritage Dictionary* defines it: "The act or process of disconnecting or detaching; separation." Not only is it different from forgiveness, but it has more of a psychological aspect to it, while forgiveness has more of a moral aspect to it.

There are many times in life where we are forced to let go of something valuable to us. Losing a wallet or purse, finding the house has been burglarized, having the car stolen . . . these are all big deals for us and create a lot of stress. But in the end, the item(s) is gone and hopefully, we let go of the anger and detach from the object itself, replacing it with another one.

However, dealing with detachment on the level of relationships, and particularly marriage relationships is extremely difficult and painful. It is often, the most difficult aspect of healing a broken heart. Even though the spouses live in separate homes, the divorce is final and there is no contact between them, it sometimes takes years before the marriage is actually let go.

The goal of this session is to define the steps you need to take in order to let go of your marriage, put the issue in God's hands and consider the fact that God's plan is what will bring you *true* happiness, whether your spouse is part of that plan or not.

# The Case

Lance describes his difficulty in letting go:

For two years after my wife and I divorced, I thought about her several times during the day . . . in the morning as I got ready for work and had coffee, the silence in our empty home was very loud and I would remember her fixing breakfast. During the day, I would think about finding a reason to e-mail her - any problem with the pending sale of our house or any detail about our son that could be discussed seemed like a valid reason to get in touch with her. It was the same thing at night. I tried hard to get thoughts of her out of my mind, but I never found anything that really helped to distract me from those thoughts.

I found this ridiculous given all the pain we had put each other through, I mean, it was pretty brutal at times. We had hurt each other deliberately and deeply during the last years of our marriage and throughout the divorce. What was I, a masochist? I knew there would be disappointment waiting for me if I reached out to her. I found my state of mind very annoying because I felt I should have been well past this stage after two years.

When we first separated, I had been angry with her. Then I became hopeful that after a cooling-off period, we could work it out. That hopefulness didn't last long when she told me she was involved with another man and I became indignant. Defiant. I became depressed about losing her; then I just got angry all over again. It seemed to be a vicious cycle.

It was hard to get it out of my mind. Even just driving around town brought back vivid memories – positive and negative ones. Seeing her when I came by to pick up or drop off my son, or meeting with the listing agent to put the house up for sale . . . it was all very difficult. Why was this happening after so long?

After two years I don't feel as though I've progressed much at all. My sister calls frequently because she's worried about me and keeps saying the best thing for me to do is let go of my marriage. I thought I did when we got the divorce, but I have to admit, I still love my wife. I don't know if I can ever stop loving her? I don't know what I'm going to do.

## Letting Go = Win-Win

Letting go is hard; no question about it. Even the strongest among us, when faced with letting go of something precious, will bury their faces in their hands and ask God, "Why? Why do I have to give it up?"

> If God causes you to suffer much,
> it is a sign that He has great designs for you,
> and that He certainly intends to make you a saint.
> — St. Ignatius of Loyola

If you think seriously about it, you can see there are certain reasons why you need to learn to let go, such as your emotional well being. You need to stop living in the past and move on, looking towards the future, no matter how painful it may be to do so. Other reasons are not as apparent, and require a lot of personal reflection and prayer. An example of this would be recognizing that letting go of something so precious to you forces you to mature as a human and spiritual being. In letting go, you learn how to practice the virtue of detachment, which is a lesson that will help you now and in the future. Detachment helps to free yourself from things that prevent you from growing and experiencing true freedom. What does true freedom represent, and how does it apply to your situation?

Well, society promotes true freedom as having the ability to do whatever one wants, whenever one wants with no responsibility for consequences. But in reality, if you live that type of lifestyle, you are actually allowing your desires to dictate your behavior and control who you are. This, instead of freedom, is slavery. Becoming a slave to your flesh and your passions.

In your particular situation, detachment helps discipline your desires, primarily the desire you may have to control things. So many people lose their focus and their reasoning because of their desire to control, but we should always place our trust in God, and not in ourselves or our desires for a specific outcome of the situation. In learning to let go of your relationship with your spouse and giving God the control, you place your hope in him and trust that he will make all things new again.

It is no secret that many of the most admired people in history were very disciplined people. Presidents, sports professionals, military leaders, etc. The freedom they experienced in disciplining their lives allowed them to excel; to be better than the average person and remembered, honored for these virtuous qualities. They are examples of having true freedom.

Enduring suffering out of love for God is very pleasing to him. Doing so promotes growth in virtue and you receive many graces because of it. By giving God control over something so dear to you, you can only win, even though you may feel at first that letting go is losing. It is important not to give in to the illusion that you have lost. In giving God the control, you can be sure that he will bless you for doing so. He will make good things come out of the bad because you have given him the control.

All this equates to learning to trust in God instead of trusting only in yourself. If you are able to give God the things most important to you and really trust him with them, you will find a freedom and a peace you've never experienced before.

The great thing about all this is that Christ wants to give you this peace *now!* He doesn't want you to become stagnant or hollow as a result of your pain and suffering - He wants to fill you with true peace, right now, no matter how painful your life is.

## What Does Scripture Say?

Never worry about anything; but tell God all your desires of every kind in prayer and petition shot through with gratitude, and the peace of God which is beyond our understanding will guard your hearts and your thoughts in Christ Jesus. Finally, brothers, let your minds be filled with everything that is true, everything that is honorable, everything that is upright and pure, everything that we love and admire – with whatever is good and praiseworthy. Keep doing everything you learnt from me and were told by me and have heard or seen me doing. Then the God of peace will be with you (Phillipians 4: 6 - 9).

Obviously God wants you to focus on the good things, the honorable and pure things. How can you do this if you cannot let go of the hurt from your marriage and divorce? When you pray, pray for the grace from God to help you let go; to give you the desire to rid your heart of the pain and resentment.

## What Now?

It's easy to talk about why you need to let go but you also need to think about how to let go, too. How do you stop loving your spouse? How do you cut the emotional ties to your married life?

Well, a good way to begin is by recognizing that letting go is a process, as is most of what you are going through. You may not be ready to start down this road quite yet, and this is not a problem. Here are a few rules of thumb about this issue:

1. Normally, a person is ready to start letting go when he feels an interior need to change or to take a step towards moving on in life.

2. Letting go is something you work on daily. It won't happen overnight and when you feel overwhelmed by your feelings you need to go back to God in prayer and seek direction from him.

3. If you are not ready to take this step yet, you shouldn't push yourself. You just need to remain prayerful about your situation and God will lead you to take the appropriate steps.

When you feel you are ready to begin heading in this direction, a good way to begin the process is by going through your things and removing all those items that tend to remind you of your ex-spouse. Photos, clothing, letters, wedding and birthday gifts are all good to start with (if you have children who live with you or visit often, you may want to remove old photos gradually, replacing them with new ones as you go so as not to upset them). Place all these personal reminders in a box and remove it from the house to the attic, basement or garage. In time, you'll be prepared for going through them again or using them as kindling.

Spending time away from home by yourself (no friends or relatives along for company) is a very effective way to begin letting go. Visiting a museum, taking a day trip of some sort . . . something you might normally do with your spouse, but this time do by yourself is a great exercise that helps you develop a healthy sense of self. It may not seem that important or desirable, yet it works very well.

It's also important to look deeper into yourself with brutal honesty and find out why you might be having a difficult time letting go, if that, indeed is the case. Are you scared of the future? Is it your pride that won't let go? Do you feel guilty? Sometimes the reluctance to let go is, in reality, the unwillingness to face the feelings at the root of the problem that broke up the marriage. This is a good subject to broach with your counselor or therapist, if you are seeing one, or just to contemplate on your own.

## Concluding Thoughts

Change never takes place without some pain. But wait – look at that from a different viewpoint – if you are experiencing pain, you can experience change. You can allow this pain to change you for the better – or for the worse. Clinging tightly to what God wants you to let go of will only prevent the change from being good. Face your difficulties bravely, protected by the armor of God's grace.

> Rest in God alone, my soul!
> He is the source of my hope.
> He alone is my rock, my safety,
> my stronghold, so that I stand unwavering.
> In God is my safety and my glory,
> The rock of my strength.
> In God is my refuge; trust in him,
> You people , at all times.
> Pour out your hearts to him,
> God is a refuge for us.
> Psalm 62: 5 – 8

# Now What?

While holding onto the past may be of some comfort to you, as it provides a sense of hope for what could be again, it is not healthy if it prevents you from embracing the future. As long as your hands refuse to let go of what has happened, you will be unable to take hold of anything new. So many times fear paralyzes us and makes it hard to take a chance, to make a leap of faith. Often the "new" is simply a new state of mind—a state of mind that has accepted the fact that your life has taken a very different path; one you never expected, or wanted. A state of mind that is open to forgiveness and open to embracing whatever lies ahead, even if you are not exactly sure what that is. Here are some ways to help foster an open heart and mind and begin the process of letting go:

1. **Be Honest**: If you are fearful of letting go, it is important that you find out why. Like children attached to their blankets, we hold onto the past because it is familiar to us and provides refuge from the present storms. On page 122 of the Workbook you will find a questionnaire for reflection. If you take the time to sit down and complete the questionnaire, you will find the answers will help you understand where you are in the process of letting go. Like any process, letting go has a beginning, a middle, and an end. A sign that you are making real progress is when you can look to the future with a sense of hope.

2. **Make a Physical Change**: It is hard to let go when you are surrounded by places, people and things that tie you to your past. If at all possible, consider moving to another part of town. This will allow you to make a fresh start without moving too far away from your children, family and friends, and still provide plenty of opportunity to create a new life and make new friends. If you are a non-custodial parent, make sure that you are still as close as possible to your children. If you are a custodial parent make sure your children are not still raw from the divorce before you make a move. You want them to see the move as a positive one. If relocating is out of the question, making other physical changes such as: redecorating your home, switching bedrooms, rearranging the furniture, getting a different car, or changing your hair style or wardrobe—maybe even a

new job or career. Making physical changes helps you become emotionally open to change and will help you in your process of letting go.

3. **Look Forward**: While thinking about the future can be intimidating, especially if there is a lot of uncertainty, looking at the future as an opportunity for more freedom to be who you really are can give you a sense of excitement and hope. While it is true that a divorce is a bitter – and usually tragic – end to something you had hoped was forever, it is also a new beginning. It is an opportunity for you to be authentic to who you really are. You are now free you to live the values and morals that are truly important to you. Marriage is about compromise from both spouses. Bad marriages usually have one spouse doing all the compromising. Maybe that was you. Now you can look forward to a future where you don't have to compromise your principles, your morals, or your faith. Grasp this opportunity to live a life that is fully authentic to who you really are and to who God is calling you to be.

4. **Create New Patterns**: It is easy to get stuck in the patterns of everyday living. Same time to get up, same time to bed, same drive to work, same drive home, same time to mass, etc. While these patterns give us comfort because they provide predictability to a life that can be unpredictable, they can also reinforce habits and attitudes that prevent us from letting go. Try creating new patterns to your life. This will help put you in a posture of letting go of the past by embracing a more promising future. Here are some ideas:

   - Commit to praying each morning for 15 minutes
   - Start new family traditions, particularly around the holidays
   - Explore a new hobby or pastime
   - Turn off the TV an hour earlier then usual each night
   - Join a gym and commit to going at least 3 times a week
   - Plug into activities at other parishes and make new friends
   - Join a men/women's group or bible study
   - Volunteer to teach religious education at your church

5. **Pray the Chaplet of Divine Mercy**: The Marians of the Immaculate Conception's web site (www.thedivinemercy.org) for Divine Mercy states: The message of The Divine Mercy is simple. It is that God loves us — all of us. And, he wants us to recognize that his mercy is greater than our sins, so that we will call upon him with trust, receive his mercy, and let it flow through us to others. Thus, all will come to share his joy. Praying the Divine Mercy Chaplet is an excellent way to tap into that mercy and to develop a strong sense of trust in Christ. So many times our inability to let go of the past is based on our inability to accept it, and a fear of the future. Praying Divine Mercy helps us receive the special graces that Christ himself offers to each of us. The grace to trust, even when we have no idea what the future holds. The grace of abundant mercy, especially when we feel the pain of being forced to let go of our dreams of what we hoped our future would be. And the grace of abundant, unending, love from God that helps us look forward with real hope knowing in our hearts that God will never abandon us. The Divine Mercy chaplet is a quick and simple way to pray for God's abundant love and mercy. Pray it whenever you can: in the morning, evening, even while driving.

# Meditation

## Mark 10: 17 - 22

He was setting out on a journey when a man ran up, knelt before him and put this question to him, "Good master, what must I do to inherit eternal life?" Jesus said to him, "Why do you call me good? No one is good but God alone. You know the commandments: *You shall not kill; You shall not commit adultery; You shall not steal; You shall not give false witness; You shall not defraud; Honor your father and your mother."* And he said to him, "Master, I have kept all these since my earliest days." Jesus looked steadily at him and he was filled with love for him, and he said, "You need to do one thing more. Go and sell what you own and give the money to the poor, and you will have treasure in heaven; then come, follow me." But his face fell at these words and he went away sad, for he was a man of great wealth (*Mark* 10: 17 - 22).

**Opening Prayer**: Come Holy Spirit and enlighten my heart and my mind. Help me to be open to your inspirations, especially now as I venture into places I am uncomfortable in. I know you are asking me to trust you. Please, Lord, show me how to trust you with the things that are so hard for me to let go of.

**Petition**: Lord, grant me an increase in faith and in detachment.

1. *Why do you call me good?*

   Let's step right into the scene ourselves and look more closely at what is happening. The rich young man calls Jesus "Good master" and Jesus' reply is "Why do you call me good?" By saying this, he places himself on the same level as the young man; Jesus wants this young man to know that he can approach him with trust and ease. Jesus wants us to approach him in the same way – with trust and with ease. Christ loves us passionately and calls us to himself, so he places himself right where we are so we can speak to him.

2. *Keep the Commandments.*

   Then Jesus asks the young man simply to follow the commandments. Because of Jesus' divine nature, he already knew that the young man was obedient to the commandments. So why would he still say all that? Because he knew that as he explained himself, the young man would recognize himself as a good person, and this was Jesus' desire. And that is the same with us. Christ wants us to understand that we are good and despite all that has happened to us in our divorces, he sees and loves this goodness in us.

3. *Sell what you own and follow me.*

   This was the tipping point, the point where his life could have changed in ways the young man never would have dreamed of! But the young man didn't follow – he walked away, sad. He was not able to let go of his possessions – the things he believed to be too valuable to give up. Christ was sad too, because someone he loved was refusing him. But, Jesus did not force the young man to follow. Jesus, himself, showed us the art of "letting go." He loved him but did not force him to stay. The young man wanted so much to follow Christ. Because Jesus was God, he knew what would make the young man happy. Even so, the young man became afraid . . . afraid of letting go of what he thought was making him happy. But in the end, he walked away, sad!

**Closing Prayer**: Lord, what are you asking me to let go of? You know me better than anyone. You know what will make me happy. Please help me to trust you with my life so I may find the happiness that awaits me. In your name I pray. Amen.

# Resolution

Spend some time with Christ at an Adoration chapel and discuss with him this issue of letting go. Ask him for his help and to strengthen you on this difficult road. Then, take at least one step towards letting go by acting upon one of the suggestions (either in the session or one that came up during the discussion) on how to let go.

# Suggested Reading

Jean Du Coeur De Jesus D' Elbee, *I Believe in Love: A Personal Retreat Based on the Teaching of St. Therese of Lisieux,* Sophia Institute Press; 2Rev Ed edition (July 1, 2001)

Lyn Holley Doucet A, *Healing Walk With St. Ignatius: Discovering God's Presence in Difficult Times,* Loyola Press (March 2003)

# Chapter Thirteen:

## Working On Forgiveness

In this session, let us address a critical issue – forgiveness. You know the meaning, you know the necessity and you are acutely aware of the difficulty in achieving true forgiveness. Even so, your forgiveness of others is important in so many ways, and your ability to move on in life is dependent upon your level of forgiveness.

The goal of this chapter is to take a good look at some reasons why forgiveness is necessary in our situation and develop some concrete ways to practice forgiveness.

## The Case

It may seem impossible for spouses engaged in a separation or divorce to forgive one another, especially if there has been infidelity. A spouse who considers the issue of forgiveness early on and understands the vital role it plays in life shows maturity and is on the right track. It is natural to say that one or both spouses have the right to be angry and insulted. This is a normal human reaction. But, the emphasis you place now should not be on blaming each other; nor on the damage that has been caused. Those things are a needless waste of your energy and will only drag you downward. Instead, let's focus on how you are to move past all this. Forgiveness is imperative if you want to move forward.

Suzanne shares her thoughts on forgiveness:

It took me a long time to be able to face this issue of forgiveness. When my husband filed for divorce, it was actually kind of surreal. We didn't end our marriage with horrible fights and attempts to hurt each other further. I think I was so much in shock that I didn't know what to say or do. It was, for all intents and purposes, a rather quiet divorce. But in the silence, I walked away with tremendous anger and resentment.

I was aware of these intense emotions, and I tried my best to deal with them. I decided I would busy myself with things; work for the distraction, the gym for the release, and the children who kept me going because they needed me. But the feelings didn't go away and at times, I felt completely overwhelmed by it all. I was consumed with anger at the way he had thrown our relationship away and the different things I tried to help me overcome these feelings were not doing much. But forgiveness was out of the question! Not only did I not want to forgive him, but I was not about to let him off the hook for his crimes, and I was just as reluctant to forgive the other people who had either played a part in the breakup or who treated me as if I were the one who had done something wrong. The whole thing was so very unjust!

I went to confession one Saturday and was able to have a good conversation with the priest who pointed out that my unwillingness to forgive my ex-husband was keeping my heart full of anger, hate and resentment. He asked me if I loved my children, and I replied, *of course!* But then he asked me, *How can you say you love if your heart is full of hatred for your husband?* He went on to say that my love for my kids was being suffocated by the intense negativity I held in my heart toward their father. How could I truly love my kids, or anyone, for that matter, if I was so full of resentment toward my ex?

He asked me how I felt at the end of the day when I went to bed, and the thought made me shudder. I was wiped out, of course, but I realized his point right away. A lot of my fatigue was due to the energy I expended during the day, despising my husband. And I knew this was correct because I was stewing over it all day.

My talk with my pastor helped me so much and I've made progress since then in working on forgiving my husband. Although I have a long way to go, I am learning how to forgive my ex-husband.

# Amazing Grace

The first step in finding forgiveness for those who have hurt us is to recognize our own constant need of mercy and forgiveness from God. Aren't we all — every human being — responsible for the suffering and death of Christ? No doubt, all of us here are good people who try to live good lives, but as human beings, we are all sinners and no different than any other human being. Therefore, we require forgiveness and mercy from God every day of our lives. How can we expect forgiveness and leniency from God if we refuse to forgive others?

Then Peter went up to him and said, "Lord, how often must I forgive my brother if he wrongs me? As often as seven times?" Jesus answered, "Not seven, I tell you, but seventy-seven times. And so the kingdom of heaven may be compared to a king who decided to settle accounts with his servants. When the reckoning began, they brought him a man who owed ten thousand talents; he had no means of paying, so his master gave orders that he should be sold, together with his wife and children and all his possessions to meet the debt. At this, the servant threw himself down at his master's feet with the words, "Be patient with me and I will pay the whole sum." And the servant's master felt so sorry for him that he let him go and canceled the debt. Now, as this servant went out, he happened to meet a fellow-servants who owed him one hundred denarii; and seized him by the throat and began to throttle him, saying, "Pay what you owe me." His fellow-servant fell at his feet and appealed to him, "Be patient with me, and I will pay you." But the other would not agree; on the contrary, he had him thrown into prison till he should pay the debt. His fellow servants were deeply distressed when they saw what had happened and they went to their master and reported the whole affair to him. Then the master sent for the man and said to him, "You wicked servant, I canceled all that debt of yours when you appealed to me. Were you not bound, then. to have pity on your fellow servant just as I had pity on you?" And in his anger the master handed him over to the torturers till he should pay back all his debt. And that is how my heavenly father will deal with you unless you each forgive your brother from your heart" (Matthew 18: 21 – 35).

Understanding the need to forgive others is not such a difficult thing to do when we take a moment to reflect on our own lives. By doing so, we will quickly become aware of the things we need to be forgiven for. Time after time, we have hurt our Lord and he never turns us away. He never puts conditions on our coming back; instead, he opens his arms wide and welcomes us back. What an awesome love he has for us!

But how do you transfer this philosophy to those who have hurt you so deeply? How can you forgive your ex-spouse?

## What Does Scripture Say?

You have heard how it was said, *You will love your neighbor* and hate your enemy. But I say this to you: Love your enemies and pray for those who persecute you, so that you may be children of your Father in heaven, for he causes his sun to rise on the bad as well as the good, and sends down rain to fall on the upright and the wicked alike. For if you love those who love you, what reward will you get? Do not even the tax collectors do as much? And if you save your greetings only for your brothers, are you doing anything exceptional? Do not even Gentiles do as much? You must, therefore, set no bounds to your love, just as your heavenly Father sets none to his (Matthew 5: 43 - 48).

You may be justifiably angry about your situation. It doesn't matter who left who or who still has the house . . . there has been a lot of hurt. You may be innocent victims of a tragedy and feel you have the right to be indignant and unforgiving. And having these feelings is the exact point where something great can take place . . . this is the exact point where you can decide if this experience will change you for the good or the bad.

No one said it would be easy. Being good isn't easy and forgiving isn't easy, but if you choose to say, "Yes, I hate the way my ex-spouse has hurt me – but yes, I will try to forgive him/her – well, I will at least think about it . . ." this is God's grace working within you and an integral part of the healing process.

## What's Next?

It's important to not just talk about forgiveness, but really look at taking some steps in that direction. Let's identify, first of all, a roadblock to forgiveness. You might feel that if you say "I forgive," once, then that is sufficient, but then realize sometime later that you are still angry and maybe you haven't really forgiven the offender of the offence. This might cause you to be harsh on yourself for not "truly" forgiving, or give up on the idea of forgiveness altogether.

But true forgiveness is not developed and put into place in a few moments, or even in a few days. Because your situation causes you to be constantly confronted with the details and bad memories every day, you need to practice forgiveness every day (PFED).

The practice begins simply by asking God to grant you the desire to forgive. It may be extremely difficult to forgive your ex-spouse, your in-laws, your own family members, the "other man/other woman," and/or any other person whom you hold captive as a prisoner in your heart, and this is why it's so important to ask God in prayer for this desire and the strength to act upon it. When you stop and remember how awesome God is, you can understand that he alone can make this desire grow within you like a tiny spark growing into a flame. Then, beginning with small and simple steps, eventually working into deeper and more sincere forgiveness, you will reach the point where you can say "all is forgiven."

Then, there are other steps to take in this process that are more immediate and practical. For example, when you are confronted with thoughts of your spouse, and the ways you've been hurt, either say a brief prayer for help such as, "Lord, please help me forgive," or say aloud, "I forgive you." There are many small steps that can be suggested, and the important thing is to start practicing one and begin the habit of forgiveness. Once a habit is formed, bigger steps can be taken and progress is made.

## Concluding Thoughts

By practicing forgiveness, you will be able to see changes in yourself for the better, and your ability to handle yourself when confronted by your spouse or other hurtful situations.

So you know you need to do your part and practice forgiveness – now comes the time to rely on Christ and let him work on your heart. This is why it is so important to stay close to the sacraments. Christ gives you the grace and the strength to forgive, and he transforms your heart when you are a willing participant. You cannot do it on your own. Go to confession frequently and receive the Eucharist as often as possible and you will see miracles happen in your life.

# Now What?

Forgiveness is not a one time event, of course, but a daily event. It is a process of assimilating what happened, accepting it and releasing the anger and resentment toward the person(s) that were involved. The old cliché: forgive and forget is too simplistic sometimes, and particularly in your case. Because traumatic events leave a permanent impression on our lives, it is likely you will never forget this wrong that has been done to you. With God's grace, some painful memories and details about your divorce will be forgotten and some just fade away as the years pass and you focus on other things. But what is possible and necessary for forgiving is to come to a better understanding of why something happened, accept it, and let go of the pain that it has caused you. Then you will be in a posture to forgive. That takes time, prayer and personal reflection. Here are some ways you can work on forgiveness:

1.  **Write a Letter:** The pain of betrayal is very intense and can last a long time. Chances are that long after you have accepted the things that your ex-spouse did which contributed to your divorce there will always be a sense of sadness and disappointment. One way to begin the process of forgiveness is to write a letter to your ex-spouse in a spirit of openness, not anger, letting him or her know the pain they have caused you and why. Tell them that you are trying to forgive them and why it is so hard to do so. Be specific. If you believe your ex-spouse will receive your letter with love, send it. If not, file it away. The point of writing the letter is to start the process of forgiveness by recognizing that it is difficult and why. It can be very therapeutic to get your feelings "off your chest" in a proactive way, not in reaction to what your ex-spouse did or said.

2.  **Pray the Our Father:** Ask God for help with forgiveness. The Our Father is the perfect prayer for this. It is a plea for help from God to help us forgive others: "...forgive us our trespasses as we forgive those

that trespass against us." It underscores the need to forgive others. It also underscores that we can't do it on our own. Say this prayer at least once a day asking God to give you the grace to forgive. While you may not suddenly feel more forgiving, know that no prayer goes unanswered. God wants you to forgive and He will help you develop a spirit of forgiveness. Ask him for it—often.

3. **Get a Personal Forgiveness Trainer**: Running a marathon takes consistent and intense training. Why? Because it is not a natural thing for your body to do. Well, forgiveness is not a natural thing for you to do, especially when the magnitude of the wrong done against you is so great. Just as a personal trainer can be very helpful by helping you understand what you need to do to get into shape and making sure you are consistent in our workout program, a priest or counselor can be equally as effective in helping you understand what you need to do to begin the process of forgiveness and to keep you moving forward. Having someone who knows you and who you can be totally honest with (and they with you), will help guide you down the path of forgiveness. Forgiveness is essential to your spiritual and emotional healing. Find someone who can help you be successful.

4. **Forgive the Intent**: If you are finding it hard to forgive, you can kick-start the process by forgiving the intent. Typically, your pain is the result of someone's action, not their intent. For example, usually someone commits adultery to seek their own personal pleasure, not to inflict pain on their spouse. If you can begin to understand your ex-spouses actions from this perspective, it may be easier for you to begin to forgive them. Once you are able to open the door to forgiveness, God will walk with you giving you the openness and courage to keep moving further down the road to forgiveness. Forgiving the intent is a significant step in that direction.

5. **Consider the Source**: You can often trace your ex-spouse's behavior back to his/her upbringing and life experiences. We are all formed by our parents and the personal life experiences we have. Poor parenting forms someone just as much as good parenting. The difference is the end result. What was your ex-spouse's childhood like? Were they surrounded

with good role models of marriage or was divorce a significant part of his/her family history? Did he/she experience unconditional love or was abuse involved? Was faith a critical part of his/her upbringing or was it ignored? Was trust and honesty a part of his/her relationship with their parents or were the relationships strained? Did they have good role models or bad examples? All of these questions will help you gain an understanding as to some of the factors that guided your ex-spouse's behavior. This is not to absolve him/her from responsibility for his/her behavior, but to help you understand that most likely the reasons for that behavior had little to do with you. As importantly, it helps you understand that you most likely could not have "fixed" your ex-spouse either. Their actions where driven by how their character was formed. And that character was formed long before you met them. This helps shed new light on why your ex-spouse did what they did and may help you realize that it wasn't about you, what you did, what you didn't do, how you looked, or how you didn't look. It was about your ex-spouse and his/her failings and shortcomings. If you can understand that, you can begin to separate the hurtful actions from your pain. The next step is to forgive those actions in spite of the pain. This is the epitome of being Christ-like as that is exactly what Christ did on the cross when, in spite of the great injustice done to him and his extreme pain, he said, "Father, forgive them, they do not know what they are doing" (Luke 23:34).

6. **Seek an Annulment**: While seeking an annulment is no guarantee you will receive a declaration of nullity, it is an excellent way to come to a fuller understanding of what caused the end of your marriage. It is in that understanding that the seeds of forgiveness can begin to germinate.

## Meditation

### Luke 23: 33 - 34

When they reached the place called The Skull, there they crucified him and the two criminals, one on his right and one on his left. Jesus said,

"Father, forgive them; they do not know what they are doing. Then they cast lots to share out his clothing.

**Opening Prayer**: My Lord and my God, you suffered for me so that I might live with you in heaven for eternity. Be with me now and teach me how to love, how to forgive through contemplation of your own unjust suffering.

**Petition**: Lord, grant me the desire to forgive those who have hurt me.

1. *The True Victim.*

Jesus – the man who loved, the man who healed, the man who fed, the man who gave hope to those suffering from despair – was mocked, beaten, tortured and killed, dying the shameful death of a criminal. Imagine being present at the crucifixion and being able to see all that is taking place. Jesus' mother Mary cannot stop her tears, nor can Mary Magdalene or the other women who are watching from afar. The soldiers are laughing and making fun of him as he suffocates and chokes on his own blood. The apostles . . . where are the apostles, but John? All those who said they loved him are hiding in fear. All those who welcomed him into their town as a king just one week before are spitting on him and shaking their fists at him. They want him dead. And during it all, Jesus is winning their salvation. Our salvation. Imagine the feelings of anger growing quickly and the tears beginning to stream down. Just then, Jesus speaks: "Father, forgive them . . . ."

2. *Christ will help us forgive.*

Sometimes, the downfall in trying to forgive is that we try to do it all on our own. Let us remember that the very fact we are willing to forgive is in fact a grace from God. So let us ask him to stoke that spark, however small, and let the desire to forgive those who have hurt us grow into a flame and set our hearts on fire with love.

**Closing Prayer**: Jesus, my Savior, thank you for all you have done for me. Thank you for all that you suffered so that I might be saved. I ask you for the grace to follow in your footsteps and forgive those who have hurt me. In your name I pray. Amen.

# Resolution

Spend time in prayer with Jesus and contemplate all that he suffered for us. Ask him to permeate your heart with the desire to forgive. Also, put your answer to discussion question #2 into practice.

# Suggested Reading

Eamon Tobin, *How to Forgive Yourself and Others: Steps to Reconciliation*, Liguori Publications (September 2006)

Immaculee Ilibagiza, *Left to Tell: Discovering God Amidst the Rwandan Holocaust*, Hay House (June 1, 2007)

*Fourteen Flowers of Pardon (DVD/VHS)*, Ignatius Press

# Chapter Fourteen:

## Gratitude

In this chapter, let's take a look at a very important aspect of getting over grief – one that, given your situation, you possibly have not focused on, and that is being thankful. The ability to be thankful to God and find the positives in a negative situation have great bearing on your outlook on life and the progress you make in healing your life.

What is there to be thankful for in the midst of a divorce? After wading through the mud of betrayal, lies, insults, lawyers, bills, custody trials, anger, depression, loneliness, how is it possible to be thankful? All these things that are a part of divorce can keep you weighed down and unable to see anything except how bad it is.

In other chapters, we talked about the poignant differences in two attitudes toward suffering: *Why do bad things happen to good people?* vs. *Why do good things happen to bad people?* And the difference in attitudes that were cited was simply realizing that even though everyone makes mistakes that cause terrible pain and suffering, God still blesses us. *Why does God continue to bless us with good things even though we offend him each day?* As we have discussed, the answer is because he loves you and wants you to be happy, even in spite of this terrible trial you are going through. Here is the perfect opportunity to begin delving into the "good things" that have happened to you, even as a result of your divorce. Impossible? Not at all.

The goal of this chapter is to step back for a while from the problems and complaints you are concentrating on. Relax your proverbial grip on these negative aspects so you can re-focus your sights on all the blessings you have been given by God.

# The Case

It may be difficult, with all that has happened, to find reasons to be thankful or grateful to God. Maybe you are at the stage where you are tired of all the negativity and are desperately looking for something positive . . . something to be thankful for, to refresh your outlook on life. Kevin talks about the gratitude he felt in the midst of one of the most terrible events in his life:

I had been through a miserable divorce. Insults, fighting, my suitcases thrown in the pool . . . and then the court dates. Those were grueling. When it was all finally said and done, I was glad. I wasn't happy that my family was torn apart – for that, I will ache till my death. But I just couldn't take it anymore. I felt gutted; like a carcass on the fence. Left for everyone to see what divorce does to a person, particularly if one is the husband. My kids wouldn't talk to me much at all. Not unless they needed something. Words could not describe how empty I felt!

Several years passed and I was doing alright when I was occupied with something. But when I was alone, I was having trouble keeping a good attitude. I couldn't motivate myself to do much. I still felt sad, no matter how I fought it. I wanted to be my normal self again, to feel like a regular person, but I just didn't know how to do that. Every Christmas after my divorce, I spent alone in my rented house with no tree, no family Christmas dinner . . . just a lot of sadness.

I went to see a counselor with much skepticism, but realized quickly that this guy had a lot of integrity. I knew he would be able to help. And one of the first things he helped me to realize was that I was focusing solely on the sadness of my situation - it was all I could see. Rather, it was all I would allow myself to see. I was not allowing these feelings to pass away naturally and let myself move on in life. I was using these feelings as a shield, as if they could block any future hurt. By clinging to this sadness, I refused to let anyone into my heart; much like an abandoned fortress, I appeared strong and impenetrable on the outside, yet I was cold and empty on the inside. I had always believed that life should be filled with love and happiness and here I was, ironically, staving it off as though it were a disease.

God has subtle ways of bringing us to himself, and I was no exception to this reality. As time passed, I began to grow restless and hungry for something, anything that could help me grab a hold of a new feeling that was emerging from within me . . . a feeling of strength; of wanting to not lay down and die from sadness and hurt. My heart was telling me I was stronger than I had been up to this point and if I would ever get my life back, I needed to give myself permission to move forward. Little by little, this hunger to change grew in my heart and I began to look for ways to open myself to life again. I decided I wanted to be happy, and although it was going to take some work, I had to begin somewhere.

One night, I saw a documentary on television about the holocaust. There were many survivors interviewed during the film, and an old man's story in particular touched me deeply. As a teenager in a Nazi concentration camp, he suffered tremendous and ongoing physical and mental tortures. He was starving to death, as all the prisoners were and he had lost his entire family to either illness or the showers. He, himself, was eventually sent to the showers to be murdered. But incredibly, he managed to escape with another young man through a hidden tunnel they found just before the gas came on. The weak and starving teenagers found the strength within themselves to run and hide, naked and frozen, for two days until they reached safety. Now, as this once young man, now very old man was being interviewed, he didn't curse the Nazis, he gave thanks to God! He gave thanks to those who saved him. His eyes showed the young man still inside him. He highlighted his story by saying that he had lived a full and happy life and although he grieved for his family every day, he had still known much love and happiness throughout his whole life.

I was so affected by this man's testimony that I couldn't get it out of my mind for days. I began to think of all the survivors of the holocaust and how they suffered unbelievable atrocities. After much contemplation, I recognized that if these people - victims of the holocaust - can pick up their lives and be happy, there was no reason why I couldn't do the same. It wasn't that I felt my suffering was meaningless compared to this man's, it was more that his example of determination and thankfulness was so refreshing . . . so motivating. I thought of my own life and realized then, how good it was, despite my divorce. True, I had suffered, but not to the degree that many people have. I began to look at life in a positive light. In the support group I was attending, instead of being in my own world of pain, I began to really listen to the others there. I heard different accounts of divorce and began to understand that, yes, my situation was painful, but could have been much, much worse. These things helped me to be grateful. And each day I was thankful was another day of healing.

## I Don't *Feel* Grateful!

Divorce is a traumatic event to suffer through. Sometimes you may feel like you are the only ones suffering to such an intense degree. Grief and sadness can easily lead to hopelessness and an "I just don't care" attitude. There are feelings of abandonment, rejection, confusion, disillusionment, etc., and it's hard to be readily focused on what is good in your life. But despite all the negativity you are experiencing, there are many good things in your life.

A great way to begin recognizing these good things you have is by taking some time to reflect on yourself – not particularly your memories or circumstances, but on *who you are*; what your talents are, your gifts, your personality, the things that make you who you are. For God made all of us beautiful creatures.

Aren't each one of us unique? We all have our weaknesses, of course, but don't we all have strengths? Especially during times of hardship, these strengths are there for us to draw upon and help us find our way through the suffering and turmoil.

And certainly we all have talents - something unique to each individual – that when offered with generosity, brings happiness to others. No one is without these gifts and you should sit down and make a list of your strengths and talents. Why is this important? First, to acknowledge some of the good things about yourself. When a marriage ends, often one or both spouses walk away with a loss of self-confidence or with a sense of inadequacy. Recognizing and claiming your winning attributes is a great thing to do and a confidence booster.

# What Does Scripture Say?

For what can be known about God is perfectly plain to them, since God has made it plain to them: ever since the creation of the world, the invisible existence of God and his everlasting power have been clearly seen by the mind's understanding of created things. And so these people have no excuse: they knew God and yet they did not honor him as God or give thanks to him, but their arguments became futile and their uncomprehending minds were darkened (Romans 1:19-20).

By learning to be thankful in times of difficulty or suffering, you will find your efforts will result in acquiring many desirable virtues:

1. maturity in your faith and emotion,
2. peace of heart and mind,
3. perseverance in our struggles, and
4. a flourishing of hope that strengthens even the dimmest view.

These virtues help your formation and strengthen you; they enable you to control your emotions, instead of allowing your emotions to control you. But in addition to your human formation, gratitude is highly instrumental in beginning the process of putting the past, with all it's pain and bad memories, behind you.

# How to Find an Attitude of Gratitude

Adopting an attitude of thankfulness is not always easy. Some days, we see blessings with every step we take. Other days, it's hard to find anything positive at all. But Christ is always at our side, regardless of how we feel, and he is always working for our good.

We can normally be grateful, of course, for very basic things such as our life, our health, our loved ones, the gift of faith, etc. But often the crosses we bear seem unfair – unjust – and this makes it harder to turn to God and say, "Thank you." But when we persevere with a positive attitude, our lives change and our hearts heal. As we've discussed previously, human suffering suddenly has meaning when we see it through the eyes of faith.

For example, a young mother dies within months of being diagnosed with cancer. She leaves her husband to take care of their three young daughters. Through her months of agony, her husband witnesses her courageous suffering and attitude of love toward God and all. There is no anger present in her, only love. This softens her husbands hardened heart toward God, and after years of separation from the Church, he is reunited to the Faith.

Another couple, headed toward divorce, buries their son whom they lost in an accident; but through hard work and communication with each other instead of turning away, they find that the loss brings them closer as a couple as they cling to each other for solace. They emerge from their suffering as different people, stronger and more loving. The loss of their only child turned their lives around. Instead of giving intotheir pain and losing their marriage, they have since renewed their vows and had more children. Their story is not typical of parents who suffer the loss of a child, but how inspiring a story it is! It is a testament to what can happen when people are open to each other and to God's grace.

Finding gratitude in the midst of difficulties is as simple as finding a positive thought to contest a negative one. For example, when the memory of a fight with your spouse comes into your thoughts, you can immediately be thankful that because you live apart, you don't have to constantly be fighting. Or if you begin to feel sad about your children and how this has affected them, be thankful that God has blessed you with children and as a family, you may comfort each other and grow stronger together because of what has happened. If you are enduring financial difficulty, be thankful to God for what he has blessed you with so far and have faith that he will take care of your family.

As you put a thankful way of thinking into practice, it becomes easier and easier to find the positive aspects of any situation. Gratitude paves the way to happiness. Think of a wrapped gift sitting under a Christmas tree, waiting to be opened. We cannot enjoy the gift until we open it. And so it is the same with gratitude – when we are thankful, we are opening of the gift of love that God shows us through all the positive events we find in our lives.

## Concluding Thoughts

Gratitude enables you to move forward, to say, "I have survived that pain and I am better for it." Gratitude heals your heart and provides a multitude of reasons to wake up in the morning and get out of bed. It enables you to recognize God's plan for your life.

> We should accept, as we would a favor,
> every moment of our lives and whatever they may bring,
> whether it is good or bad, but the crosses
> with even greater gratitude than the rest.
> Crosses release us from this world and by doing so bind us to God.
> – Venerable Charles de Foucauld

## Now What?

Trials demand your attention and focus. It is easy to get consumed with the internal struggle that comes as a result of these trials, and loose sight of those things you can be thankful for. Here are some ways you can begin to develop a sense of gratitude, despite the crushing pain of divorce or separation.

1. **Make a List**: To help focus on the positive aspects of your life, use page 142 of your Workbook to make a list of those things you are truly thankful for. This can be anything, but don't be afraid to list the obvious like your health, your kids' health, the roof over your head, heat in the winter, running water, etc. Also include any talents or gifts that you have. When the pain is present on a daily basis, it is easy to take for granted the basics of life – those things that being without would make our lives even more difficult. When your list is ready, post it in an obvious place (like your bathroom mirror) so you will have a frequent reminder of the blessings God has given you.

2. **Retrace Your Steps**: Only by looking back can we see how far we have come. Of course, it takes a grand soul to be thankful for the struggle, itself, but it may be easier to be thankful for the positive things that have resulted from the struggle. Divorce is a detour from our plan for life. Yet, like any detour, we will experience things we might not have otherwise. Some of these things will be positive. In the Work-

book companion, reflect on this question and write down what comes to mind:

*How did my divorce result in experiences or changes that were positive to me or to others in my life?*

While it is true that divorce results in many negative experiences and painful changes, it is also true that in that rubble some gems can be found. Think and pray about it. Did you go back to school as a result of your divorce? Did you learn a new skill? Did you make a new friend that has helped you or added to your life in some positive way? Did you draw closer to your faith? Did you renew/repair an important family relationship? Are you seeing your family more often? Are you able to help other divorced people because of your experience? Looking back helps you gain perspective that there is always some good that comes out of something bad.

3.  **Fast**: Fasting has been a cornerstone of the religious life since before Christ. It is used as a means of humbling ourselves by reminding us of our dependence on God. It is also considered one of the highest forms of prayer since we are offering our self-induced suffering up to God. Fasting doesn't have to be done just during Lent★. Given that going through a divorce is painful enough, how can it be helpful to introduce more suffering into your life? Fasting is a powerful way to reshape your attitude toward your present life. Simply put: going without makes us really appreciate what we do have. If you can't fast for health reasons, or you just can't get your head around the benefit of fasting, try doing without something else for a day or two: take the stairs instead of the elevator, go without TV, drink water instead of coffee or soft drinks, give up your iPod, or take the bus instead of driving your car. When you fast or give something up, be sure to offer that suffering up as a prayer to God and ask for the grace to see your blessings and the gratitude to always be thankful for them.

4.  **"Carpe Diem" – Seize the Day**: Everyday is an opportunity: an opportunity to try again, an opportunity to make a difference in someone's life, an opportunity to make an improvement in your life. Seize those opportunities every chance you can. It is so easy to live in the pain of yesterday, or be overwhelmed by the uncertainty of the future,

that you can miss the promise of today. Try and develop an approach of focusing on what you can do, instead of what you can't. The more you do that, the more you will develop a positive, hope-filled, outlook as you see how what you can do day after day, no matter how small, leads to a real improvement in your life and those you love.

5. **Psalm 136**: Pray and mediate on these words from Psalm 136, verses 1-8:

> *Give thanks to Yahweh for he is good; for his faithful love endures forever;*
> *Give thanks to the God of gods; for his faithful love endures forever;*
> *Give thanks to the Lord of lords; for his faithful love endures forever;*
> *He alone works wonders, for his faithful love endures forever;*
> *In wisdom he made the heavens, for his faithful love endures forever;*
> *He set the earth firm on the waters, for his faithful love endures forever;*
> *He made the great lights, for his faithful love endures forever.*

This entire psalm is filled with gratitude and praise to God for all the things he has done for us, great and small. As you reflect on this psalm, think about all the good things that God has done in your life, both in the past and in the present. If any of them cause you to exclaim "Praise God!" write them down and remember them. There will be times in the future you will need these powerful reminders to remind you that despite the pain in life, there is always something to be thankful for.

# Meditation

## Luke 17: 11 - 19

Now it happened that on the way to Jerusalem he was traveling in the borderlands of Samaria and Galilee. As he entered one of the villages, ten men suffering from a virulent skin-disease came to meet him. They stood some way off and called to him, Jesus! Master! Take pity on us. When he saw them he said, Go and show yourselves to the priests. Now as they were going away they were cleansed. Finding himself cured, one of them turned back praising God at the top of his voice and threw himself prostrate at the feet of Jesus and thanked him. The man was a Samaritan. This led Jesus to say, Were not all ten made clean? The other nine, where are they? It seems that no one has come back to give praise to God, except this foreigner. And he said to the man, Stand up and go on your way. Your faith has saved you.

**Opening Prayer**: Dear Jesus, Healer of all infirmities, I approach you now with faith and a desire to know you more intimately. I know the healing of my wounds is part of your plan and I listen attentively to your words that they may soothe my heart and bring me peace.

**Petition**: Lord, grant me the grace to always be able to see your blessings in my life.

1. *Jesus! Master! Take pity on us!*

   The suffering men begged Jesus to pay attention to them. We are suffering, Lord! Our lives are in shambles! We are outcasts! Lord, help us! Heal us! They did not even dare approach him, they stayed at a distance and called to him. We may feel quite the same . . . . When we suffer, we long for someone to acknowledge our pain. At times, we might go to mass and stand in the very back of the church because we feel distant - we hurt, we feel like outcasts, or just simply lost and we call to Christ from a distance . . . *Take pity on me, Lord!* Christ loves us and will always give us what we need to heal from our wounds. He loves us with the greatest love and cares for us as if no other existed.

2. *One of them turned back . . . and thanked him.*

   This man, was a Samaritan. Samaritans knew that – according to they Jews – they counted for nothing. They were outcasts. Samaritans then worshipped other gods, and many of them. But this man, the most unlikely of the bunch, recognized what a great miracle Jesus had performed for him. We can identify with this man. We need healing! We may feel disenfranchised from our parish, our family or friends because of our divorce. And we must recognize the great things God is doing for us. Sometimes, even the smallest of ways are not actually small at all. They can be life-changing. But we need to be on the look-out for these things, for recognizing God's blessings will bring hope. Hope that God will take care of us.

**Closing Prayer**: Lord Jesus, I thank you for all your blessings; those I can recognize and those I can't. I know that you are beside me, loving me, protecting me, guiding me. Help me to see all the good things you have done for me. In your name, I pray. Amen.

## Resolution

Every day this week, take ten minutes to thoughtfully write down more than one thing you are thankful for. Keep this list with you and look at it when you're feeling particularly negative. On Sunday, bring the list with you to mass and offer your mass in thanksgiving for these things.

## Suggested Reading

Jorge Cardinal Medina-Estevez, *Lord, Who Are You? The Names of Christ*, Ignatius Press (February 2004)

# Chapter Fifteen:

# Sex and Dating as a Divorced Catholic

Growing up, you were probably told the same thing about sex that most kids where told: "Don't have sex until you are married because it's a sin." What you may not have been told was why. That gap of understanding is a problem, especially now that you find yourself divorced. Without a fundamental understanding about what the Church teaches about sex, dating, and marriage, it is hard to embrace and live its teachings. It simply becomes a set of rules that you better not break or "you're going to hell." While that might have worked to keep you on track when you were fifteen years old, it is hardly an effective means to ensure a life of peace and joy and an eternity in heaven when you are an adult. Further still, it is easy to become very cynical about living a chaste life after divorce since you are no longer a virgin. No doubt, this is a highly charged issue filled with emotion. When explained, the Church's teaching on sex and dating provides a very hopeful message for divorced Catholics.

## The Case

Claire describes her experience with dating after her divorce:

When my husband and I split-up I was completely numb. I couldn't believe it was happening to us! In the several months that followed, I was trying to adjust to this new life I hated. The life I knew and loved, being married, was gone forever and I was having trouble making the change.

Much to my dismay, I found it difficult at first to keep from crying and I cried in the most awkward situations - a board meeting, getting my hair done . . . it was all I could do to control myself. A few of my friends at work took me out on my birthday and kept the margaritas coming. They assured me as I was crying even then, that I just needed to forget about the whole thing. I needed to go out and date! They encouraged me to find some guy who had a lot of money and would treat me well. One of them even tried to set me up with a friend of hers. But, I couldn't do it. My heart wasn't ready for someone new. I wanted my husband. But I never could have expected what would happen next.

I had taken a job in the evening to help pay for legal costs, etc. and became friends with one of the business consultants working in the office named Ian. He and I hit it off well and after several weeks of working there my opinions about dating began to change. I liked Ian and he paid a lot of attention to me. I felt attractive around him – as if I was worth something. We began dating ever so casually and I was really enjoying myself. I was able to ignore the pain and loneliness of my divorce when I was with him.

I had been raised by my parents to value a chaste dating relationship and remained a virgin until I had met my husband. But when we began dating, he pressed me so hard to become intimate with him that I finally gave in. I knew that part of the reason why marrying him was such a mistake was because we were sleeping together before we were married. I became completely wrapped up in the emotional highs that resulted from the physical intimacy we shared. I was so blinded by these emotions and could not bring myself to acknowledge all the warning signals I received during our engagement.

One evening as I got ready to meet Ian, I was inspecting myself in the mirror. I always wore something conservative, no super low necklines or really suggestive clothing. I didn't want to make any statements that would give him the wrong impression about me. I was not interested in the slightest in having this guy think I was going to jump into bed with him. I knew there would be heartaches in the future with trying to find my place in the world; I had no clue if I would be able to marry again or not, but I hoped that in comparison to my divorce, these disappointments would be kept to a minimum. And if there was one thing I knew without a doubt, it was that I didn't want to go through a divorce ever again. I looked at myself in the mirror and gave myself a nod of approval. I was attractive, yet modest.

But there were already interior warnings signals that were trying to get my attention and I could not see them because I was allowing myself to be carried away with the emotions I was already feeling. Well, the more likely scenario was that I would not see them. There was no chance, not even the slightest, that I was ready for a relationship of any type. My heart had been broken beyond belief and I had a long way to go until I was healed. I also had a lot of work to do on myself before I was fit to give someone else what they needed in a relationship. But being with Ian felt so good and I couldn't see the wisdom in stopping the progression of the relationship. I couldn't see what was happening

Later that evening after dinner, we went over to his corporate apartment and he showed me around. We sat and talked for a while and then he began to make the moves. It started to get a little too heavy, and I asked him to stop. I sat back and told him that I was in the process of a divorce and really had no interest in getting into anything serious just yet. I still had a lot of healing to do and didn't think getting intimate with him was the right thing to do. He listened with interest and said, "You're right!" when I was finished. "Come on, let's go!" and he grabbed my hand and out we went. We had a great time and I never wanted my time with Ian to end.

Ian was off to another consulting job within a few days. We saw each other almost every night during his final week in town and sadly, I allowed myself to succumb to his advances in the end. Each time we were together, I became weaker and weaker until I my resolve crumbled and we woke up together the next morning. Unfortunately for me, he left my house with many "thank you's" and a sincere "I had a wonderful time," but no, "I'll call you" or any promise of ever seeing him again. And I realized what a fool I had been. I felt lower than ever.

Mike describes his experience with dating after his divorce:

I fought hard to save my marriage, but in the end my wife decided that she wanted to be single again. I was devastated. The end of my marriage was the last thing I wanted. She may have wanted to be single again, but I didn't. The thought of being single again made my stomach turn. I pretty much swore off women for the rest of my life.

It was less than two months after our divorce proceedings began that I began to get phone calls and emails from single women wanting to go out on a date. I was shocked! I was in the midst of grieving the loss of my marriage and I was being pursued by other women. I was not ready for that. I made it very clear that I was not dating and had no desire to date. Guys at the office told me I was nuts. They told me now was my chance to live it up, to get all the sex I wanted. All I could do was shake my head in disbelief. It was as if they were trying to live vicariously through me.

Although I made it quite clear that I was not dating, there was one woman, Amy, who continued to stay in touch with me during my divorce. Amy had been our friend when my wife and I were married. She was so kind and caring to me during this difficult time and often offered to help me with my kids. The closer it got to my divorce being final, the more open Amy became in her interest in me.

While I was still smarting from my divorce, I was also lonely. Physical intimacy had been almost nonexistent in my marriage and the thought of someone actually being interested in me was very appealing. Amy would always compliment me on my looks and tell me what a great person and father I was. Having been beaten down in my marriage and subsequent divorce, here was someone who was praising me and lifting me up. I had to admit it made me feel great. I was like a sponge soaking up the attention and compliments.

My faith had always been central to my life and who I was. I knew that even though I was getting a civil divorce, I was still married in the eyes of the Church. I also knew that even after my civil divorce was final, if I had sex it was considered adultery. That really stung because from my perspective, I had been through tremendous pain and suffering during and after my divorce, and now I had to suffer even more after it. Didn't the Church care about me? After all I had been through, wasn't I entitled to enjoy life? Why wasn't the Church more compassionate about my need for intimacy? After all, it wasn't like there was any of that happening in my marriage. Plus, I wasn't a virgin anymore. I have to admit, I became somewhat cynical toward the Church and its teachings on marriage, sex and dating.

My divorce took over a year to be finalized. I held firm to my resolution to not date during my divorce. In my mind as long as I was legally married I had to honor my marriage. However, I had made up my mind that after my divorce I was free to date and even have sex. Less then a week after my divorce was final, I met Amy for dinner. Afterward, we went back to her place. Amy made it very clear that she was interested in more than just having dinner. After all I had been through, I couldn't resist. I stayed overnight and we had sex. Afterward while I was driving home, I tried to tell myself that I deserved that intimacy and that it was great, but deep down I felt empty. I figured it was just because I was still attached to my ex-wife in some way so I ignored it.

Amy and I continued to date for several months and we continued to have sex. I kept justifying it because I felt I deserved to be happy after all the misery I had been through in my marriage and divorce. While I was dating Amy, I was continuing to get emails and phone calls from other single women I had known. It was unbelievable to me how aggressive women had become since I was in high school and college. Here I was a forty-year-old man who had done alright for himself financially and it was like the women where coming out of the woodwork. I didn't have to do anything – they were pursuing me. Talk about getting validated. It felt great!

Over the course of the next year, I continued to date Amy on and off. We mainly got together to have sex. During this time, I also started dating a woman I knew from college. As with Amy, this woman wanted a sexual relationship as well. I was living "the dream" that my colleagues had talked about. I was dating whoever I wanted and I was having sex whenever I wanted. Yet, the more I did this, the emptier I felt. I kept trying to ignore it, but the feelings of emptiness and shame kept coming back, stronger and stronger each time. I was more confused than ever. *Why wasn't I happy?* I was living the life that society had promised would bring me great happiness and fulfillment and yet I felt anything but. Some dream!

# A Reason for Hope

In spite of all the uncertainty after divorce, there is reason to be very hopeful. God has many good things in store for you, despite your pain and suffering. But you need to understand something very important; that your ultimate destination in life is heaven, not earth, and so your ultimate and lasting happiness will be found in heaven, not on earth. However, while you are here on earth, God wants you to have a life filled with as much peace and joy as humanly possible. And better still, he has given you a way to get it. Once you understand what that way is, your moral guidelines become a "map" that leads you closer and closer to God and happiness, instead of being just a list of do's and don'ts. As you draw closer to God, you realize more fully his promise of abundant peace and joy.

Before you start off on your journey toward the land of peace and joy, let's make sure you understand how to use your "map." It begins with the basic truth that only in God will you ever find true, lasting, peace and joy.

The bottom line is that unless what you are doing is part of God's plan for you, you will always be searching and never find true peace and joy. You will never be truly "happy." That is a very black-and-white statement, and yet many people live their entire lives never really understanding it.

# God's Design for Sex

You may be saying to yourself, "Well, God made people and he made sex, so why will sex in-and-of itself not bring me closer to God?" Good question. The short answer is: because when people have sex *outside* of marriage it is outside the context which God planned. God created sex as a wonderful, sacred, gift to married couples to not only create life, but to draw them closer to God. Which means sex *inside* of marriage is holy. When sex is pursued outside of that context, it is unholy and it will draw you further away from God. The further away from God you become, the further away you are from finding the peace and joy you are seeking. It's that simple. Whether or not you believe it, doesn't make it any less true. You can ignore it only to find that your relationships are empty and superficial, and your peace, fleeting.

In his groundbreaking work, *Theology of the Body,* Pope John Paul II gave a true gift to the Church. In that series of teachings, the Pope revealed God's design for our sexuality, our bodies, and how sex is part of God's glorious plan for our salvation. He discusses how instead of being dirty or wrong that sex, when pursued within God's plan, is not only a great thing, it leads us to holiness. Imagine that! Many people want to separate sex and God as if they are opposed to each other. The Pope shows how God created sex as an integral part of His plan for us. The key is to understand that plan and then commit to living it.

Entire books have been written on the Pope's writings on *Theology of the Body,* so no attempt will be made to fully cover that material here. Instead, here is an overview of the basic teachings so you can better understand the answer to the question of "What is so wrong with sex outside of marriage?" Here are the basic points of the Pope's teaching:

- The Trinity is the eternal sharing of love between the Father, the Son, and the Holy Spirit. In essence, love is what binds the Trinity together. Marriage is a visible sign (sacrament) of this love here on earth modeling the Trinity because it is the permanent sharing of love between a man, a woman, and God.

- God created us to share in this eternal, unbroken, always faithful love.

- God created sexual desire to be the very power to love as he loves—in a free, sincere, and total gift of self.

- Sexual love becomes an icon or earthly image of the eternal exchange of love in the Trinity.

- Only in marriage can the purpose and power of sexual love be realized because sex isn't just a biological reality. It's also a spiritual and theological reality.

Some of the above seems rather theological. Maybe looking at it in a more concrete way might help to understand it. In Christopher West's book, *Theology of the Body for Beginners,* he describes how when sex is separated from God's plan for it, sex actually becomes the god. And that society's obsession with sex is actually the human desire for Heaven gone haywire.

The bottom line is that we are all searching for God. We all desire the abundant peace and joy associated with heaven. The problem is we look for God in all the wrong places. We have plenty of earthly options available to us to try and fulfill this craving – money, sex, sports, work, clothes, houses, cars, television, vacations, etc. Yet, we find the more we pursue those things the more they leave us feeling empty and unfulfilled.

This is particularly true with sexual relationships. The more we pursue sexual relationships outside of marriage, the more elusive the peace and joy we are seeking in those relationship becomes. If we are honest with ourselves, what we really find is disillusionment, anxiety, emptiness and regret, none of which comes from God. It seems the harder we try to find fulfillment in these types of relationships, the more elusive it becomes. It is like trying to fill up on cotton candy. While the initial experience is sweet, it quickly fades. It doesn't satisfy our hunger, but instead leaves us wanting more. We can never seem to get enough; we can never get full. We simply get stuck in the vicious cycle of trying to find happiness but it never lasts.

West goes on to say that our sexual desire, when used as God intended actually helps "propel" us toward Heaven, stating our sexual desire is akin to rocket fuel that's intended to launch us to the heavens, and only when this takes place as God intended, does marriage become truly a sacrament. God's plan for sex is to help sanctify married couples and give them a taste of heaven on earth.

*A taste of heaven?* Hold on! For many, their marriage was anything but a taste of heaven. Yet, for every married couple, **that is the promise that marriage holds**. That is all well and good for married couples, but what about divorced men and women? Are they shut out from this promise? Are they doomed to a life of emptiness and sorrow? What now is *their* path to peace and joy?

> **As we draw closer to God we realize more fully his promise of abundant peace and joy.**

## The Path to Peace and Joy

The Church's teaching on sex is very clear: it is reserved for marriage.

That fact is the reason why many divorced Catholics feel bitter and disconnected from the Church. They feel a great injustice has been done to them. For many, they have to suffer yet another rejection, they have to give up the promise of the taste of heaven. Whether they ever experienced that level of peace and joy in their marriage or not, the Church's teaching can be interpreted as making it impossible to attain outside of marriage. They feel betrayed, abandoned, and alone. The future seems to be a choice of following the Church's teaching and dooming oneself to a life of loneliness and self-deprivation, or to set out on a path apart from the Church in search of peace and joy.

But, wait! There is great news! The Church really is the ONE place that holds the path for all people to true peace and joy. While marriage is one pathway to the fullest union with God, it is not the only way. For a divorced Catholic, it is not a matter of choosing a path inside the Church or a path outside the Church, but choosing a different path within the Church. One of the biggest struggles for a divorced Catholic is not in taking that new path, but in surrendering to the truth that a new path must be taken. It is in trying to accept this truth that many divorced Catholics either abandon their faith or get stuck in trying to be true to the Church while still pursuing their personal happiness. Either place is not good as it is full of turmoil and struggle, not peace and joy.

What is this new path? How can you firmly plant your feet on it? Well, this new path is actually not new at all. It is the same path offered to all: a relationship with Jesus Christ. Jesus Christ always has been and always will be "...the way, and the truth and the life" (John 14:6). As a divorced Catholic, you must make the switch from focusing on your marital relationship as being the pathway to God to focusing on your relationship with Christ as being that pathway. Remember, the closer you draw to God, the more abundant your peace and joy. Nurturing your relationship with Christ is how you can draw closer to God. The Gospel of John underscores this:

"I am the Way; I am the Truth and Life. No one can come to the Father except through me. If you know me, you will know my Father, too. From this moment, you know him and have seen him" (John 14:6-7).

# The Challenge Ahead

It is time to take a new path, the path of Christ. The challenge is to surrender the old path. Taking on this challenge is usually very difficult. The struggles and the suffering come because this is not a natural thing for humans to do. It is not natural to let go of yourself, your dreams, your desires, your wants, and give it all to Christ – especially after a divorce when it seems that those are the only things you have left. However, this is the exact point that meaningful growth takes place.

At this point, you may be saying to yourself: "All of this seems like just more suffering, more struggle, what's the point? It is much easier to just start dating again and 'enjoy the moment.'" That is certainly understandable, but as C. S. Lewis points out in his book *Mere Christianity*, it is not a recipe for peace and joy. He explains in that book that the struggle of trying to serve two masters, ourselves and God, is a far greater struggle than surrendering our lives to Christ.

True, surrendering our lives is a scary proposition. Most people work hard every day to gain control of their lives, not give it away. This is especially true for people who have experienced divorce.

No doubt, embracing this new path and giving it all to Christ is not easy. But the truth is that any other path, while initially seeming easier, more exciting, or more fulfilling, in the end will not bring you the peace and joy you are searching for. Only a life centered on Christ will.

The point of surrender is not to wake up each day expecting Christ to have left you a calendar of events for the day on your pillow. The point is to change your attitude about your life and your future. Instead of trying to be in control of every situation, you invite Christ into all aspects of your life and follow his lead. When you give your life to Christ, you can expect your trust to be rewarded hundred-fold and incredible things to happen.

> "And there are those who have been sown in rich soil;
> they hear the word and accept it and yield a harvest, thirty
> and sixty and a hundred fold" (Mark 4:20).

# Sex and Dating

What does this have to do with addressing the issue of when and if it is okay to pursue dating relationships? To answer that question unequivocally, let's put all the above pieces together.

As previously addressed, the Church teaches that sex is reserved as a sacred act for married couples. The reason the Church teaches this is because God uniquely designed the act of sexual union for two sacred purposes: the unitive and the procreative. It is natural to feel cheated, perhaps even angry, when you read that, especially if you were not the one who caused the divorce yet, must now suffer the consequences everyday by having to abstain from physical intimacy. That is true, yet fortunately, Christ and the Church provide you with a new path that leads to the peace and joy you used to get through physical intimacy.

The Church also teaches that until and unless you receive a decree of nullity, you are still bound to your vows of marriage. Breaking your marriage vows is considered adultery. That may be a bitter pill to swallow, but it is the truth nonetheless. So, given that, can you date after divorce? The answer is, "it depends." If you have already received a decree of nullity regarding your former marriage, the answer is "absolutely." You are no longer bound to your former spouse, and therefore, dating is not an issue.

If you have not received a decree of nullity, you are still bound by your marriage vows and therefore it is not advised that you pursue a romantic relationship for several reasons. First and foremost, if you do choose to pursue a serious relationship before getting a decree of nullity, you are taking a real risk. If you don't receive a decree of nullity, you have invested in a relationship that you cannot pursue and still remain in full communion with the Church. In that case, you will be forced into the horrible position of choosing between your relationship and the Church. That is a risk you don't want to take.

That being said, the Church does not expect you to live as a semi-cloistered religious doing nothing but working and praying. You are called to be an apostle, a beacon of light, drawing others closer to Christ. But the Church also understands the human heart and its tendency to draw near what is pleasing. Pursing a serious relationship and being sexually active will not do that. However, relationships among friends of the opposite sex where you are honoring your vows and being an example for others on how to live your faith as a divorced Catholic certainly do.

Second, know that being in a serious relationship provides an on-going opportunity to be tempted and will make it very difficult to honor your vows. Finding another person who is equally committed to helping you preserve your existing vows is a real challenge. More often than not, one person is more committed than the other to preserving chastity, creating tension in the relationship. It is very hard, if not impossible, to maintain a commitment to being chaste in a relationship when one person is not committed to it. So, while the Church does not expect you to live like a hermit, it does expect you to honor your vows. Doing so inside of a dating relationship can prove very difficult, even for the most committed couples.

No doubt, pursuing new relationships after a divorce and living the Church's teachings can be difficult. However, through the virtue of chastity, there is a way, and one that promotes true happiness and virtue.

## The "C" Word

The word "chastity" not only sounds medieval, it conjures up medieval imagery of chastity belts and other practices to protect purity at all costs. In the eyes of the world, the word has a negative connotation. However, in the eyes of the Church, chastity is a gift to everyone—married or not—to help us master ourselves, maintain our dignity, and draw us closer to God.

Suffering the loss of physical intimacy is one of the greatest struggles for a divorced Catholic; a real and valid source of pain. This struggle is compounded by the uncertainty of how long they will have to endure the loss of physical intimacy. It is one thing to abstain from something for a finite period, but to abstain indefinitely can be a very difficult, seemingly impossible, burden to bear. And, in the case where a decree of nullity is not granted, the divorced person is required to abstain from sexual intimacy for life (unless, of course, he or she reconciles with his or her spouse). The virtue of chastity can be a tremendous help in shouldering this burden.

The *Catechism of the Catholic Church* describes chastity this way:

> Chastity includes an apprenticeship in self-mastery which is a training in human freedom. The alternative is clear: either man governs his passions and finds peace, or he lets himself be dominated by them and becomes unhappy. "Man's dignity therefore requires him to act out of conscious and free choice, as moved and drawn in a personal way from within, and not by blind impulses in himself or by mere external constraint. Man gains such dignity when, ridding himself of all slavery to the passions, he presses forward to his goal by freely choosing what is good and, by his diligence and skill, effectively secures for himself the means suited to this end" (*CCC* 2339).

Notice the word "peace" is used to describe the benefit of chastity. That is quite a paradox to how the world views chastity. The worldly perception of chastity is denial; that chastity only means suffering, injustice, and sacrifice. Not surprisingly, our Church teaches us something quite different. By being chaste, you actually help speed yourself down the path toward peace and joy. You are able to do your part with Christ in living God's will for you. Looked at in this manner, chastity is a very hopeful thing to obtain.

The *Catechism of the Catholic Church* goes on to describe that chastity is a virtue that takes time to be formed. You don't wake up one day being totally chaste and loving it. It is an on-going process to integrate into your life.

> Self-mastery is a long and exacting work. One can never consider it acquired once and for all. It presupposes renewed effort at all stages of life. The effort required can be more intense in certain periods, such as when the personality is being formed during childhood and adolescence (*CCC* 2342).

In addition, notice that the Church in her infinite wisdom, knows that there are going to be times in your life when being chaste is going to be more difficult. Life after a divorce is one of those times. This is a period of intense "re-forming" of your life. You can expect the pursuit of chastity during this time to require much more intense effort. It will not be easy. It is important to stay close to the sacraments during this time, particularly the sacrament of reconciliation. It is not uncommon to stumble and fall during the pursuit of chastity. However, never forget that God knows your heart and your intent. He blesses you with an abundance of graces when he sees that you are suffering for him. Remember his promise:

> None of the trials which have come upon you is more than what a human being can stand. You can trust that God will not let you be put to the test beyond your strength, but with any trial will also provide a way out by enabling you to put up with it (*1 Corinthians* 10:13).

It is very hopeful to know that through chastity you are able to develop relationships with members of the opposite sex that ultimately draw you closer to God.

Chastity is expressed notably in friendship with one's neighbor. Whether it develops between persons of the same or opposite sex, friendship represents a great good for all. It leads to spiritual communion (*CCC* 2347).

What the Church is saying is that friendship between two people is a good thing, not just for those two people, but for the greater good of all people. By sharing in friendships, you fulfill Christ's commandment to love your neighbor as yourself and in so doing lead society closer to God. Chastity is not only about you living a virtuous life and getting to heaven; it is about helping your entire community experience the love of God. It is chastity that allows these friendships to form and flourish, free from the prospect that they could disintegrate into a self-serving relationship.

Understanding what chastity really is should help you see that you are called to be chaste not just to keep you from sinning, but also to help further God's kingdom. As a divorced Catholic, you are NOT called to stay home and avoid relationships, but rather the opposite. You are called, with God's help in the virtue of chastity, to cultivate relationships with everyone and be a witness to all of God's love and kindness.

Chastity leads him who practices it to become a witness to his neighbor of God's fidelity and loving kindness (*CCC* 2346).

That is a reason to be VERY hopeful. Use your divorce as an opportunity to let your life speak—to be a witness to others—that in spite of the pain and brokenness of divorce, your life has profound meaning and purpose: to draw others closer to God.

## Living a Chaste Life

It is so easy to focus on what you can't do regarding sex and dating after divorce. What about what you CAN do? Here are some guidelines for living a chaste life:

Whether you have received a declaration of nullity or not:

- Meeting the challenges of a chaste life, especially when in a relationship, is almost impossible without the help of Christ. Pray daily for the strength and grace to live chastely. St. Joseph is looked on as a model of chastity as he honored the virginity of his wife, Mary, for his entire life. Pray to St. Joseph for the grace to live a chaste life as he did.

Before you receive your declaration of nullity:

- You certainly can go out socially in groups. This is a great way to remain socially active after divorce and yet honor your marital vows.

- You can go out socially with the opposite sex. Approach the relationship with the same respect and level of intimacy as you would a family member. Not romantic, for sure, but that is the best way to play it safe. Also, try to avoid one-on-one alone situations.

- Don't be afraid to talk about your chaste approach to dating after your divorce with your family and friends. By being an example to others, you actually may inspire them to lead a life more aligned with the Church. Moreover, you will be a sign of hope to other divorced Catholics.

- Initiate the annulment process. Allow your heart to heal as it will in this process, and hopefully you will become free to pursue serious dating relationships by receiving a declaration of nullity.

After you receive your declaration of nullity:

- Pursue relationships with like-minded people. To be successful, both people have to be equally committed to a chaste life. If you sense the relationship has the potential to become serious, bring up your commitment to chastity early in your dating relationship before strong feelings are formed. While it may be awkward and uncomfortable, it is the best way to avoid tension and heartbreak.

- Set yourself up for success by avoiding temptation. If you are a woman, dress modestly. If you are a man, don't spend time around a woman who is deliberately dresses with the intention of keeping you focused on her body.

- Pray for the strength and grace to live a chaste life. The virtue of chastity is formed and lived with the help of the Holy Spirit. Call on him regularly.

# Now What?

Here are some great ways you can get come to know the truthfulness of the Church's teachings and tap into the peace and joy it promises:

1. **Pray**: Prayer is the cornerstone to finding a new path to Christ, and staying on it. Commit to daily prayer. Start out small and build up to at least fifteen minutes a day. It is very important to create this quiet time of prayer each day.

2. **Stay Close to the Sacraments**: The Sacraments are the cornerstone of our faith and in them, Christ will give you an abundance of strength and mercy as you forge this new path. Instead of seeking your solace in dating, find it in Christ by immersing yourself in the sacraments. Go to mass, receive the Eucharist, and go to reconciliation routinely. The peace and joy you are searching for is there because that is where Christ is.

3. **Give yourself to others**: The fastest way to move along the path of Christ is to love others. That was Christ's great commandment. Look for ways at home, at work, in your community or church to help or serve others. It will take the focus off you and be the spark that lights the flame of hope.

4. **Seek to Understand**: Unless you really understand the Church's teaching on sex, dating, and chastity, it will be very difficult to embrace and live them. They will seem like a set of rules that must be followed to avoid Hell, instead of the pathway to peace and joy on Earth and ultimately Heaven. Read Sections 2337-2372 in the *Catechism of the Catholic Church* for a detailed explanation on chastity. The book, *Theology of the Body for Beginners* by Christopher West, is an excellent resource to learn about God's plan for our sexuality. The first encyclical by Pope Benedict XVI, *God is Love*, will give you a great insight into how physical and spiritual love unite together to form the foundation of God's love for his people. These are all great resources to help you understand how God's plan for love and sexuality are embodied in the Church's teachings.

5. **Take Stock**: Reflect upon where you stand regarding these teachings. Do you agree with the Church? Do the Church's teachings seem out of date to you? Have your personal experiences with sex and dating after divorce led you to peace and joy, or despair and sorrow? Be honest. Is it hard to be hopeful about the future when it is so uncertain? Does the idea of living a chaste life seem impossible to you? Does it anger you? Is it hard to see how living these teachings is the pathway to peace and joy? Using the journal pages in the *Workbook* companion for this chapter, try to identify those areas that are most difficult for you to live.

6. **Take a Leap of Faith**: As was made clear by this chapter, the more we seek our own personal peace and joy, the more elusive it becomes. Peace and joy are the fruits of a life committed to Christ. To receive these fruits, take the first step by surrendering those things to Christ those things that you are holding onto the tightest. Is it fear of being alone? Is it the desire for physical intimacy? Is it the anger over your divorce? Is it your personal pursuit of happiness? Identify what those are and give them up everyday in prayer to Christ. This act of trust is the "on ramp" to the path to peace and joy.

7. **Cling to Christ**: Christ's teachings have always stood in paradox to the world. This is never truer than when living a chaste life. The world screams that personal pursuit of happiness is the pathway to peace and joy, while Christ teaches that a life surrendered to him is the pathway. Cling to Christ through daily prayer and the sacraments. As you draw closer to Christ, you will experience a depth of peace and joy that words alone cannot describe. You will experience that taste of heaven that you are looking for.

8. **Be a Role Model**: When you live a life of authenticity you radiate Christ. People can sense this in you without you even saying a word. If you have children, let your authentic commitment to chastity be an example to them. Letting them know that you are living the same standard you expect of them is a tremendous act of love. They will be emboldened to live the Church's teachings because of your example. With your witness, you can help them avoid the pain and despair that you have suffered. If you don't have children, let your commitment to chastity shine a bright light in a world darkened by sexual sin. Your

example will be a guiding light to all those you meet. You may never know how many lives you influenced and led closer to Christ by your commitment to chastity.

# Meditation

## John 4: 3 - 26

He left Judea and went back to Galilee. He had to pass through Samaria. On the way he came to the Samaritan town called Sychar near the land that Jacob gave to his son Joseph. Jacob's well was there and Jesus, tired by the journey, sat down by the well. It was about the sixth hour. When a Samaritan woman came to draw water, Jesus said to her, "Give me something to drink." His disciples had gone into the town to buy food. The Samaritan woman said to him, "You are a Jew. How is it that you ask me, a Samaritan, for something to drink? – Jews, of course, do not associate with Samaritans. Jesus replied to her:

> "If you only knew what God is offering
> and who it is that is saying to you,
> 'Give me something to drink,'
> you would have been the one to ask,
> and he would have given you living water."

"You have no bucket, sir," she answered, "and the well is deep: how do you get this living water? Are you a greater man than our father Jacob, who gave us this well and drank from it himself with his sons and his cattle?" Jesus replied:

> "Whoever drinks this water
> will be thirsty again
> but no one who drinks the water that I shall give him
> will ever be thirsty again:
> the water that I shall give him
> will become in him a spring of water, welling up for eternal life."

"Sir," said the woman, "give me some of that water, so that I may never be thirsty or come here again to draw water."

"Go and call your husband," Jesus said to her, "and come back here." The woman answered, "I have no husband." Jesus said to her, "You are right to say, 'I have no husband,' for you have had five and the one you now have is not your husband. You spoke the truth there."

"I see you are a prophet, sir," said the woman. Our fathers worshipped on this mountain, though you say that Jerusalem is the place where one ought to worship." Jesus said:

> Believe me, woman, the hour is coming
> when you will worship the Father
> neither on this mountain nor in Jerusalem.
> You worship what you do not know;
> we worship what we do know;
> for salvation comes from the Jews.
> But the hour is coming – indeed is already here –
> when true worshippers will worship the Father in spirit and truth:
> that is the kind of worshipper
> the Father seeks.
> God is spirit,
> and those who worship
> must worship in spirit and truth.

The woman said to him, "I know that Messiah – that is, Christ – is coming; and when he comes he will explain everything." Jesus said, "That is who I am, I who speak to you."

**Opening Prayer**: My Lord and my God, I believe that you are waiting to reveal yourself to me in these few moments I spend in prayer with you. Help me to be attentive to your word and let my heart be open to your inspirations.

**Petition**: Lord, grant me the grace of purity of heart and mind and the desire to please you in all that I do.

1. *If you only knew what God is offering . . .*

If only we knew . . . if only we knew! We would forget every care we have, every concern, every worry, every need. If we only knew what

God was offering us, we would beg him to give us only his love and his grace. That would be enough for us. The Samaritan woman wanted and needed love and she was willing to go the unconventional route to get it. She had already been through five husbands looking for that love she needed and was living with another man that she was not married to. After five marriages and divorces, and now a live-in relationship, is it likely she found the love she was looking for? Yes it is, but not in the way she thought it would happen. The love she found was a stranger, a Jew, sitting at the well in the hot sun asking her for a drink. This woman was drawn in by Jesus, most likely his gentle nature; of course by the fact that he was a Jew and a male who normally would have ignored her as if she were worth nothing; yet he spoke to her, he drew her to himself, he spoke the words of everlasting life and touched her soul in a way no one else could. And Christ wants to do the same for us. Christ wants to show us that he knows . . . he knows the love we are looking for. He wants to give it to us.

2. *You worship what you do not know.*

So many times, we believe we know the answer, have the answer to our prayers and yet we couldn't be more off base. We hope and pray for things that may provide some brief happiness or consolation, but in reality will bring us more pain than anything. This is why we need to give everything to Christ, especially the things that are most important to us. Is this easy? No! It is not easy to loosen our grip and let go of the things that are so important to us. But the harder it is to let go, the more we need to do it. Let us learn to trust Christ and his plan for our lives. Let us place our whole lives and everything we love in his hands and sit back and watch. He will make us happier than we could ever imagine!

**Closing Prayer**: Thank you, Lord, for all you have done for me. Thank you for the ways you guide me and instruct me. Please grant me the grace to see that your plan for my life is what will make me happy. I ask this in your name. Amen.

# Resolution

Spend time in Adoration and ask the Holy Spirit to help you reflect on your own personal situation and how these issues of dating and chastity fit into your situation.

## Suggested Reading

Jackie Kendall and Debby Jones, *Lady in Waiting: Developing Your Love Relationships,* Destiny Image Publishers; Expanded edition (December 1, 2005)

Eric Ludy and Leslie Ludy, *When God Writes Your Love Story: The Ultimate Approach to Guy/Girl Relationships,* Multnomah (January 8, 2004)

C. S. Lewis, *Mere Christianity,* HarperOne; New Ed edition (February 6, 2001)

Christopher West, *Theology of the Body for Beginners,* Ascension Press (April 2004)

Pope Benedict XVI, *God is Love,* USCCB Publisher (February 14, 2006) or see also: http://www.vatican.va/holy_father/benedict_xvi/encyclicals/documents/hf_ben-xvi_enc_20051225_deus-caritas-est_en.html for a downloadable version.

# Chapter Sixteen:

# Mary, Our Mother and Role Model

These days, there are many different people who present themselves as leaders . . . all of them propose their opinions and ideals as important for us to embrace. But who is the best choice to uphold as our role model? In this chapter, let us observe a worthy and true role model in every sense of the word, our Blessed Mother, Mary.

In previous weeks, you have read about the type of person you don't want to become. Now let's focus on the type of person you *do* want to become. And you may be thinking, Mary is an obvious role model for women, but why Mary as a role model for men? The answer is simple. Mary lived virtue perfectly. As Catholic men and women, we are to be examples to others, and so we need to practice living these virtues as well. So why not let ourselves be led by, Mary, someone whose example is perfect in every way?

The goal of this chapter is to learn more about who Mary really was and the characteristics and virtues she possessed that, through your imitation of them, will help you become the man or woman you were created to be; happy, strong and holy.

## The Case

Catherine relates a life-changing encounter she had a short time ago:

I met a really nice woman some time ago, Valerie, and I can honestly say I have never been more impressed by someone than I was by her. I met Valerie at a Women's Guild meeting one night and we had a very pleasant conversation. She was friendly, easy to talk to, and I couldn't help but notice that she seemed to have great inner peace. I left that evening remarking to myself that it was refreshing to meet someone like her.

Over the next six months, I had more opportunities to get to know Valerie as we worked together on a guild-sponsored fundraiser. I enjoyed my conversations with Valerie and began to notice other things about her . . . the fact that she was always so helpful and concerned about others. The fact that she never said anything bad or negative about anyone; her comments were always on the positive side of things. She was a very gentle woman, yet she gave the impression that she was as strong as steel.

The night of the fundraising party, Valerie showed me pictures of her four children. "What a nice family you have!" I said as I viewed the photos. I never noticed a ring on her finger and realized suddenly that in all our discussions, I had never really asked Valerie much about herself. "Your boys look like great kids!" I commented. "Was your husband unable to make it this evening?"

"My husband and I are divorced," Valerie said with closed eyes and a softened tone in her voice. "And I lost my oldest son, Brad, early last year in an accident." She looked at me and smiled with a tear in her eye. Her eyes suddenly revealed the depths of suffering she had endured and she sighed deeply. "But the boys and I are doing well," she reassured. "We've learned so much during these last few years and we've become much closer than I could have imagined. That is something I prayed hard for."

I was horror struck to think that such a lovely woman had been suffering so terribly . . . and silently. Suddenly all my own hardships seemed to look small and ridiculous.

"How did you survive those terrible losses and still be such a nice person?" I asked, thinking about my own depressed and angry feelings. "I don't know many people, if any, that would have come through this as gracefully as you have!" I suddenly realized that maybe I could be doing a lot better than I was.

"Well," she answered, "it's been a rough couple of years . . . and there have been times when I thought I couldn't make it. I was on the verge of giving up, but I found my strength in God. Some days I would wake up and I felt I wouldn't be able to get out of bed, but I knew my boys were counting on me for strength. If I didn't have my faith, we would have fallen apart."

I felt terrible, yet uplifted at the same time. Valerie looked at me and said with a smile, "I prayed a lot to the Blessed Mother and that really helped. She is a wonderful model for me. You know, I just kept thinking about how she watched her own innocent Son die . . . how painful it must have been. And how she lived her later years without Joseph. She's a lot like me" she said. "Mary and I have grown very close." I realized at that moment how similar Valerie was to Mary . . . beautiful, peaceful, graceful, charitable, always focused on others, not herself.

Valerie's example brought a new perspective into my life, and I began paying more attention to the role the Blessed Mother had as mother of the Church. It made such a huge difference in my life. These friendships helped me become a much better person myself.

## The Makings of a Role Model

It seems there are very few good role models these days despite the fact there are many people who want to be considered as someone to look up to. Not everyone who says "follow me" or "do it the way I do" are not very good choices as role models. What is it exactly that makes a good role model?

Virtue is what sets role models apart from other people. Virtue enables a person to do the right thing, regardless of the cost to themselves. Think for a moment of someone who has demonstrated virtue, your parents, maybe a friend, your pastor . . . it was the virtue these people have shown that has a positive affect on others. Society wants you to follow the mainstream trends and popular viewpoints. It's probably safe to say that because of her virtue, Valerie did not follow the mainstream example of someone tempted to despair because of tragedy.

According to the *Catechism of the Catholic Church*:

A virtue is an habitual and firm disposition to do the good. It allows the person not only to perform good acts, but to give the best of himself. The virtuous person tends toward the good with all his sensory and spiritual powers; he pursues the good and chooses it in concrete actions (*CCC* 1803).

That statement alone begins to separate the current role models from those who simply make noise in society. But what are these virtues that are practiced that help you become a good example?

First, there are the **Theological Virtues** of faith, hope and love. They are the key virtues and all other virtues stem from these. Then, there are the Cardinal Virtues which stem from faith, hope and love, but are set apart because they play a pivotal role in human formation. The Cardinal Virtues are: prudence, justice, fortitude and temperance.

**Spiritual and Human Virtues** fall under the umbrella of the Cardinal Virtues:

| Prudence | Justice | Fortitude | Temperance |
|----------|---------|-----------|------------|
| Pure Intention | Obedience | Faithfulness | Humility |
| Integrity | Forgiveness | Patience | Chastity |
| Wisdom | Authenticity | Tenacity | Poverty of Spirit |
| Discernment | Care | Magnanimity | Sobriety |
| Pure Thought | Kindness | Perseverance | Purity |
| Circumspection | Sympathy | Constancy | Modesty |
| Common Sense | Reverence | Diligence | Meekness |
| Right Reason | Piety | Courage | Self-Control |
| Sagacity | Sincerity | Vigilance | Sacrifice |
| Caution | Patriotism | Nobility | Detachment |
| Prudence | Justice | Fortitude | Temperance |
| Deliberation | Loyalty | Conviction | Long Suffering |
| Industriousness | Cooperation | Persistence | Self-denial |
| Initiative | Veracity | Fidelity | Self-discipline |
| Responsibility | Truthfulness | | Simplicity |
| Astuteness | Respect | | Abandonment |
| | Goodness | | Docility |
| | Gratitude | | Joy |

| | |
|---|---|
| Honesty | Flexibility |
| Courtesy | Moderation |
| Fairness | Balance |
| Generosity | Optimism |
| Graciousness | Cheerfulness |
| Compassion | |
| Mercy | |
| Friendship | |
| Social Justice | |
| Understanding | |
| Dutifulness | |

When you look at the Blessed Mother, Mary, you can see a great woman who possessed many virtues. Some of the most obvious ones are her charity, humility, purity, patience, self-denial, courage and fortitude; the same virtues that have built the role models mentioned earlier.

Although Mary lived 2,000 years ago and society has changed dramatically since then, you can relate to her in your own life journey.

You can relate to Mary because she relates to you. Mary faced the possibility of being divorced by her betrothed spouse. After Joseph died, she was a single parent, working hard to make sure Jesus had what he needed while he was home with her. She understands you because during her life, she experienced many of the same joys and endured many of the same sufferings and hardships that you do.

Take, for example, the way she trusted God and his plan for her even though she didn't understand the details; even though it all seemed impossible to her (*Luke* 1: 26–38). Or the fear and anxiety she experienced when she and Joseph lost Jesus on the trip from Jerusalem (*Luke* 2: 41–52). She suffered the grief of a mother's broken heart as she watched her innocent Son suffer at the hands of the government and die a criminal's death on the cross (*John* 19: 25–27). She experienced the awesomeness of her fear being changed to indescribable joy with the apostles in the upper room when the Holy Spirit descended upon them (*Acts* 1: 13–14, 2: 1–4).

As Jesus died on the cross, he gave his mother to us to be our own and this is how Mary loves us. She wants to love us, protect us, help us and lead us to her Son. She leads us to Jesus in many ways, primarily through her example of virtue in times of joy and suffering.

And here is another important point for men to consider: every man needs a woman in his life. Call it part of man's nature . . . men are made to long for a fulfilling companionship of a woman. That's why Mary is so important for men. She is not just a great, historical figure and example of heroic virtue. Mary is your mother *par excellence*, living, listening to you, encouraging you and loving you. So don't let this great gift of God - a woman to love who is perfectly lovable - go undervalued in your life. A relationship with Mary will make you a better man.

Mary is the Mother of God and our mother. She calls us to herself because she loves us and she wants us to be closer to her Son. She is interested in us and wants to help us with the concerns of our hearts. And she calls to us as a mother calls to her child to come sit by her side and talk about the day.

Do not be troubled or weighed down with grief.
Do not fear any illness or vexation, anxiety or pain.
Am I not here who am your Mother?
Are you not under my shadow and protection?
Am I not your fountain of life?
Are you not in the folds of my mantle?
In the crossing of my arms?
Is there anything else you need?
- Words of the Virgin Mary to Juan Diego in 1531

## What Does Scripture Say?

On the third day there was a wedding at Cana in Galilee. The mother of Jesus was there, and Jesus and his disciples had also been invited. And they ran out of wine, since the wine provided for the feast had all been used, and the mother of Jesus said to him, "They have no wine." Jesus said, "Woman, what do you want from me? My hour has not come yet." His mother said to the servants, "Do whatever he tells you" (John 2:1 - 5).

There are so many facets of beauty that Mary displays in this passage that you can draw from. First, she was the only one who noticed there was no more wine. Imagine running out of alcohol at a wedding! She knew the newly married bride and groom would be embarrassed and took great care to go to her Son quietly and without making a scene.

She petitioned her Son with great trust, knowing he could take care of the situation. And finally, when his only answer was, "My hour has not yet come," she simply told the servants, "Do whatever he tells you," showing us all how to have complete and total faith in God, that he will take care of everything. She did not demand answers, she did not demand that her Son obey his mother, she simply trusted he would take care of it all. And of course, he did, out of the desire to please his mother.

What a beautiful gift you have in Mary, that she is your mother, cares for you as a mother cares for her child, and petitions her Son on your behalf, obtaining graces and all good things for you.

## Comforter of the Afflicted, Pray For Us!

Mary loves you with the greatest motherly love. She wants nothing more than to see you happy, to see you resting in the arms of her beloved Son, Jesus. She longs to help you by leading you to that point, and she does so through her example to you.

Mary's impressive spirit of prayer and union with God is important to take note of. The Gospel always shows her meditating and reflecting on the things of God. This intimate interior relationship with God was what allowed Mary to hear the message of the Angel, what enlightened her in moments of darkness and incomprehension, what strengthened her in moments of sadness, and, finally, what maintained her hope when, at the end, all of the apostles fled from the shadow of the cross.

Imitate Mary in this sense of prayer and interior life because it will always provide you with the climate in which to hear God, the light and strength with which to walk on your Christian journey. Learn to love silence, recollection and humility, as a means to live a deep closeness to Christ. Make room in your heart for prayer so the vanities of the world and concern for external things cannot hold back your hearing the voice of God who is present in our souls.

In imitating Mary, you will find a richness and elegance that is lacking in many "role models" of today. You will come to know a trustworthy and caring friend that you can always rely on. And you will discover a source of happiness in your heart that brings peace, stability and confidence.

If you follow her guidance, you will not go astray.
If you pray to her, you will not give up hope.
If you think of her, you will not go wrong.
If she upholds you, you will not stumble.
If she protects you, you will not be afraid.
If she leads you, you will reach the goal.
- St. Bernard

## Concluding Thoughts

Measuring any potential role model or mentor is easy when you apply any of these virtues mentioned as a litmus test. If the would-be role model demonstrates these virtues, then he or she is someone whose imitation will lead to eventual happiness. If not, then the road diverges such that it will never arrive at true happiness.

That is where Mary comes in. Get to know her, because she is the ultimate role model. What's more, she is the ultimate mentor. Talk to her and measure your progress in virtue against hers. You cannot go wrong.

> In imitating Mary, we will find
> a richness and elegance that is lacking
> in many "role models" of today.

## Now What?

Christ gives us the ultimate example of how to live, and he did this to perfection because he was equally God and equally man. He also gave us his mother, Mary, to be the finest role model for her example of a human being who lived virtuously. If virtue was a sport, Mary would be the Michael Jordan of virtue. She is the one you can always turn to for inspiration and motivation.

With the exception of the theological virtues (faith, hope and love), all other virtues must be formed. This formation typically takes time, sometimes a long time. Here are some ways you can be inspired through Mary's example to form new virtues in your life.

1. **Learn More about Mary**: St. Louis de Montfort was a priest who lived in the late 17th and early 18th centuries. He had a very special devotion to Mary, and spent his life writing and preaching about her. His books, *The Secret of Mary*, *True Devotion to Mary*, and *The Secret of the Rosary* are classic written works. They give great insight into Mary and her power in Christian living. Learn more about Mary by reading any one, or all of these great books.

2. **Choose a Virtue to Work on**: Identify a particular struggle in your life, and then using the list of virtues on page 162, identify one that will counteract your struggle. Determine ways you can begin to integrate that virtue into your daily life. For example, if you are struggling with anger, working everyday to form the virtue of forgiveness is a way to overcome your anger. If you are struggling with lust, work on forming the virtue of purity. A virtue, like any good habit, takes time to form. Expect to struggle as you work on forming a virtue. That is where Mary can help you. Pray to her everyday to help you form the virtue you have identified. The *Workbook* has an excellent exercise on page 160 to help guide you through identifying your struggles and develop a daily program to help form virtues that will take over in these areas.

3. **Pray the Rosary**: No discussion about Mary would be complete without the rosary. You can read an excellent description of the rosary when you visit www.theholyrosary.org.

There is so much power in praying the rosary. It has been tied to so many graces. Not only does praying the rosary unite your prayer with Mary's, it has the power to get you to Heaven. Praying the rosary can provide both partial and plenary indulgences. There are so many meditations that have been written to be used when praying the rosary. To learn more about these mediations and about the rosary go to your local Catholic bookstore, or search the Internet. Tap into the power of the rosary by praying it often—daily if possible. If you need help with the basics of praying the rosary, you can find help on page 185 of the

"Excellent Prayers" section of the *Workbook* companion.

4. **Pray the** *Memorare*: The *Memorare* is a very powerful prayer to Mary. Use this prayer to bring your special requests to the Blessed Mother. She will bring these requests to Jesus in a very powerful way. This is a great prayer to memorize and pray whenever you need extra special help (like when you are going to be around your ex-spouse, or you are experiencing a great deal of stress). You will find it on page 162 in the "Excellent Prayers" section of the *Workbook*. Pray the *Memorare* and then tell the Blessed Mother exactly what you want her to pray for. You will be amazed at the power of this prayer!

5. **Consecration To Jesus Through Mary**: St. Louis de Montfort in his book, *True Devotion to Mary*, describes a powerful 33 days of prayer by which one is consecrated to Jesus through prayers to Mary. Pope John Paul II said, "Reading this book (True Devotion to Mary) was the turning point of my life . . . This Marian devotion . . . has since remained a part of me. It is an integral part of my interior life and of my spiritual theology."★ This consecration is a perfect renewal of your baptismal vows. Consider this consecration as a great way to draw closer to Christ and Mary.

# Meditation

### John 19: 25 - 27

Near the cross of Jesus stood his mother and his mother's sister, Mary the wife of Clopas, and Mary of Magdala. Seeing his mother and the disciple whom he loved standing near her, Jesus said to his mother, "Woman, this is your son." Then to the disciple he said, "This is your mother." And from that hour the disciple took her into his home.

**Opening Prayer**: Lord, you are my helper, my loving support. You draw me to you now, and I love this time with you. Help me to leave all concerns behind for these few precious moments I spend with you.

**Petition**: I pray for help, Lord, to grow in virtue, especially in those virtues in which I know I need the most . . .

1. *Woman, this is your son.*

   Mary was the most delicate and sensitive of mothers. She knows the pain and suffering that comes with loving others, yet she always treated others with the greatest care, with the greatest love and humility. She never sought an eye for an eye her concern was always first with loving God and being one with him, and secondly, how she could help others. Someone who can truly detach from their own concerns and seek only the happiness of others is not only honorable, but worthy of imitation. And imitation of Mary will only lead us to Christ, her beloved Son, upon whom all happiness and peace rests.

2. *This is your mother.*

   If a child shows her love for its mother by behaving well, visiting her and bringing her gifts, we should try to honor Mary by being faithful to Christ, praying with fervor and attention, telling her our difficulties, asking her advice, never forgetting to say good night to her and asking her to guard our fidelity.

# Resolution

Sit down this week and make note of some of the areas you would like to improve upon in your self . . . then pick a virtue to counteract the problem. Write down how (a practical means) you will work on it and ask Mary for her help. Continue to work on that virtue until you feel you are ready to move to another problem area. This is something that we can all do, every day of our lives.

# Suggested Reading

Don Dolindo Ruotolo, *A Month with Mary*, translation: Msgr. Arthur Calkins, The Catholic Company

Rawley Myers, *Embraced by Mary*, The Catholic Company

Thomas A. Kempis, *Imitation of Mary*, Catholic Book Publishing Company (September 2005)

# Chapter Seventeen:

# Hope for the Future and Your Vocation in Life

You have come very far in the time you have dedicated to this book. Hopefully, you have made progress in your life and with God's grace, you've gone from nursing your broken heart and grieving the loss of your marriage to getting back on your feet and finding a new person emerging through the rubble. So what about the future? Where are you headed and what do you have to look forward to?

Divorce is not the end of the world, although it may very well feel like it many times. It is important to remember that time will continue to march on and you can either get left behind in a pit of misery, or you can seize the day and begin anew, leaving the pain and the need for healing in God's loving hands.

In order to make sure you find the right path to take so you don't end up in this position again, you need to discern a very important aspect of your life; you need to reflect on the events of your life up to your divorce, contemplate that to the point you are at now, and finally, take a look ahead at what possibilities your future holds. Ask God to be part of the process. After what you have been through, you want to make sure you begin including God in all your decision-making processes. When you invite God, not just for guidance to make the right decision, but also to remain completely open to him and his plan for your life, it is impossible to go wrong.

The goal of this chapter is to find hope in your future through understanding that God has a plan for your life, one that has been there for all eternity. Begin to discern, in light of all the changes that have taken place in your life, which direction God wants you to take.

# The Case

Lisa explains a significant moment in her life, six years after her divorce:

With all the time to ponder what had happened in the years since my divorce, all the time to discuss things with my therapist, and all the time I had to myself to pray about my situation, I was able to come to a truly helpful realization, which was actually one of my crucial mistakes. It was simply that when I married my ex-spouse, I had been completely wrapped up in myself and what I wanted. *I* wanted to get married. *I* wanted a big wedding. *I* wanted to have children. . . *I, I, I!* Since I mistakenly believed this was what my spouse wanted (due to poor communication), it never occurred to me that I should confer with anyone else. But I could have brought my hopes, my deep desire for a good marriage before God. However, I never once considered asking God what he wanted for me, I simply assumed that because *I* wanted it, that was all that was necessary. It never occurred to me when I married that God might have had a plan for my life. I should have asked the question: *Is marrying this man part of God's plan?* I was certain getting a divorce was not part of his plan, but, what about getting married? Was it possible that God had really wanted me to consider some other vocation? Maybe a vocation to the religious life? I didn't feel I was meant to be a nun or live in a religious community, but nevertheless, this doubt in my vocation grew stronger and I pushed it away each time I thought of it. It was not what I wanted, I wanted to be a wife and mother.

And that was the amazing thing . . . now, after the failed marriage, the divorce, all the lessons I learned from the annulment process – I was making the same mistake again, despite all that had happened, despite all my previous mistakes. Without realizing it, I was completely wrapped up in *me* and what *I* wanted. All I could think of was meeting the right man and getting married. I wasn't allowing myself to consider that maybe God's plan involved something other than that; something other than the dream I was clinging to so tightly to. The more I demanded to have what I wanted, the more I became possessive and fearful of not getting what I wanted – what I believed would make me happy. I didn't consider that maybe God knew better than I did. I wasn't trusting him. I was trusting only in myself and my ability to make things happen.

One day, I was sitting in my car at a red traffic light, waiting for it to turn green. In front of me, there was a family crossing on the crosswalk . . . a dad with a kid on his shoulders and a mom pushing a stroller. Very sweet. I watched them, not with envy, but certainly with longing. My mind began to wander off to a day when I would get married and have children, I hoped. And then, the thoughts of becoming a nun tapped me on the shoulder once more. I pushed those thoughts away immediately, adopting that stubborn attitude of a selfish, self-centered child; *I want it my way!*

No sooner had this occurred than everything seemed to get very quiet. It was as if I was suddenly drawn inward, right into my very soul and it was completely still. All the other noises and distractions seemed to fade away quickly, and in that gentle silence, I heard a voice. It was not an audible voice, but I could hear it in my heart very distinctly. Very gently, the voice said, *Why won't you give Me this part of your life?* I knew without a doubt who was speaking to me and I was so moved by the request, so touched, that I burst into tears right there at the traffic light.

That voice I heard was the voice of the Holy Spirit and now I know why people refer to him as *the sweet guest of the soul.* God was speaking to me, and he wanted me to give up this power struggle.

By this point, I sincerely believed I had given over most of myself already. I had let go of my marriage to my ex-spouse. I had released my anger toward everyone over the divorce and miscarriages. I had let go of my home, my friends, and the life that was familiar to me. And most importantly, I had given my heart back to God. Each time I had taken a step in that direction – giving something up and allowing God to handle it – He blessed me. He took care of me and I was always happy. How could I not trust him with this? How could I not believe that he knew how to make me happy? With all the mistakes I had made over the years, how could I think that I could do a better job than God could?

My heart, although still clinging to my dream, was filled with peace because I clearly knew the direction I needed to go in. I also felt great love that came from truly hearing God's voice. I knew what needed to be done and I felt strong. I felt that I would finally be able to hand over this last, but most important part of my life to him.

The next morning, I got up as usual and went to mass. It was here that I would make a formal dedication of my life to Christ. I was going to do it once and for all and be happy with whatever God brought into my life. During the consecration of the bread and wine, I visualized my wedding dress thrown over the altar in an act of sacrifice, and as the paten was lifted into the air, I imagined my desire to be married and a mother lifted with it and offered to God. It may have been a simple thing, but it was the best way I knew how to drive the point home to myself. I had given up the power struggle. Now, it was truly in God's hands.

Of course, now that I had done that, I believed God was going to lead me to a convent somewhere. It's funny, sometimes, how we think we can second-guess God and know what his plans are. I thought I knew what the game plan was, but again, I was missing the point that God was trying to make, and I couldn't have been more wrong about what was going to happen.

Two weeks later, I was still doing what I normally did . . . working. I was buried in a file of bills that needed to be paid when the front door of the office opened and a co-worker from the office next door entered my office with another gentleman.

"Hey, Lisa!" a scratchy voice called. That was Sandy, one of the department heads. I looked up to see Sandy and another gentleman standing at the front door, waiting, while Sandy was pointing around the room and describing things to the gentleman. I put my file aside and walked up to meet them, smoothing the wrinkles out of my suit as I walked.

"Lisa, this is Jim. Jim, Lisa." We shook hands and smiled politely at each other. Unbeknownst to me, I had just been introduced to the man I would marry one year later. But I didn't recognize Jim as anything more than a new co-worker. I think God planned it that way. I believe God wanted to turn my intense fascination with finding the "right one" away from it all, so he could introduce me to the one who would truly make me happy.

. Jim has been more than the perfect husband, and he has shown me more happiness than I ever could have imagined. Oh yes, and we now have three beautiful children.

## Your Mission, Should You Choose to Accept It

We were all created by God with a purpose, a mission, and one that only we can fulfill. We have been given the gifts and the talents we have to help us fulfill this special mission.

Everyone wants to be happy. This is a fundamental part of our being. "Life, liberty and the pursuit of happiness . . ." basic human rights, right? But how do you actually go about pursuing happiness? What steps are necessary for you to take in order to find true, lasting happiness?

Well, there are several steps to take, and the most basic step is discerning your purpose in life. Not simply discovering a career, such as being a doctor, an artist, a social worker, a coach, etc. You need to go much deeper than that. The question you need to contemplate is, *Why was I put on earth to begin with?* Why did God choose *me* to be who I am and alive at this point in history? Is it by accident that I am a man or a woman, a Catholic, a citizen of the country I am from? Is it a coincidence that I have the parents I have or my particular siblings and relatives? Is it by chance that I have the use of all my faculties, my arms and legs, my eyes, my ears and mouth, my mind when others don't? These are very basic issues, yes, but why are you who you are?

The Catechism teaches:

> God put us in the world to know, to love, and to serve him, and so to come to paradise" (*CCC* 1721).

So many people puzzle endlessly over what the meaning of life is, and there it has been in the Catechism all these years! The Catechism teaches us that our ultimate goal in life is to spend eternity in heaven with God. This goal is not only for Catholics or only for "religious" people; it is the same goal for everyone no matter who we are or what our circumstances are. When you look at your life through this perspective, you begin to realize the only real happiness you will have on earth is in doing those things that bring you closer to this goal. What you do with your life while you are here on earth is of extreme importance.

The things you have to do everyday keep you focused on smaller details. Details are important, but they are not all-important. You need to step back from time to time and refresh yourself by looking at the bigger picture and refocusing on your ultimate goal. It's not just about getting what *you* want in life as society wants you to believe. How many wealthy people have everything they could ever want and are still bored and dissatisfied with life because they do not know God?

The big picture is about living your life to the best of your ability within the vocation God gave you. This is why you need to discern your true vocation because within it you will find God's plan, and within God's plan you will find happiness. Ask yourself these questions:

- Do I believe there is a chance to reconcile with my spouse and restore our family?
- Do I feel that marriage is not for me any more and I will be single for the rest of my life?
- What does being single for the rest of my life mean to me?
- Do I feel called to consider some other direction for my future?

Some of these questions may conjure up feelings of fear or anxiety. But you shouldn't be afraid to ponder these questions and answer them honestly. Why? Because finding your true purpose in life is what will make you happy here on earth. Often times, we believe that one specific thing will make us happy, but how do we know that's what will happen? You may spend a good portion of your life chasing that one thing and when you finally get it, you are not happy. Think of all the people out there who have been married three, four or even more times. They are pursuing what they want, but they never find love that brings true and lasting happiness. Instead, they end up lonely, bitter, unhappy and have left a trail of destruction and broken hearts in their wake.

Their example is reason enough for you to seek guidance from God in prayer in all your choices, asking God to show you his will. In doing so, God will show you happiness beyond anything you could ever imagine.

# What Does Scripture Say?

Ask, and it will be given to you; search, and you will find; knock, and the door will be opened to you. Everyone who asks receives; everyone who searches finds; everyone who knocks will have the door opened. Is there anyone among you who would hand his son a stone when he asked for bread? Or would hand him a snake when he asked for a fish? If you, evil as you are, know how to give your children what is good, how much more will your Father in heaven give good things to those who ask him! (Matthew 7: 7 - 11).

As we have previously read in this beautiful gospel passage, Christ is trying to make it plain that he wants you to come to him with your concerns and desires. He wants us to talk to him about your life and give him the opportunity to make you happy.

When the two disciples were on the road to Emmaus after the crucifixion, feeling disillusioned and afraid, Christ came to them and pretended not to know any of the events that had taken place. Of course, he knew, because they happened to him, but he pretended because he wanted to hear it from the disciples themselves. He wanted to hear their take on it, their opinions, their fears and concerns. After they had told him all that had happened, he enlightened them with his teaching and eventually revealed himself to them. Their hearts had been burning within them as he spoke to them.

Jesus did so out of love for the disciples and he does the same for you. He wants to hear it all from you, your perspective, and then he wants to show you the way. The passage assures you that he will give you the good things that will make you happy.

# A Few Things to Help . . .

So how do you begin discerning God's plan for you? Here are some simple steps:

**Be Open**: Be open with God and truly offer him your heart. You need to allow him to be in charge and show you which direction to take.

Each day when you pray, tell Christ he is welcome in your heart.

**Be Honest**: Be honest in your relationship with God by not ignoring his voice in your heart. Discuss everything that is important to you with God in prayer. Then ask him what is important to him.

**Be Courageous**: Being open to God's plan takes faith and living faith correctly takes courage. This is what makes life exciting!

**Be Active**: You can't just sit there and wait for the answers to just drop into your hands. You need to be proactive. If you feel you should consider a different vocation than marriage, check out your options. For example, go on a silent retreat, for example, where there is plenty of time to be alone with yourself and with God. Give him the opportunity to speak to you. And then, *listen.* Listen to the gentle words he will speak. And then, take a step forward. Remember, God has the steering wheel and if the car is not moving, he cannot steer us in the direction you need to go.

What you seek is happiness and love. God has known your desires and your longings. He knows what you want better than you do yourself, for he is our Creator and Savior. Ask Christ for light so you may know him more intimately and recognize his will for you. Ask him to show you what he desires of your life – now, and in the future.

I know, Lord, that without you I can do nothing.
Amid the fatigue and turmoil of every day,
I often forget that you alone are the one who strengthens me.
Lord, give me the grace to walk beside you always.
Help me to practice the virtues which brought me to you:
faith, hope and love.
God wishes not to deprive us of pleasure;
but he wishes to give us pleasure in its totality;
that is to say, all pleasure . . . .
What greater pleasure is there than to find myself
the one thing that I ought to be, and the whole thing that I ought to be?
-Blessed Henry Suso

# Concluding Thoughts

What all this comes down to is very simple:

- Communicate with Christ through prayer.
- Trust him and place all concerns, worries and hopes in his hands (and leave them there!)
- Allow him the opportunity to direct you according to his plan for your life.

Christ will never let you down, he will always show you the way. Today can be a completely new beginning for your life, if you simply open your heart to the love of Christ.

# Now What?

No two days are ever exactly the same. Each day holds a fresh opportunity to live the life that God has planned for us. We are not bound by our past. We have the ability to cooperate with God in shaping our future. Here are some ways to continue the work you have started and claim the peace and joy God has promised you.

1. **Pray Everyday**: Get in the habit of praying everyday. It is your direct link to God. Find at least fifteen minutes each day to turn the world off and turn your mind and listen to God.

2. **Stay Close to the Sacraments**: The sacraments are God's gift for every day living. Go to mass at least every week, if not more. Receive the Eucharist as often as possible. Tap into the incredible power of reconciliation by going every month. The Church is not only your greatest source of healing it is your greatest source of hope. Make Christ, through the Church and its sacraments, the center of your life.

3. **Read**: Form the habit of reading scripture everyday. Take advantage of the

daily meditations that are available in subscription form either in print or via e-mail. The <u>Magnificat</u> (www.magnificat.com) and <u>The Word Among Us</u> (www.wau.org) are but two of the many publications that provide daily reflections on scripture. There is also a variety of e-mail meditations on scripture. You can find a daily meditation, plus so much more at www. usccb.org, which is the official web site of the United States Conference of Catholic Bishops. Regnum Christi, a lay apostolate movement within the Church provides an excellent daily gospel meditation (www. regnumchristi.org). There are many others. A search of the Internet will give you a plethora of options.

There are also many great works of literature by Saints, Doctors of the Church, Popes, and lay people. Keep learning and keep opening your mind by reading these works. In each chapter of this book appear books for suggested reading. Seek these books out. So many people have gone before you and have great wisdom to share. Leverage their knowledge and use it to help you improve your life and discern God's will.

4.  **Journal**: In the bombardment of life, it is easy to get caught up in the routine of everyday living. Patterns of thought and patterns of behavior get lost in the noise of life. Journaling is an excellent way to record your thoughts, record your struggles, and record your joys. By forming the habit of journaling, you give yourself a gift by recording your life. Only by looking back can we learn and create a better future.

5.  **Follow the Peace**: The more you open yourself up to God, the more he, through the Holy Spirit, will guide your heart. The Holy Spirit is your advocate, your guide, in daily living.

> The Advocate, the holy Spirit that the Father will send
> in my name – he will teach you everything
> and remind you of all that (I) told you (John 14:26).

The more you work to center your life on Christ and doing God's will, the more sensitized to a feeling of peace you will become. Let that feeling of peace, or the lack of it, be your guide. As a general rule, when you are doing God's will you will find peace. If you are not, peace will be fleeting or nonexistent. While it is true that God leads you through difficult times to form you and strengthen your faith, through prayer and reflection, you will come to know if the struggle is leading you closer or further away from God.

# Meditation

## Matthew 13: 44-46

Jesus said to his disciples: "The Kingdom of heaven is like a treasure buried in a field, which a person finds and hides again, and out of joy goes and sells all that he has and buys that field. Again, the Kingdom of heaven is like a merchant searching for fine pearls. When he finds a pearl of great price, he goes and sells all that he has and buys it."

**Opening prayer**: Lord Jesus, you are my light and my life. Help me now to spend these moments with you and forget everything else that competes for my attention. Let me find my direction for today in being with you now.

**Petition**: Lord, I ask your guidance and your wisdom, that I may find the direction you want to lead me in.

1. *Buried Treasure.*

The parable of the pearl of great price, the kingdom of heaven, implies that we must go in search of it. We must seek it with our own efforts, for if it simply falls into our hands, it doesn't mean that much. We have worked hard in this period after our divorces to rid ourselves of the things that keep us at odds with Christ and with others. This hard work brings us peace and confidence and we are approaching the point where our efforts are most needed – knowing God's plan for our lives. To a degree, we can experience the kingdom of heaven while we live on earth by walking the path God has chosen for us, the road that will lead to the most happiness we can experience before we die.

2. *Sell all that we have!*

There is no comparison in life to the joy we experience when we are firmly ensconced in the life Christ chose for us – when we are fulfilling our mission. The joy that God gives us truly changes our lives and we become new creatures in Christ. We sell all that we have in a sense because our joy in finding God is so great, we don't want anything to take it away from us, to steal the peace we have been given.

**Closing Prayer**: I thank you, Lord, for your love for me, and for creating me with a purpose. I pray that you will grant me the grace to remain open to you and your will each day of my life, so that I may be one with you, now and in eternity. I ask this in your name. Amen.

## Resolution

Spend some time in Adoration and think about your future. Contemplate the gospel of the rich young man with yourself standing in the scene as an observer. Think about what Christ might turn to you and say. Tell him you are open to his inspirations and will trust him.

Then, set a direction and start heading there. God will take care of the rest, because he wants us to be happy even more than we do.

## Suggested Reading

Thomas D. Williams, *Spiritual Progress: Becoming the Christian You Want to Be*, FaithWords (February 13, 2007)

Ralph Martin, *The Fulfillment of All Desire*, Emmaus Road Publishing (July 1, 2006)

Visit
## www.divorcedcatholic.org

For a variety of resources for divorced Catholics including:

## Journey of Hope
a 13-week divorce recovery program designed just for
Catholics

JOURNEY OF HOPE

# Acknowledgements

Lisa would like to acknowledge and thank the following people:

The Blessed Trinity. Thank you for never giving up on me.

Jim, my incredible husband; they always say "behind every great man is a great woman." I tend to believe the exact opposite. Without your encouragement, wisdom and guidance, this book would not have been possible.

To Christina Grace, Ryan Christopher and Monica Claire, the true miracles in my life.

To my parents, for the gift of my Faith and my wonderful family who prayed for me and supported me during the most difficult time in my life.

To Patrick for his generosity and outstanding guidance.

To Vince, for his tireless efforts, great writing and patience, and especially to Vince and Monica for their tremendous faith and beautiful example to all.

★   ★   ★

Vince would like to acknowledge and thank the following people:

Jesus Christ, my Lord and Savior, for always pursing me,

The Holy Spirit for giving me the words,

My children, Caroline, Kaitlyn, Riley, and Vincent Peter for showing me the face of God,

My wife, Monica, for her love, her faith and her passion for serving divorced Catholics,

Our children, Caroline, Kaitlyn, Emily, Riley, Austin, Maria, and Vincent Peter for showing me the face of God,

My mother for giving me the gift of my Catholic faith,

My father for being home each night when I was a kid,

My brother, Anthony, for being my rock in my darkest days,

My grandmother, Nonni, for her unceasing prayers, and

My sister in Christ, Lisa, for her initiative, insight, and wisdom.

Lisa Duffy has more than 15 years of both personal and professional experience in helping others deal with their divorces. Born and raised in Southern California, Lisa suffered through the pain of being a divorced Catholic in the early 1990s and knew that after seven years of intense struggle, spiritual growth, personal triumphs, and finally remarriage in the Church and the birth of three miracle children, her one desire was to help others who were suffering find hope and healing.

Lisa has worked for the Church in a variety of roles, and is the past President of Journey of Hope Productions, a program in the Archdiocese of Atlanta, which she authored and upon which this book was based. Lisa has given workshops for the North American Conference for Separated and Divorced Catholics (NACSDC) national conference and a part of their speaker panel. Lisa lives in Summerville, SC with her husband and three children.

---

Vince Frese, a lifelong Catholic, is a father, a ministry leader, a catechist, and a business leader. After experiencing first hand the pain and difficulty of divorce, Vince felt a calling to help serve other divorced Catholics. He has worked with the Archdiocese of Atlanta and the United States Conference of Catholic Bishops to help create programs and resources for divorced Catholics. Vince founded the Embrace Ministry, a ministry serving the on-going needs of divorced, separated, and single-parent Catholics. Through this ministry he has hosted a variety of spiritual, educational, and social programs that have helped many Catholics rebuild their lives after divorce. He is the President of Journey of Hope Productions Corporation, and is active in his parish as a catechist, ministry head, and program facilitator. He has been President and CEO of Tridia Corporation, a software development company, for twenty years.

Vince lives in Cumming, Georgia with his wife, Monica, and their seven children.

Made in the USA
Charleston, SC
28 April 2016